Warm Hearts For Cold Noses

Unusual *Tails* of a Young Veterinarian

ABIGAIL

THIS BOOK IS FOR YOU AND THOSE LIKE YOU WHO HAVE THE WARMEST OF HEARTS FOR COLD NOSES

Edward Dionne

Edward R. Dionne Jr. VMD

Illustrations by Emily Dennis

Copyright©2013 by Edward R. Dionne Jr. VMD
Book Design by Edward R. Dionne III
Cover Artwork and Illustrations by Emily Dennis
Back Cover Photograph by Steve Williams

Author's Note

This book is a work of fiction based on actual cases. Most of the names, identifying characteristics, and places in this collection of short stories of people and animals have been changed.

However, the veterinary hospital, Somerset Veterinary Group, in Somerville, New Jersey, exists. Dr. Richard Coburn, the late Dr. Arthur North, Margot Roebling and John DeHope are also factual.

The stories represent my recall of events aided by extensive notes of what I felt were unusual cases. A liberal sprinkling of fiction has also been added. Any resemblance to actual persons, living or dead is entirely coincidental.

... To the memory of my mentor,
Dr. Arthur North

... To Tina, my wife, and my son, Edward
without their encouragement the
stories would not have been told

... To Terri and Michelle, my daughters
who lived the stories and
later assisted in our office

... To my grandchildren,
Desiree, Emily, Zachary, Kestrel and Aziza
so that they can have some understanding
of what their grandparents did a long time ago

Out of the Earth
I sing for Them
a Horse Nation
I sing for Them

Out of the Earth
I sing for Them
the Animals
I sing for Them

~ *Teton-Sioux*

Contents

The Author - 2013

The Author - 1968... The story begins...

Prologue ~ The Question

Every story has a beginning...

"Hey dad, have you ever treated a turtle with a cracked shell?"

I was sitting on a wooden stool in front of a computer screen in the small library in Black Mountain, North Carolina. I smiled when I saw the e-mail from my son, Ed. Even though I had been retired from my veterinary practice for several years now, there was no hesitation with the reply.

Most of my patients, especially the unusual ones, have become permanently deposited somewhere in the recesses and convoluted folds of my cerebrum. A simple question like this brings that distant memory right back to life as if it were only yesterday. Such is the nature of veterinary medicine. The unique triangular relationship of owner, pet and veterinarian produces many stories.

Animal Doctor Joins Infirmary

BRIDGEWATER—Dr. Edward R. Dionne, formerly of Arlington, Mass., has joined the staff of the Somerset Veterinary Infirmary, Route 22.

Dr. Dionne began working

DR. EDWARD R. DIONNE

with animals as a veterinary nurse in the Angell Memorial Hospital for Animals in Boston.

After completing his three years of undergraduate studies at Penn State he enrolled at the Veterinary College at the University of Pennsylvania from which he was graduated cum laude in May.

1

Eggbert the Turtle

I like turtles because they're so chill.
They don't hurt anyone. They're just like,
"Hey man, I want to swim, and maybe eat
some lettuce..."

Unknown

Strolling into the office after lunch I needed to pick up my afternoon appointment schedule. A cloud of cigarette smoke rushed toward the opened door hoping to somehow escape into the stratosphere. Having encountered this pungent smoke ball on numerous other occasions, I remained unperturbed. In 1968, smoking in the workplace was quite common, especially in our veterinary office.

The source of this carcinogenic brew was emanating from our intrepid office staff, Rosalee, Doris and Mike. Sitting at their desks, the trio were busily preparing and bracing themselves for the hectic afternoon. Over the next five hours, a steady stream of clients and pets would flow through our doors.

Rosalee was in charge of greeting and directing clients to the proper exam room. Today, like most afternoons, there would be three veterinarians and their patients to manage. A wall with an open window separated Rosalee from the masses. Sticking her head out the window, Rosalee, with the aid of her oversized, tortoise-shell spectacles, had the uncanny ability to recall clients' names and faces after only one visit. The returning clients loved the recognition.

"How are you today, Mrs. Fritzinger? Doctor Dionne will see Mittens shortly."

Having reached the age of senior citizenship, Rosalee, a widow, could have easily retired to a quiet life. Instead, she opted for the action and stress of a veterinary receptionist. Her usual immaculate attire was not complete without an assortment of rings, bracelets and necklaces. Fixed neatly in some sort of bob or French twist, her blond hair revealed extensive streaks of gray. One or two pencils were always nestled into the once golden locks for rapid deployment.

In addition, the ever lively hours of 2-7 p.m., brought further hordes of clients to pick up (or drop off) their pets for boarding, surgery or other medical problems. The comings and goings, ins-and-outs of cats and dogs, kittens and puppies, and other assorted critters--all attached to family members--could have been handled with a certain efficiency if it were not for one item.....the *telephone!* Mr. Bell's invention contained three very active lines into the hospital. The small, square, plastic buttons, attached to the base of the telephone were always in a state of frenetic flashing. As a result of the incessant ringing, the stress levels of the office staff were elevated to where an artery or two might blow at any moment.

Even with a valiant effort, Rosalee would soon become overwhelmed and strands of hair would sneak out of the once tidy bob and point aimlessly hither and yon. The previously nestled pencils would randomly disappear into a sea of patient records, reminders, call backs and notes now strewn about her desk.

The unraveling of the pencil-less hair, was Doris's cue to rescue Rosalee before heart palpitations set in. Doris, the mother of two high school-aged children, was in charge of the daily bookkeeping and receipts. Whatever the chaos, she, at least outwardly, remained unruffled and congenial. Doris was the type of person who just begged to be teased incessantly by a young veterinarian like myself. Her desk was often the home to a variety of tasty treats; my eyes were conditioned to quickly scan the desktop for a lonesome cupcake, cookie or lost piece of candy. It was rather simple for me to abscond with one or two delectable samples.

For more than twenty years, Mike, our office and hospital manager, had seen the hospital grow from a small one man veterinary practice to the present five veterinarians on staff. Using a no nonsense approach, he kept everyone in line which included the three full-time and four part-time kennel help, plus the surgery and laboratory technicians. Mike delicately handled the various whims, fancies and personalities of each veterinarian.

It was no wonder that he was starting to lose his hair. His once jet black hair, now gray at the temples, was combed straight back across the top of his head. Sitting at a desk in dress slacks, brown loafers and dress shirt opened at the collar with no tie, he was able to direct and orchestrate the ebb and flow of each day. A pack of his favorite Marlboro cigarettes was safely stashed in his shirt pocket. The essential cup of coffee on his desk was always within easy reach.

The daily routine tended to make Mike somewhat portly around the middle. Speaking softly and calmly to clients on the phone, he deftly answered their questions and concerns. On the other hand, if a kennel boy made a blunder, he could quickly change to a stern and vociferous taskmaster. However, showing a soft and patient side, Mike was a great help to me personally during this critical first year out of veterinary school and still wet behind the ears so to speak.

Loitering in the office smog, I teased Doris while glancing through my list of appointments. On the surface it looked like a fairly routine afternoon: rabies vaccination, new puppy checkup, cat with diarrhea, booster shot, injured turtle, itching dog...... *Wait a minute, did I just read injured turtle?*

Yes!

There it is, injured turtle, my 4:15 p.m. appointment with Mrs. Terrapin – a new account.

Looking up, I said, "Hey Mike, what's with the injured turtle? I don't know anything about turtles!" I was hoping that he would then switch the turtle case to one of the other veterinarians.

No such luck.

Instead Mike said, "Don't worry Doc, no one else knows anything about turtles either. You'll do just fine."

Making one last plea, I asked, "Mike, are you talking about Doris's chocolate covered turtles?"

Politely turning and lifting his head slightly, he wafted a plume of smoke toward the ceiling. Standing up from his desk chair, the 200 lb., five-foot-eight-inch office manager turned and pointed to the door.

"Doc, get out of here," Mike ordered, as small puffs of smoke continued to sneak out of each nostril.

Obeying orders and feeling like a crumpled cigarette butt, I left the office, wondering what kind of an injury could a turtle have? Maybe he was run over by an automobile or just sprained his ankle while out jogging. Nervously checking my watch, I had fifteen minutes to my first afternoon appointment. Racing up the stairs to our second floor, two bedroom apartment above the veterinary hospital, I tried to recall where my school notes were on our only lecture on amphibians and reptiles. Seven years of college and I knew next to nothing about turtles.

Looking up from feeding our one-year-old son, my surprised wife, Tina, smiled to see me back so soon. Sitting down on the floor in front of the bookcase filled with my veterinary books, I frantically started rifling through my notebooks looking for the amphibian and reptile lecture.

"Looking for something, honey?" my grinning wife asked.

"Yes, do you know anything about turtles?" I asked.

"Hmm... They're slow," answered my non-helpful wife.

Having now finished his lunch, my son,Eddie, waddled over to help in the hunt. "Da, da," he squealed.

I instinctively patted him on the head and told

him, "Good boy, sit, stay!" The well-trained toddler sat and began to shuffle through the scattered notebooks.

Time was flying swiftly along, and it was now less than five minutes to the start of afternoon appointments. Just before giving up the search, good fortune smiled, and there was the elusive lecture. Quickly scanning for the turtle section, I found the following:

Turtles: 1. Disease- Salmonellosis- a bacterial disease found in pet turtles, contagious to man

2. Cracked shells- repair with glue

"That's all I have?" I muttered as a tight knot started to form in my stomach. "Great, not enough time to check the library either."

"Ed, did you say something to me?"

"No, dear."

I then turned my attention to my son who was happily tearing pages out of various notebooks.

"Tina! Come get Eddie, he's eating my notes on ferrets," I cried.

Armed with my impressive turtle knowledge, I raced out of the apartment, down the steps and through the kennel to the exam room. I checked my appearance before entering the room. Our doctors' uniforms were similar to what the attendants wear in an insane asylum-- white pants and matching white shirt top with snaps at the collar. One front pocket held my stethoscope and the other held a pair of bandage scissors, suture removal scissors, forceps and one or two stolen goodies from Doris.

The medical profession had not yet learned how *chic* it was to drape the stethoscope over one's neck signifying stature and importance to the non-stethoscope wearing public.

My afternoon appointments were moving along fairly smoothly, but each one brought me that much closer to the dreaded 4:15 p.m. appointment. Intensifying with apparent glee, the knot in my stomach signaled me that it was almost *show time*.

My assistant, Ann, finally spoke up and asked, "Dr. Dionne, why are you so quiet today? Is everything okay?" I confessed that I was worrying about my upcoming turtle appointment.

"You'll do just fine," she confidently exclaimed.

Isn't that what Mike said? I thought.

Meanwhile, Mrs. Terrapin and her family were waiting in their automobile to cross the highway. Located in the heart of central New Jersey, Somerset Veterinary Group is a two story, ivy covered, brick building which overlooks the very busy Route 22. This four lane highway, separated in the middle by a grassy median was the main thoroughfare for trucks and cars going west to Pennsylvania or east to New York City.

Our veterinary hospital faced the eastbound lane. Mrs. Terrapin, traveling to the hospital on the westbound lane, had to make a u-turn and cross the median island. Exhibiting great bravery, she revved her automobile's engine and raced in front of the endless stream of oncoming traffic. Propelling her family and pets into the parking lot, it was time for the Terrapins to see the animal doctor.

After the necessary new patient forms were filled out, Ann directed the Terrapin family to Exam Room 2. Still running on schedule, it was now 4:15 p.m.-- *turtle time*. Trying my best to look confident and filled with turtle expertise, I entered the exam room. There in the middle of the exam table stood Eggbert having a casual look around the room. Eggbert appeared to be staring at my diploma hanging somewhat crookedly on the far wall.

Mrs. Terrapin and her two young kids flanked the table to keep Eggbert from tumbling off. Coming along for a rabies shot, Maxwell, a large golden retriever with long blond hair, was amusing himself by sniffing every inch of the room.

First clearing my dry throat, I announced, “Hello, I’m Dr. Dionne, and I assume this is the injured Eggbert.” Venturing a guess, I also uttered, “He looks like a nice box turtle.”

The youngest Terrapin, a six-year-old, freckled-face pixie with long red pigtails informed me, “Eggbert is not a box turtle. He’s a red-eared slider!” (All hopes of pretending to be a renowned turtle veterinarian were effectively dashed by a six year old.)

Trying to make light of the situation, I replied, “Excuse me, I stand corrected, but isn’t the *Red-eared Sliders* the name of the Russian bobsled team?”

There were blank stares and no smiles on the faces of the Terrapin family. I could only assume that this crew must either be in shock or have some humor deficiency problem, and I would have to be more serious.

Making matters even worse, Maxwell now turned his attention to the embarrassed veterinarian. He started his exploration at my shoes which were annointed with a cornucopia of old blood, urine and poop smells from a wide variety of beasts. Maxwell had found *smell* heaven, but soon tiring, moved up to check out Dr. Dionne’s private parts. Trying to stay calm and focused, in spite of the pesky Maxwell’s sniffing and probings, I leaned over the table.

Looking down at Eggbert, I could not help but notice the good-sized dent in the top of his shell. Pretending to ignore Maxwell was becoming exceedingly more difficult, since his nose was now lodged halfway up my backside. Carrying on with the exam, however, I carefully picked him up for a closer look. Eggbert hastily retreated into the safety of his damaged home. Turning him over to inspect his underside revealed a long crack running the length of his shell.

"How did this happen?" I asked.

The Terrapin family all turned and looked at the guilty party-- Maxwell. Mrs. Terrapin then admonished her pet for probably the hundredth time, "Maxwell is a bad, bad boy."

The heartbroken dog put his tail between his legs and skulked over to the corner of the room and laid down with a sigh. A slight smile appeared on my face; I now knew that there would be no more *sniffings and probings* from the inquisitive canine.

I reviewed my brief lecture notes in my head-- *cracked shell-- glue*. And I explained to the Terrapins my game plan for fixing their pet turtle. Eggbert was listening carefully inside his shell, and if he heard any mention of *turtle soup*, he was going to make a run for it. Mrs. Terrapin left their turtle in my care. Carrying Eggbert in his box, I stopped for a moment so Ann could take a look.

"Oh, what a cute red-eared slider!" she exclaimed.

"Huh, how did you know that?" I inquired.

"I've had several pet turtles," she admitted.

"Now you tell me," I said with a smile.

"Please ask Dr. Coburn to see the rest of my patients until I get back."

Smiling back, she replied, "I already have."

I proceeded straight to the surgery room on the second floor. Sandy, our surgery technician, was busily cleaning and sterilizing instruments from this morning's surgery. Opening the door and quickly asking, "Hi, doing anything right now?"

She turned, looked in the box, and asked, "What's up, Dr. Dionne?"

"Sandy, meet Eggbert, he has a cracked shell that we are going to fix, hopefully." The young assistant, still in her twenties, was taking courses and studying to become a certified animal technician. Every case was of interest to her and this was no exception. Pulling back her long brown hair, she peered down on the turtle.

"Don't worry, Eggbert. Dr. Dionne will fix you up."

Why do I keep hearing such optimism? I asked myself.

Placing Eggbert on the surgery table, I turned on the bright overhead surgery lights to illuminate Eggbert's cracked shell. Sandy quickly placed forceps, hemostats and some dental instruments on the surgery tray.

Very carefully, I started to lift the broken shell fragments back into place. Sandy kept a hand on Eggbert to keep him from moving. Halfway through the procedure, Eggbert stuck his head out and gave me a look like, *How's it going, Doc?*

"Did you ever hear of Humpty-Dumpty and all the king's men and horses?" I mumbled.

Eggbert retreated back into his shell of a home

and prayed to all the turtle gods. Finally after thirty minutes of fumbling and lifting shell fragments back into place, the first phase was complete. The next step was to glue the broken pieces together. Mixing tube A with tube B, I prepared the epoxy adhesive which is similar to today's superglue. I squirted a thin layer on all of his many cracks. I was being very careful not to touch the glue, or else Eggbert and I would be stuck and going home together. I imagined the comments, *Hey buddy, is that a turtle on the end of your finger?*

The three of us breathed a sigh of relief when it was over. Placing Eggbert in a box, I kept him overnight in the hospital while the glue hardened. The next day, his shell was solid and good as new.

Taking a few moments to study and observe Eggbert, I couldn't help but notice that he was quite a handsome fellow. His head was a bright mixture of green, yellow and black colors arranged in wiggly, thin, horizontal stripes running from his nose down along his neck and disappearing underneath his shell. His legs were similarly marked.

There were two oval, bright red spots on each side of his head. His eyes were round with a horizontal black band crossing the yellow iris. In the center of the black band was a small round black pupil. The top part of the shell was decorated with swirls of yellow and green in no particular pattern as if the artist was having fun just dabbing colors here and there. The bottom or lower shell was arranged in several uneven yellow rectangles with distinct black borders.

Eggbert was a visual delight. The smiling Terrapin family, including Maxwell, arrived at the hospital and picked up their superglued Eggbert.

Happy to finally be out of the dog house, Maxwell, wagging his tail and barking excitedly, poked his head in the box and greeted his playmate.

I stood there like a proud father and expected big things from Eggbert with his new aerodynamic shell. The *Turtle Olympics* were certainly not out of the question. I daydreamed of him blazing across the finish line in the 50 ft. dash breaking the Olympic record by an astounding twelve minutes. Or maybe in the swimming events; Eggbert was a natural back-stroker. I am also sure he could crush his competitors in the 25 yd. turtlefly. Disney would probably then want to make a movie of his life, and I would guest star glueing his shell back together. Then, it would be on to action movies such as *Super Turtle*.

But sadly the dream ended; I never did see Eggbert or Maxwell again because the Terrapin family moved out of the area. I did receive a Christmas card from them and enclosed was a picture of Eggbert and Maxwell dressed in their best holiday outfits lying beside the decorated tree. Maxwell wore a green bow on his collar, and Eggbert wore a festive red bow on top of his good-as-new shell. A short note in the card read:

Merry Christmas, Dr. Dionne

Love,
Eggbert

PS: I tell your joke about the red-eared sliders to all my turtle friends. It cracks them up!

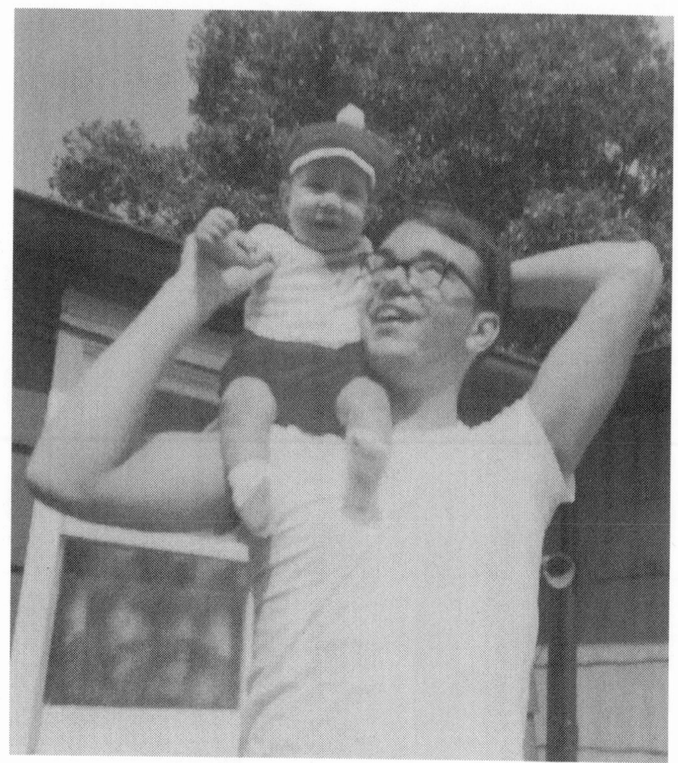

The Author with son, Eddie

2

Salty

Live in such a way that you would not be ashamed to sell your parrot to the town gossip.

Will Rogers

After the resounding success of my first turtle shell repair, the office staff of Mike, Doris and Rosalee felt that I would be the perfect vet on our staff to handle the appointments involving *unusual* animals, like turtles, as well as birds. Being that I was the new graduate with not a lick of experience did not bother the staff one bit.

My protests were met with the usual reply. "Doc, you'll do just fine."

Their decision made it possible for me to meet Salty, resulting in a case so bizarre that I was never to have another quite like it.

Taking care of the occasional parakeet was

not as bad as I had expected; it became a refreshing break in the seemingly endless stream of dogs and cats. Then came my first parrot case. One afternoon my appointment sheet read: *2:30 p.m. N/A (new account)-- Lucy Silver-- Salty (parrot)-- sick.* Questioning Rosalee, the appointment secretary, as to the nature of the parrot's illness was not at all helpful.

"Dr. Dionne, Mrs. Silver wouldn't say specifically; all she kept saying over and over was that Salty was a sick, sick bird!"

"Okay, Rosalee, I know you tried," I replied with obvious disappointment. This was my first parrot case, and I was hoping to have some clue as to the nature of the problem. It would have been nice to be able to fret about the parrot's illness, and worry about how to treat it prior to the actual exam.

Oh well, I'll just play it by ear, I thought.

Entering Exam Room 3 at exactly 2:30 p.m., there was the sick Salty, a large and magnificent looking Amazon parrot. He was sitting in the middle of the exam table in his worn and battered traveling cage. Paying no attention to me, Salty was busy climbing the side of the cage pulling himself up with his strong claws and beak.

The colors of his feathers were a bright green with accents of blue on his head and wings. Yellow feathers decorated his face in a colorful swirl that swept below each eye and down onto his neck. His green tail was long and broad with a few blue feathers here and there in no particular pattern. Salty appeared to shine and radiate as the sunlight streamed through the office window and reflected off his body.

His bill looked very strong and powerful which is needed for opening up seeds, nuts and fruit.

Parrots and their parakeet cousins are found in numerous flocks in the rain forests of Central and South America. I wondered if Salty was captured or bred and raised by professional breeders.

On first glance, I was not able to pinpoint any obvious illness. Salty had now reached the top of his cage and appeared to be quite content hanging upside down. Mrs. Lucy Silver was the one who did not look well. Standing in the far corner of the exam room, she was wringing her hands and mumbling something that was not audible enough to be understood.

I guessed her age to be in the neighborhood of seventy years or so. Lucy was rather short in stature, about five foot nothing and closing in on 100 lbs. with her shoes on. Her short once gray hair was now molting into a blue-white color, but still had an impressive array of curls circling her head like a crown. She wore a pair of wire-rimmed bifocals, a green cotton skirt, a white blouse with a large green and red parrot emblazoned on the front and a pair of black penny loafers.

She looked like my grandmother!

After introducing myself, came the usual introductory remark. "How are you today, Mrs. Silver?"

"Very worried, doctor."

No kidding, I thought. Trying to ease her discomfort, I started with a few questions.

"Salty is a handsome Amazon. How long have you had him?"

"Six months," came the reply.

"Oh, how old is he?"

"Salty is about 45 or 46 yrs. old," answered the still nervous, hand-wringing Mrs. Silver.

"Wow! Gee, he doesn't look a day over thirty-five," I replied like an idiot.

There was no smile or laughter from Mrs. Silver in response to my joke. Some parrots can live a longtime in captivity, 50-60 yrs. and even longer. There are a few reports of parrots having reached the century mark.

Despite my best efforts, the tension in the air was still palpable.

Continuing on with the history part of the exam, I asked, "If you had him for six months, where did he live before? Who had him?"

Lucy went on to explain. "My older brother Frank died, and left Salty to me because I had agreed to take care of him. Salty has lived in Nome, Alaska, almost his entire life. Frank ventured out to Nome in 1908 during the big gold rush and opened up a saloon. A few years later, he won Salty in a poker game." The story was becoming fascinating, and the tension was easing a bit.

"Please continue, Mrs. Silver, this is very interesting."

"Frank kept Salty in the saloon because it was good for business. The miners would come in to see Salty and drink, of course. Those nasty miners would get drunk and teach Salty some *very bad* words. As a reward, they would give Salty sips of beer for saying those awful words. After a few sips too many, he would fall right off his perch. *Drunk!* And this made them laugh all the more. Poor Salty."

I turned and looked at the very healthy looking Salty who was now eating some pumpkin seeds. "Do you still swear, Salty?" I kidded.

"Awk, go to hell," came the reply. And, Salty spoke very clearly, quite loud and with impeccable diction.

Somewhat stunned and at a loss for words, I mistakenly told Salty, "That wasn't a very nice thing to say."

Salty countered my reprimand with "Awk," followed by the mother of all swear words. Speechless, I turned to Mrs. Silver who now had her ears covered with her hands. She was mortified; so I helped her to sit down in the lone exam room chair to *un-mortify*.

Realizing that there would be no further conversation with Mr. Salty, I gave Mrs. Silver a few moments to compose herself. Meanwhile, I now realized what she meant by a *sick, sick bird.*

From across the room, still slumped in her chair, Lucy calmly and quietly asked, "Dr. Dionne, please help me stop the swearing. Last week, it was my turn to have the bridge club at our house. Salty must have thought that he was back in the saloon in Nome. He started saying many, many bad words; so I put him in the hall closet. But, even in there we could still hear him squawking. He made a terrible mess and racket. It was so disturbing that all the *girls* left early."

Tears were now welling up in her eyes. "My husband, John, wants to open the window and let him fly away. What can I do?"

At this point my eyes were also getting misty.

The curious Salty had returned to his perch. Cocking his head back and forth, he appeared to be listening intently to Lucy's sad tale. Thinking for a moment, I tried to come up with a solution for *old foul mouth.*

Two ideas came to mind. First, wash his beak out with soap; an idea which I quickly scratched. It didn't work when my parents tried that one on me when I was a kid. So chances were mighty slim it would work on Salty.

Plan two seemed more reasonable, call a veterinary school and speak with a bird specialist for a second opinion.

"Mrs. Silver, I'm sure that there must be something we can do to help Salty," I half-heartedly assured her. I explained plan two and promised to call her in a day or two. Mrs. Silver smiled and said thank you and good-bye.

Lucy had a ray of hope as she carried her cage out to the waiting room, stopping at the reception window to pay her bill.

Rosalee pleasantly said, "Good-bye and have a nice day, Salty."

Salty, of course, told Rosalee and the rest of the crowded waiting room what he thought of her nice day using another colorful swear word from his extensive Alaskan saloon vocabulary. Fortunately, Doris had smelling salts in her desk, as we all did, and was able to revive Rosalee after a few whiffs.

The next day, I called Dr. Macaw at Cornell University and explained the situation. He laughed and was of no help. After two restless nights' sleep, I had a brainstorm. Parrots and parakeets are often taught to speak and learn words with records. So maybe by using records continuously, we could override what he had learned in Nome with a new vocabulary. It was worth a shot.

I called Mrs. Silver and explained the plan. I wanted to use some upbeat, popular music with lots of singing. I chose the Beatles because they were the most popular group at this time.

Lucy was skeptical, but said, "Doctor, I'm willing to try just about anything for Salty. I'll get the records right away."

* * *

Three months had past, and I had not heard a word from Lucy. Being curious as to how the experiment was going I called to find out.

The phone rang and it wasn't long before John Silver, her husband, answered. "Good morning,"exclaimed a very happy John.

"This is Dr. Dionne. I'm calling to see how Salty is doing." I could hear *A Hard Day's Night* blasting away in the background.

"Well Doc, Salty is right here on my shoulder and he's doing great! Want to say hello?"

"Sure," I said, hoping there would not be a relapse. John held the phone up to Salty's head. With a little trepidation I asked, "Hi Salty, this is Dr. Dionne, remember me?"

This was the first time I ever conversed with a *bird* on the phone. I braced myself for the response.

"Awk, Salty loves you, awk, awk, awk." He sang somewhat off-key, but it was heavenly music to my ears.

A laughing John got back on the phone and asked, "How did you like that, Dr. Dionne?"

"Amazing! And how is Mrs. Silver?" I asked.

"Lucy is just sky high with joy. I even bought her a new set of diamonds. Let me get her, Doc."

Lucy picked up the phone and thanked me profusely. She was no longer the nervous, hand-wringing grandma that I first met in the office.

Lucy went on to say, "Salty has been a perfect gentleman, no swearing for three months! I've bought all the Beatles records and have joined the New Jersey Beatles Fan Club. Salty is an honorary member as well."

After a few more minutes of conversation and one more thank you, we said good-bye.

I spent the next couple of weeks humming Salty's version of various Beatles' tunes, especially *She Loves You*—his favorite.

Raise the Jolly Rodger, Salty was cured!

* * *

PS: If you are ever in Bound Brook, New Jersey, drive down Maple Street. You may still be able to see the life-sized cutouts of the Beatles on Lucy's lawn.

In the past, visitors would often take souvenir photographs of John, Paul, George, Ringo, and the fifth Beatle, dancing on his keyboard, wearing his custom-made Nehru jacket, with a few green feathers combed down over his eyes.

Awk, Awk, Awk...

3

Siamese Twins

Dogs have owners, cats have staff.
Anonymous

My first weekend on emergency duty resulted in a secret that I kept for several years. It had to do with both *magic and mystery*. I refer to it as the curious case of the Siamese Twins. Let me explain.

Being fresh out of veterinary school, I was being coddled and groomed by my first employer, Somerset Veterinary Group. I was like a newborn baby chick with several attentive mother hens. The majority of my office appointments consisted of vaccinations, physical exams, and suture removals. In other words, all the easiest office calls were given to this baby chick. The same held true in surgery. I gained valuable and much needed experience doing cat and puppy spays, neuterings and declaws. Help, if needed, was always close at hand.

After four weeks of employment without any major *faux pas* on my part, the honeymoon was apparently over. The unexpected note in my office mailbox was very brief.

It read, *Dr. D, I have put you on emergency duty this weekend.*

Mike, our office manager and author of the note, had the authority to make such proclamations. I read the note a second time while panic settled in and upset various bodily organs.

I muttered to myself, "Mike can't do this to me; I'm not ready for emergency call all by myself!" No back-up, or mother hens to rescue me, my agitated mind felt that a major disaster was looming.

With note in hand, I charged into the office to plead my case. Mike was sitting at his desk enjoying his morning cup of coffee and the first of many cigarettes. He heard the office door swing open with a thud and the patter of anxious feet. Before I could vocalize my first syllable of protest, Mike quickly raised his hand signaling me to halt.

"Oh yes you are Doc."

"But..."

"And furthermore, Dr. D, you are ready."

"But..."

Doris and Rosalee, our two secretaries, pretended to be busy doing paperwork, but all the while listened intently with great amusement to our very one-sided conversation.

Mike continued, "I also have a little extra job for you this weekend. On Sunday, Miss Davida Copperfield and her sister, Agatha, will be picking up their cat, Houdini. So please make sure he is ready to go home by 12:30 p.m."

"But..."

Mike re-raised his hand signaling me to stop again. "Doc, do you know who Miss Copperfield is?"

"No."

Mike knew we had a few thousand clients, and I had only been here a month. He proceeded with much pleasure to illuminate his new young vet.

"Davida Copperfield is a wealthy, English heiress from Far Hills who also happens to be very close friends with Dr. North, your boss. So we bend the rules a tad about releasing boarding animals on Sunday."

I was now illuminated.

Rosalee, with an obvious smirk, chimed in, "Dr. Dionne, your first appointment is here. They are waiting in Exam Room 3."

Mike returned to his paperwork and half-smoked cigarette. I stood there momentarily and realized that any further whining would fall on deaf ears. I turned slowly and left the office, closing the door quietly; a trail of muffled laughter followed me out.

Speaking aloud to myself, "I really have to work on my communication skills. Three buts and one no are not very persuasive." But, I had good reason to be nervous.

Emergency duty commenced on Friday at 7 p.m. at the conclusion of our office appointments and finished at 8 a.m. on Monday morning when the office re-opened. Many of the surrounding veterinary clinics happily closed up for weekends and holidays. Their clients were referred to us if they had an emergency.

Our hospital, Somerset Veterinary Group, was located in Somerville, N.J., but our clients and emergency referrals came from many towns like Bridgewater, Raritan, Bound Brook, Manville, Martinsville, Plainfield, Bedminster, Far Hills, Clinton, Whitehouse and so on.....

At least my little extra chore of releasing Houdini Copperfield on Sunday didn't seem like much of a task; little did I realize how wrong I could be.

As it turned out my first emergency weekend was not as stressful as I had anticipated. All the hospital cases were doing exceptionally well. As expected, I had an assortment of emergency office calls to keep me busy-- two HBC's (hit by car), the first of which was Rex, a one-year-old German shepherd. The untrained Rex decided to bolt out the kitchen door to visit a lovely Irish setter lass who lived just across the street.

Unfortunately, love is often blind and so was Rex. He raced in front of a station wagon filled with mom and several kids. Chaos ensued. Rex was rushed to our hospital with several cuts, bruises, and a fractured femur. He would survive, but surgery with a pinning would be needed to repair his leg. The other HBC was a nameless, possibly homeless cat, "Tom Doe", that arrived DOA (dead on arrival).

I also had two minor surgeries, a cut foot pad on an Airedale terrier and a nasty bite wound on Mimi, a miniature poodle. The twenty pound Mimi tried to boss around a much larger Rottweiler and got bit in the butt for her trouble. She went home rather sleepy from the anesthesia with her pink bows on her ears and a new matching set of six stitches in her *derriere*.

I also had an inquisitive puppy with a fishhook in his lip. Fishhooks are not an uncommon problem in both dogs and cats. Under sedation, the hook has to be pushed through the lip, or whatever body part it is stuck in to expose the barb. The barb is then cut with a pair of wire cutters which allows the fishhook to be withdrawn, thus freeing *The Catch of the Day*.

An ear infection and two vomiting and diarrhea cases rounded out my Saturday afternoon. But, there was much more to come.

On Sunday morning, feeling quite proud of myself, I strolled into the treatment room with a stack of patient records. I had three kennel workers to assist me in checking and treating each patient. Dan, the youngest of the trio, was a senior in high school. His plan was to attend college with aspirations of pursuing a career in veterinary medicine. My other kennel boys, Henry and Rocky, had no such lofty aspirations. Lengthy careers as kennel help seemed quite likely.

After finishing ward rounds, while waiting the arrival of the Copperfield sisters, I decided to introduce myself to our star boarder, Houdini. F ward is just for felines, a quiet place away from the more vocal and stir-crazy canines. I was surprised that a blue-blood like Houdini didn't have his own private suite. Instead, he was in F ward with all the other house cats and a few ragamuffins.

Entering the ward, I immediately noticed something was amiss. The door on cage 32, Houdini's home, was slightly ajar. On further inspection, the only inhabitants were the plethora of stuffed animals and assorted playthings left by the Copperfield sisters.

"Holy crap, where's Houdini?" I gasped.

It took only a few seconds for my adrenal glands to pucker up and start to spit out all the stress hormones it could muster. My watch added to the misery.

12:02 p.m. Tick, tick...

I had only twenty-eight minutes to find the missing feline before Davida and Agatha arrived. Gathering the troops, we searched high and low with no luck.

12:12 p.m. Tick, tick...

We expanded the search to the outside dog runs. A sturdy chain link fence surrounded the kennel area. The fencing was further partitioned into numerous individual runs complete with a chain link top to prevent any nimble pooch from climbing over and out.

12:15 p.m. Tick, tick...

No Houdini in the runs.

Trying to remain calm, hopeless as it was, I wondered if he could have escaped by squeezing under the fence. It would have been quite a feat if he had. Rocky and Henry were sent out to scout the grounds while Dan and I re-checked the inside of the hospital and kennel.

12:20 p.m. Tick, tick...

An out-of-breath Rocky reported back, "Doc, I think I found Houdini!"

"Think! What do you mean you think?" I shouted.

On the west side of the hospital was a rather large dense hedge some 8-9 ft. tall. The hedge served as a privacy barrier between the hospital and the home next door. Mike, our hospital manager, lived in this house which happened to be owned by Dr. North, the boss.

Rocky continued to explain, "Well, Dr. Dionne, there are two Siamese cats on Mike's back patio!"

I suddenly remembered that Mike had a Siamese cat, Harry. Mike was still at church so I couldn't have him identify and retrieve his pet. I raced around the rear of the hedge with kennel boys in tow and into Mike's backyard. Sure enough, there were two identical looking Siamese cats sitting calmly on the patio. They were about two feet apart and eyeballing each other.

Siamese cats originated in Siam which today is known as Thailand. The Siamese breed is differentiated by various coloration markings found on the ears, face, paws and tail. A Siamese may be referred to as seal point, chocolate point, blue point or lilac point depending on the shade of their markings. The seal point is by far the most common color.

There are differences in body size as well. The original Siamese has a stouter body conformation with sort of an apple-shaped head. By means of selective breeding, a leaner, finely- boned Siamese has emerged having a head that is more wedge-shaped. Both types have beautiful blue eyes, soft luxurious coats, and a distinctive high-pitched meow that has been likened to a baby's cry.

Harry and Houdini were both the stockier seal point variety and mirror images of each other. But, who was who? I quickly devised *Ed's snowball's chance in hell* plan.

12:24 p.m. Tick, tick...

We would all *sneak* up as quickly as possible

and capture both cats. Then let Davida choose the right Houdini.

The plan might have worked if it wasn't for two things. First, all animals have a flight zone which is an invisible line that once the predator crosses, they promptly head for the hills. I was hoping that this wouldn't happen being that we were not really predators.

Uh huh.

And second, the other main obstacle was that Harry and Houdini had been having their own private conversation which to our untrained ears sounded simply like a meowing contest. I imagined that the conversation went something like this:

So Houdini, you actually broke out of the kennel?

I jolly well did and it wasn't at all easy mate.

Hey man, you talk really funny, replied the perplexed Harry.

That's my English accent. Did you know that I'm an aristo-cat and live in a mansion?

Harry replied with a bit of jealousy, *No, my owners are not at all wealthy. In fact, I even have to pee and do my business outside. I usually dig a hole in the flower garden right over there next to the irises. Last winter it was so cold that I even got frostbite on my butt!*

Heavens, how uncivilized, Harry. I have eight litter boxes that the maid keeps sparkling clean. Sadly though, I never get to go outside.

That's a real bummer, Houdini. There are so many cool things outside. I never get tired of chasing bugs, birds and mice. I bring them all home just to hear everyone scream. It's a hoot.

Being rich has its drawbacks, replied a somewhat dejected Houdini. *As the old saying goes, the catnip is always greener....*

Hey Houdini, not to change the subject, but what are we going to do about those four guys trying to sneak up on us? asked Harry.

Who's the one babbling, here kitty, kitty - nice kitty, kitty?

That's the new vet; he probably won't last long though, bit of a nerd.

Harry and Houdini whispered softly to each other, *Okay, here's the plan.*

Now back to the predators. We observed one cat running toward the back door of the house and the other toward the hospital. I quickly deduced that the Siamese cat that was now going under the hedge had to be Houdini.

12:26 p.m. Tick, tick...

I pointed and authoritatively yelled at the boys, "That's Houdini, don't let him get away!"

The kennel help smartly ran toward the back of the hedge. I, on the other hand, had now reached full panic mode and spotted a narrow four inch break in the hedge row. I then *non-smartly* blasted through this break at considerable expense to my body.

I tumbled onto our hospital driveway landing awkwardly on my right knee resulting in more pain. I also landed with a torn shirt, pants and a host of scratches which decorated my body with an array of crimson tattoos. The largest and deepest wound on my forehead was now bleeding, and a small rivulet of blood was flowing south toward my right eye.

12:27 p.m. Tick, tick...

I lifted my battered body up just in time to

observe two very important events. The first was a long, shiny black limousine pulling into the front of the hospital—the punctual Copperfields.

The second observation was a slinking seal point Siamese scampering down a short flight of stairs to our storeroom under the hospital. The storeroom door was closed so Houdini had reached a dead end.

Lucky me!

I gave chase limping on my injured leg. My adrenal glands were still pumping out the juices but were coming close to meltdown. I jumped down the last two steps further aggravating my tender knee and scooped up Houdini with my right hand, holding his front legs at the elbows. I then securely tucked his body under my right arm and pressed it against my chest.

"Don't try anything funny," I warned the captured Houdini.

In the meantime, Dan let the two elderly sisters into the waiting area as I hobbled up the steps and into the hospital. The Copperfield sisters were anxiously pacing and chatting about their little baby, "Houdie."

Davida and Agatha also looked and dressed like twins with matching pairs of spectacles. They wore identical black dresses with long sleeves, hemlines ending at the ankles, and a very conservative neckline. Their shoes were also black, matching and very out of vogue. Each sister had a necessary shawl draped over the shoulders in case a chilly breeze arose on this 85 degree summer day. An over-sized hat with two long colorful feathers completed their attire.

They looked like excited spectators at the Kentucky Derby.

I, on the other hand, looked like something out of a Stephen King thriller. Davida was shocked to see her "Houdie" held by a limping, bleeding young man with torn clothing.

"Young man, where is the doctor?" Davida demanded.

"I'm the doctor, Miss Copperfield."

"No, I want the *real* doctor!" Davida cried.

"That would still be me," I sheepishly replied.

Davida adjusted her trifocals for a better look. "But, you are a mess!" as she pointed at my torn clothing with a slightly bent arthritic finger.

After apologizing profusely, I explained that my appearance was the result of a heroic rescue of a nest of baby robins that had fallen into a briar patch. The sisters seemed to accept this explanation with nodding approval.

I knew this was an outlandish fib, okay lie. But, there was no way the truth would be revealed on this day. My adrenal glands just couldn't take any more stress.

Houdini was then snatched from my hands, smothered with kisses and hugs, and placed lovingly into his fancy cat carrier for the ride home. After a thank you and a few *Cheerios*, the Copperfield sisters headed for the waiting room door.

Peering out the back window of his fancy carrier, Houdini calmly stared at me with his piercing blue eyes, and said telepathically, *Are you sure you got the right cat, Doc?*

My pupils instantly dilated to saucer size, and my bowels were preparing to bail out into my torn pants. The worrying started anew as the Copperfields drove out of the parking lot.

After visiting the bathroom, I gathered the kennel boys and swore them to secrecy about the *great escape*. We all took a blood oath. I provided the blood.

The following week, I pestered Mike about his cat, Harry.

"How's your cat, Mike?"

"Is Harry eating okay?"

"Acting peculiar?"

Finally, Mike had had enough questions about Harry and threatened to put me on permanent emergency duty if I didn't stop asking about the well-being of his cat.

The week slowly went by and to my relief, no word was heard from the Copperfield sisters about Houdini acting strangely or anything else. This was good *non-news*. Thinking that I had put the matter to rest, I relaxed and didn't toss and turn in bed at night any longer; even the nightmares disappeared.

That was the case, until I was having lunch ten days later in our apartment above the hospital. From our kitchen window, I could see over the hedge to Mike's house. There in the second floor window was a Siamese cat.

Hopefully, Harry.

He was looking at me and smiling like a Cheshire cat. I yelled to Tina, "Quick, look out the window at Houdini's twin." But, faster than you can say abra-cadabra, he just disappeared.

It was magic.

I don't know how Houdini got out of his cage, or how he got out of the hospital and past the enclosed fencing. These are the trade secrets of all the great illusionists. But, I still felt fairly confident that we sent the right “Houdie” home with the *girls*.

In time, all my tattoos healed nicely. I could now walk without a limp. My adrenal glands were recharged. (And best of all-- no more diapers.)

Cheerio, mates.

4

Peyote

Live and let live.

Scottish Proverb

Reflecting back over the years, the following case was the only one like it that I would ever encounter. In fact, I would venture a guess that only a few other veterinarians have had a similar case. It was a Wednesday evening in May of 1969, and my usual day for emergency call. After being in practice for almost one year, I was now used to the daily routine of surgery, ward rounds, office appointments, and emergency call. Being fully aware of my inexperience, I realized that there was still a great deal more to learn about veterinary medicine. And tonight would be one of those memorable evenings where knowledge was gained through experience.

Let me start at the beginning.

Trudging up the stairs after a very hectic day, I was both tired and hungry. Our apartment was on the second floor above the hospital and directly across from our surgery and lab/x-ray rooms. It was 7:30 p.m., and all was quiet for a change.

My very pregnant wife, Tina, was re-heating my dinner, and my one-year-old son, Eddie, was amusing himself in the playpen. After greeting them both, I picked up my son and plopped down on our comfortable blue couch. It was time for a little father-son bonding before night-night.

"So, Eddie, how was your day?" I asked. Since his verbal communication skills were still somewhat limited, here is the translation.

"Dad, I went for a stroller ride, mommy pushed me, and I saw some big trucks and a spider!"

"Gee, that must have been very exciting," I exclaimed.

"Yes, I tried to stand and walk a few times, but I fell down a lot and cried. So mommy picked me up."

"Oh, don't worry Eddie, you will learn to walk pretty soon," I said.

Tina suddenly appeared and handed me Eddie's night-time bottle of soybean formula. I held him while he slurped and chugged it down. Upon finishing the bottle, he grimaced and his face turned a bright red.

"Oh, no!" I cried as he proceeded to let out a tsunami of a poop completely overwhelming his diaper. I knew that this poop was one that only a mom has the necessary skill to clean it all up properly. Tina walked in with dinner, and I quickly handed off my son to the expert.

"Thanks honey. Could you turn on the television before you leave? Channel 5, please." (no remote in those days)

"And what's wrong with you?" she asked holding *Stinky* with one hand.

"My legs are broken," was my grinning answer.

I then settled in with a warm dinner to watch my favorite television programs, *Hawaii Five O* and *Mission Impossible*. After a while, I fell asleep on the comfy couch only to be awakened at 10:30 p.m., by the first and only call of the evening. I hobbled on my *broken legs* and answered the disquieting telephone, (no answering machines either).

It was Angel, my favorite answering service operator. The service screened all our late night calls and was permitted to deflect any non-medical calls to the next day. Practically everything else was put through to the tired vet for medical advice or to be seen in case of an emergency situation.

Angel pleasantly said, "Hi, Dr. Dionne, sorry to bother you, but I think you have to see this one. Mary Cannabis called, her dog got into her tranquilizers and ate them." Angel then gave me the telephone number of the Cannabis family, Mary and Juan.

"Okay Angel, thanks, I'll call her right away," I replied.

Dialing the phone, I mumbled, "Well Ed, you know that this is one you are going to have to see. There goes my good night's sleep."

The phone rang only once and a very excited Mary answered, "Hello. Is this the vet?"

"Yes, this is Dr. Dionne at Somerset Veterinary Group."

"Doctor, our dog got into my tranquilizers and ate them. Should I make him puke?" The excited Mary sounded like she could have used one or two tranquilizers herself.

"How long ago did he eat them?" I inquired.

"Oh, uh.... Maybe two hours ago or so."

"What's he doing now; is he awake?" I wondered to myself, *Why didn't you call sooner?*

"Yes, he's awake, but he's acting all weird and stuff."

I quickly interrupted, "Okay, Mrs. Cannabis, you need to bring him in right away, and bring the empty bottle of tranquilizers with you."

I needed to check both the strength and the name of the tranquilizer. Relying on the owner to remember is risky; you may only learn that it is a red and yellow capsule.

Mary replied, "Okay, cool, but we can't pay you until next week when Juan gets his unemployment check."

"Don't worry about that, just bring him in now," I interjected.

This sure didn't sound like any overdose of tranquilizers or sedatives that I was familiar with. Still in my work clothes and putting my shoes on, I told Tina not to wait up for me.

* * *

I re-trudged back down the stairs and as usual, waited in Exam Room 1 with the lights turned off until the clients arrived. This room was a quiet, peaceful refuge, and I stared out at the late night traffic still whizzing by on the highway. This was my thinking time, and my thoughts were directed at what this case might actually be. Certainly, it had the earmarks of something *unusual.*

Fifteen minutes later, a well-used, bruised and dented VW Bus came roaring into the parking lot. As the headlights illuminated the room, I rose on my now healed legs, turned the lights on, and unlocked the door. Mary, holding her dog securely in a blanket, and Juan rushed into the office.

Introducing myself again, I had them put their wide-awake pet on the exam table. Being a new account, the essentials of name, address and telephone number were needed to start a record.

Both Mary and Juan were very young, as I had already guessed, maybe in their early twenties. Mary was quite attractive with long blond hair hanging down to below her waist. Her eyes were a bright blue and seemed to sparkle when she smiled. She was of average height, maybe five foot six inches, and slim of build. The lack of makeup or lipstick seemed to enhance her fresh youthful appearance. A pair of necklaces hung from her slim neck. One necklace was made of cowrie shells, and the other was gold with the word *LOVE* attached at the bottom. She wore a simple white ruffled blouse with a long, loose fitting, red skirt extending down to her ankles. Wearing no shoes, her small bare feet peeked out from beneath the skirt.

Juan was much taller, about my height, six feet, and maybe 180 lbs. His eyes were a dark brown, and his long, jet black hair was pulled back into a pony tail. A pair of sunglasses was perched atop his head, which I hoped were not for any night-time driving. Juan wore a multicolored tie-dyed tee-shirt covered by a large, thick silver necklace with a two inch *Peace Symbol* medallion attached and hanging at about mid-chest level. Wearing a pair of tattered blue jeans, Juan, like Mary, was barefoot.

They were what I would call *Beatniks*. But now in 1969, the new more fashionable term was *Hippies*, whatever that meant.

Turning my attention to the patient, I asked Mary what her dog's name was.

She replied, "Peyote."

I thought that's an unusual name. I couldn't remember any other dog or cat with the same name as his.

Peyote was a relatively small dog about twenty-five pounds with short hair and three color markings. He was mostly brown with black, drooping ears and splashes of white decorating the front of his chest and abdomen. His tail was also black with a pronounced white tip. Peyote's paws and *stockings* were black except for one, the right rear paw was all white. Some people would refer to him as a *mutt*, but I preferred *All-American*. He was a blend of many breeds, mostly some type of terrier.

* * *

Mary held Peyote lightly by the collar as he stood on the exam table during my initial questions. He appeared to be very interested in something on the ceiling. Without moving, he just stared upward, so much so, that I also took a peek at the ceiling as well. My eyes didn't spot anything unusual.

I proceeded to examine Peyote and found his eyes to be glassy with markedly dilated pupils. His heart rate seemed faster than I expected and his temperature was 101.5 degrees, which is normal for the dog and cat. No other problems were apparent on the rest of the physical exam.

Wanting to see him walk, I asked Mary to put Peyote on the floor. He walked quite well, right over to the waste basket and stared into it.

Asking Mary for the bottle of tranquilizers, Juan chimed in, “Hey man, we left in such a hurry that I forgot the bottle.”

Trying to be stern, I said, “Listen guys, let’s cut the charade. What’s going on here? Peyote is not sedated or tranquilized. I need to know what he ingested so that we can help him.”

The guilty Mary and Juan looked at each other for a brief moment. “Oh Juan, just tell him!” said the upset Mary.

“Man, if we tell you, are you going to call the fuzz?” asked the non-eloquent Juan.

“No, that’s not my job. Plus, we have doctor-patient confidentiality.”

Actually, I didn’t know if this applied to animals or not, but it sounded good.

“Cool, see Mary made some brownies, and I dropped some acid into them,” confessed Juan.

“Do you mean, LSD?” replied the totally square vet.

“Right on, dude. It’s best to put the acid in right after baking while the brownies are still warm,” replied *chef* Juan.

Thinking to myself, *Oh, thanks for the information, I’ll be sure to mention it to Tina.*

Juan continued on, “I tossed a brownie square to Mary, but she dropped it, and Peyote got it instead. Man, he just scarfed it down.”

So the truth finally came out, and I likewise

confessed that I didn't know what the treatment for LSD (aka *Acid*) ingestion was. I felt it would be best to hospitalize Peyote, and I would contact the Somerville Hospital to see how they treated their two-legged patients.

"Far out," replied Mary and Juan almost simultaneously.

I then stated, "So I'll call you tomorrow morning to let you know how Peyote is doing."

"Hey, Doc, could you make it after 11 a.m.?" asked the unemployed one. "We usually sleep late. I need my zzz's," said Juan.

After whacking Juan on the arm, Mary said, "No, call anytime!"

I now suspected that Juan may have also had a few nibbles of Mary's brownies as well.

Holding Peyote in my arms, we watched Mary and Juan leave. I couldn't help notice all the colorful artwork on the VW Bus, plus the numerous bumper stickers proclaiming: *Peace Now, Get Out of Vietnam, Legalize Weed, Make Love not War and Burn your Draft Card.*

Waving a good-bye, Mary flashed the two-fingered peace sign out the front window. After a few tries, Juan finally got the Bus started, and they drove out of the parking lot.

* * *

Looking at the stoned Peyote, I said, "Well, it's just you and me, buddy."

Totally groovy, Doc, answered Peyote telepathically.

"I'm going to find you a nice cage with a thick blanket and a bowl of water. How's that?" I asked.

Cool.

After Peyote was made comfortable, I told him, "I'm going to call the hospital now, and I'll be right back."

Cool.

I contacted the emergency room and spoke with Doctor Timothy Stoner. After explaining the situation, Dr. Stoner informed me that there is no treatment for LSD (Lysergic Acid Diethylamide) intoxication. LSD is non-addictive and produces altered thinking for usually 6-12 hours. Visual displays of radiant colors and patterns are often experienced.

A bad trip can also happen in some cases with hallucinations, and those patients are put into a bed and strapped down until the LSD wears off.

"Oh yes, sometimes flashbacks of the LSD trip can occur without taking any more LSD," warned Dr. Stoner.

Thanking Dr. Stoner, I hung up and was relieved that Peyote was having a good trip. Walking back into the kennel to explain this to Peyote, I found that he spilled his water and was standing in his bowl.

"Peyote, why did you do that?" I asked.

Doc, thanks, this is a great beach! Awesome waves, man, replied old acid-brain.

"Okay, I'll put you in a new cage while I clean this one up," I patiently said.

Peyote showered me with *kisses* as I moved him next door to a clean cage. Halfway through the cleaning, I smelled the putrid aroma of a freshly made poop. Peyote turned out to be the aroma producer and had merrily danced all through the excrement, splattering the cage door, walls and himself with tiny mounds of feces.

"Holy crap, Peyote," I complained, which also described the situation perfectly. "Now you are going to need a bath."

Turning on the lights to give Peyote his bath, also woke up the kennel sentinel. There is always one dog in the kennel who has the life-long mission to stand guard and protect. He is always the last one to rest and the first to rise, but he never really sleeps, only dozes. The slightest sound or movement, and the ever-alert sentinel is up and barking until hoarse.

Our sentinel, whom we will call Paul, after the famous horseman, heard Peyote and me.

Quickly he raised the alarm. *Bark, bark. The British are coming!*

All the rest of the troops in the kennel joined in resulting in a non-harmonious chorus reaching a cacophony of ear-splitting noise that even woke the toy poodle that had been in a coma for the last two days. The noise also produced a splendid headache in my already weary brain.

However, Peyote was especially happy and said, *Hey Doc, look at the beautiful rainbow. Oh, here comes a shooting star. Wow!*

Finishing the bath and drying him, I turned off the lights and returned him to the third new cage of the evening. I pulled up a chair to watch him and rest. Starting to nod off, I was awakened by a howling scream.

Help, help! cried Peyote.

"What's wrong, Peyote?"

The bogey-cat is after me, he cried.

"What?"

The bogey-cat, he lives under the bed, and sometimes I even see him in the closet. He scares me!

I tried to reassure him that it would be okay. Realizing that Peyote had now entered into a bad trip, I was not about to strap him down.

Taking him out of the cage, we sat in my chair together, and I rocked him in my arms like a baby. About 4:30 a.m., the LSD appeared to have worn off. Peyote was returned to his cage, and I fell asleep in the chair to be close by in case a relapse occurred.

Early that morning, the kennel crew came in and found me asleep in the chair. I was relieved of duty, Peyote was fine, and I re-trudged again back up the stairs for a two hour nap before my first appointment of the day.

* * *

Later, Mary and Juan arrived to pick up Peyote. Mary brought me a bouquet of freshly picked daisies. I explained to them what happened and about possible flashbacks. But basically he would be just fine.

Mary then invited me to a *pot*-luck party they were having this Saturday.

"Please come, you can meet all our friends," and with a wink, "I'm making a *special* mushroom casserole."

Laughing, I asked, "What's for dessert, brownies? I'm sorry, Mary, thank you for the invitation, but I won't be able to make it."

"Okay, it's cool," and she gave me a hug, and the three flower children left happily for home.

I really would have liked to go to the pot-luck party, but I could just see the headlines now,
Local vet admitted to the hospital.....had to be strapped into bed.....the bogey-cat was after him..... wanted another one of Mary's brownies...

PEACE
LOVE

5

Arthur

It's all in a day's work.
Anonymous

Not one, but actually two very *unusual* memories are recalled in this story. First, there was the rather unique venue--a place not suited for the faint of heart or for a recently graduated veterinarian like myself.

Second, there was the *simple* surgical operation that in the end, was not so simple.

Borrowing an old military saying, this experience might have been likened to a trial by fire. I barely survived the whole ordeal. Over the ensuing years, I went to great lengths to scour each new textbook and thoroughly scan my many veterinary journals for any mention of a similar surgical finding. The search, however, was all to no avail.

Asking my friends and colleagues, if they had ever seen anything quite like it, the answer was always one of the following, *No,* or *Are you kidding?* or simply, *No way!*

Based upon this very unscientific poll, I concluded that it may happen, but only rarely. Let me explain from the beginning.

* * *

There was good reason to celebrate in August of 1968. My son, Eddie, had just turned three months old. Tina, my loving wife and mother, had settled comfortably into our two bedroom apartment above the hospital. And, I had passed my New Jersey State Board exams; a brutal sixteen hours of mind-numbing questions spread out over two days. It would have been terribly embarrassing to face the staff of Somerset Veterinary Group if I had flunked my State Boards.

Dr. North, my employer, was the first to congratulate me with a firm handshake and a *well done!* As an apparent *reward,* he said, "Dr. Dionne, since you are now a fully licensed veterinarian, how would you like to accompany me to the New Jersey State Fair this Friday afternoon?"

"Sure!" I quickly replied.

Then thinking to myself, *A half-day off from work—popcorn, cotton candy, roller coaster--definitely a no-brainer. Count me in!*

Dr. North went on to say, "The New Jersey Veterinary Medical Association (NJVMA) is conducting their very first surgical demonstrations for the general public at this year's fair. You and I are going to be spaying two dogs this Friday as part of the demonstration. I'll fill you in on all the details on our ride down to Trenton." Then he rushed off to his next appointment.

My bubble was slightly deflated as far as the reward and *good time* at the fair. I also couldn't help but wonder to myself, *Exactly what are those details that he was speaking about?*

* * *

Dr. Arthur North was a man that I and many others greatly admired. He was past-president of the NJVMA, and one of New Jersey's two representatives to the American Veterinary Medical Association (AVMA). He also served on various New Jersey Boards such as the Veterinary Ethics Board and Board of Examiners. Arthur was also a consultant for Johnson and Johnson in their Veterinary Surgical Products Division. I couldn't help but think how fortunate it was to have him as my first boss and mentor.

Arthur, or simply Art as his friends called him, was in his sixties, five foot ten inches or so and maybe 170 lbs. with a very athletic build. He had lost most of his hair on top of his head when male pattern baldness set in. The neatly trimmed, gray-white hair on the sides and back of his head gave Arthur a very dignified appearance. He had light blue, twinkling eyes with a prominent nose and chin. His large, strong hands were starting to show the wrinkles and wear that accompanied years of hard work.

A cheerful and pleasant smile seemed to always be in place and a pair of bifocals hung by a cord from around his neck. He had reached an age where the bifocals were necessary for his examining of patients and performing surgery.

In 1968, Dr. North also wore the same white uniform that all the veterinarians did at Somerset Vet.

He might have dressed rather blandly in the office, but *out on the town*, he was dazzling. His sport coats were brightly colored, almost psychedelic and his trademark plaid pants and non-matching tie completed his unique ensemble.

Only Arthur could get away with such an outfit and still look good.

* * *

Friday morning arrived quickly, and the note in my office mailbox read like a grocery shopping list.

Ed, we need:
2 surgical masks
2 surgical caps
4 gowns
2 sterilized instrument packs
4 pair of sterile surgical gloves (size 8 for me)
2 sterile drapes
2 sterile no. 10 scalpel blades
assorted packs and sizes of chromic cat gut sutures
nylon skin sutures and sterile surgical needles
Thanks, Dr. N.

Being busy with morning appointments, I quickly passed the note along to Sandy, our surgery technician. She could go *shopping*, instead of me.

The morning flew by and soon it was time to leave. Not surprisingly, Dr. North was running a tad behind in his office calls--1 1/2 hours and counting. Waiting patiently in our doctors' lounge, I curled up with my latest non-medical journal--
Sports Illustrated.

Finally, bursting into the lounge, Dr. North announced, "Okay Ed, let's go!"

Driving out of the parking lot and onto the busy Route 22, Arthur promised, "Don't worry. I know the roads very well. We can make up the time."

Five minutes down the road, there was a foul odor in the car. Hoping that it wasn't what I thought it was, I asked, "Dr. North, what's that smell?"

"Uh, oh! I brought two dead dogs in for cremation from the house call that I made on Wednesday. I put them in the trunk and forgot to take them out!"

Hmm, I thought, *let's see, that was two days ago, it's August and quite hot. No wonder it stinks in here!*

Making a quick u-turn, we zoomed back to the hospital and discharged our *passengers* from the trunk. Then it was back onto the highway, and *not to worry*, he knows the route. Thinking that this might be an appropriate time to get the left-out *details* about the State Fair, I asked, " Dr. North, what is it exactly that we are going to be doing today?"

While still zipping down the highway, he patiently explained, "The NJVMA has a campaign to educate the public about the high technical standards and professional competency in veterinary medicine. For this we have enlisted the help of sixty veterinarians to volunteer their services in various surgical demonstrations at this year's State Fair. We will be doing a total of thirty-three operations in afternoon and evening sessions over a nine day period."

"What kind of surgeries and where will they be?" I asked.

"Well, we have several dog spays scheduled, and that's what you and I will be doing as you know. The dogs are provided by various local humane societies to help their owners who can't afford to have their dogs spayed."

"That's good," I said.

Arthur continued, "Some vets will be doing other types of surgeries such as mammary tumors, hernias, plus there is one femoral pinning. Oh yes, and one canine heart surgery to remove heartworms from the right ventricle and pulmonary artery."

"That's quite a complicated heart surgery."

"And to answer your second question, the fair has provided a tent. And inside the tent we have a portable, 12 x 12 ft. surgery room with glass windows. The spectators can watch from the two bleachers that are set up along the outside of each window. We also have a closed circuit television set up for those who want to see it close up. Everything will be state of the art including the surgery table, surgery lights and anesthesia machine."

"Sounds impressive."

"Each operation has a four-man team, a veterinarian who will be a commentator/narrator, a veterinary technician to monitor the anesthesia, a surgeon and an assistant surgeon. I will be the surgeon for our first dog, and you will be the assistant, then we will switch; you will be the surgeon and I will be the assistant."

That's when I thought, *Uh oh!* I then nervously asked, "How many people will be watching?" I was secretly hoping for none.

"Oh, they have been averaging close to two hundred spectators per session so far," said the proud Dr. North. "And guess what, Dr. Dionne?" Arthur asked.

"What?" I squeaked while rolling down the window in case my stomach decided to relieve itself of lunch.

"You have the honor of being the newest and youngest veterinary surgeon at the fair," exclaimed my smiling mentor.

"Wow, I'll do my best," I weakly promised.

Having provided all the details, Dr. North glanced at his watch. "Oh my, I'm going to have to pick it up a bit, or we're going to be late!"

Blasting down the highway like a runaway *freight train*, we caught the attention of a state trooper. Clocking us at 79 mph, he pulled us over and asked for license and registration. Still dressed in our white office uniforms, the trooper eyed us questioningly. Apparently we must have looked like two off-duty bakers or something similar.

The trooper asked, "Why are you guys dressed like this?"

Dr. North explained about being veterinarians from Somerset Veterinary Group and not wanting to be late for our surgery demonstration at the State Fair.

"Hey, Dr. North, I know you!" said the now friendly officer. "You take care of my mom's dogs, Trixie and Penny!"

"Oh yes, of course," Dr. North agreed.

I was a bit skeptical that Dr. North actually knew who Trixie and Penny were.

"Listen Doc, you're about ten miles from the Fair, so just follow me."

With his light flashing, the trooper escorted us directly into the middle of the fairgrounds. The ticket-less Arthur waved thanks and good-bye to the officer. Arthur and I then ran to the surgery tent carrying all our supplies. We just made it with a whole two minutes to spare.

* * *

Dr. North quickly introduced me to the other members of our four-man team. Dr. Tom Casey, the narrator, was Arthur's longtime friend and veterinary colleague. Amanda, his technician, would be monitoring the anesthesia.

Dr. Casey responded, "Glad to meet you Dr. Dionne." Then turning to Art, "I was getting a little worried that you weren't going to make it."

The tent and bleachers were already filled to capacity. The crowd was jovial, excited and curious to see a real operation. I was sick to my stomach, non-jovial and nervous.

The first dog, Heidi, was a small, 20 lb., orange and white spaniel of some type. She was still a very young puppy about six months old.

The crowd let out a collective, "Oh...she's so cute."

Dr. Casey and Amanda quickly prepared her for the operation. She was given a preoperative sedative and atropine, followed by a short acting, intravenous barbiturate which put her to *sleep*. An endotracheal tube was then inserted into her trachea, and Heidi was connected to the gas anesthesia machine. Oxygen and the gas anesthesia flow through the endotracheal tube right into the animal's lungs.

Amanda shaved the hair with an electric clipper, then washed her abdomen with a surgical soap, and finally sprayed an iodine disinfectant over the entire surgery area. Meanwhile, Dr. North, wearing a cap and mask, scrubbed his hands and forearms up to the elbows, then donned his sterile gown and gloves. I had already opened the instrument pack, adding the necessary suture material, drape and scalpel blade.

Then I scrubbed up. We were ready. Arthur waved to the audience. It was *show-time*.

* * *

The surgery went off without a hitch. Dr. Casey, the narrator, explained each step to the crowd. The speedy Dr. North had to slow down the surgery in order to give the crowd their money's worth. Once the Y- shaped uterus and ovaries were removed, Arthur held them up so that the picture taking spectators could either *ooh* or *yuk*, depending on their individual preference. Many were either disappointed or impressed by the lack of blood and small 1 1/2 inch incision. After the surgery was completed, Heidi was awake within 6-7 minutes. Dr. North, the consummate showman, held his groggy patient in his arms and had her *wave* a paw to the applauding crowd.

A short break was then taken so that one group could exit and a new crowd could be ushered in. Now it was my turn, and I was feeling pretty good after the *show* put on during act one. Amanda went to fetch the next dog, Bertha.

* * *

Expecting another tiny, cute puppy, Bertha was none of the above, as she waddled into the surgery suite. A more appropriate name would have been, *Big Bertha.*

Her body looked like a long *torpedo* with short legs, a head and a tail. The torpedo was also very unhappy and about to *explode* at any moment.

I guessed her to be part Basset hound and part grizzly bear. She weighed 76 lbs. which was somehow crammed into a 40 lb. frame. Her record said she was seven years old and never had puppies.

Favorite hobby: eating.

Bertha was all black with white patches, droopy ears and big paws. She was also a bit miffed about having to fast overnight for her surgery today.

Tom and Amanda got her sedated, then anesthetized without too much trouble, except for lifting her up onto the surgery table. Amanda then prepped Bertha for the surgery.

Dr. North covered the patient with a surgery drape, and opened the instrument pack and suture material. Everything was ready to go. Being right-handed, I preferred to stand on the right side of the surgery table.

It was a hot day. And it was even hotter inside the tent, and adding to our discomfort it was hotter than hot under the surgery lights.

We were both sweating and hadn't even started yet. With shaky hands, I made a three inch incision on the mid-line of the abdomen, an inch or so behind Bertha's *belly button.* I was greeted with a deep layer of fatty tissue some two inches deep. Dissecting down through this fat is troublesome because once this grease gets on your gloves and instruments, they become very slippery.

The goal is to find the *white line* or linea alba which is the juncture of the left and right main abdominal muscles. This is the exact mid-point and contains no blood vessels or muscle fibers. Using a scalpel, a small nick is made in the white line. Inserting a thumb forceps into the nick, to push away any small intestine that might be hanging out in the area, the incision can be enlarged both forward and backward with a scalpel.

Dr. North was encouraging, "So far so good, let's find the uterus, partner," and handed me a spay hook.

The spay hook is about seven inches long with a smooth blunt *hook* on the end. The uterus lies deep in the abdomen up along the back, and the ovaries, about the size of a lima bean, are just behind each kidney. The two *horns of the uterus* join together into the main body of the uterus producing a Y shape.

After two or three tries, I was able to hook the left and easiest horn. With a little help from my assistant, I could lift the horn and ovary up to our incision line and tie off the blood vessels.

Still encouraging, Dr. North said, "Nice job."

Unfortunately this is where things started to become unpleasant and unnerving for the Fair's youngest vet. Even after several attempts with the spay hook, I could not find the right horn.

My assistant whispered, "Enlarge your incision a couple of inches," but still no luck.

"Make it bigger," I was told.

I did.

Dr. North assured me that, "It has to be there," as we both peered down into Bertha's abdomen.

"Okay, let's trace the left horn back to the body of the uterus and get the right horn from there," he suggested.

We did and there was no right horn attached to the body of the uterus! It was AWOL.

At this point, Dr. Casey walked over and asked, "What's going on guys? I'm running out of things to say to the spectators."

The sweat was now starting to drip into my eyes and stinging quite a bit.

Dr. North assured me again that, "It has to be somewhere," as we both peered down into the now *Grand Canyon*.

"Let's take out a few feet of small intestine," suggested my boss.

I scooped the slippery small intestine out of the abdomen and onto the surgery drape, while Dr. North tried to keep them from slithering off the table.

At this point, a few gagging people had to leave the tent. The rest started to take pictures with their flash cameras. It was starting to feel like the Fourth of July with all the flash bulbs popping.

Suddenly, by some miracle, I spotted the elusive, detached horn and ovary. The horn was free-floating so the spay hook wasn't able to retrieve it. Reaching in with a forceps, I yelled, "Gotcha" as the horn and ovary were *captured* at last.

After pulling them out and tying the vessels off, now I just had to close our eight inch incision. There would be no bikini for Bertha this summer. Dr. Casey explained to the remaining brave spectators what had happened, and they gave us a standing ovation for our effort.

Everyone left happy.

* * *

Afterwards, Dr. North gave me a pat on the back and said, "Now let's go have some fun."

I said, "Okay," even though I wasn't at all sure what exactly his idea of fun was.

We treated ourselves to a large beer and a *Big Bertha-sized* hot dog and wandered across the midway to the most popular site at the fair......The Exotic Dancers' Tent!

Drinking our beers and munching our *dogs*, we were finally having that *reward* and *good time* that Arthur promised.

I did see Big Bertha one more time. Her owners lived fairly close to our hospital and brought her in so that I could check her incision and remove her stitches. They told me that she was hit by a car when she was two years old. Bertha was bruised and tender on her right side, but they didn't take her to a vet because she was still eating.

I thought to myself, *Bertha would have to be dead or comatose before she missed a meal.*

"Ah ha," I said to her owners. "That's what happened to Bertha. She ruptured her uterus in that accident and it healed all by itself, but the right horn remained detached."

Mystery solved at last!

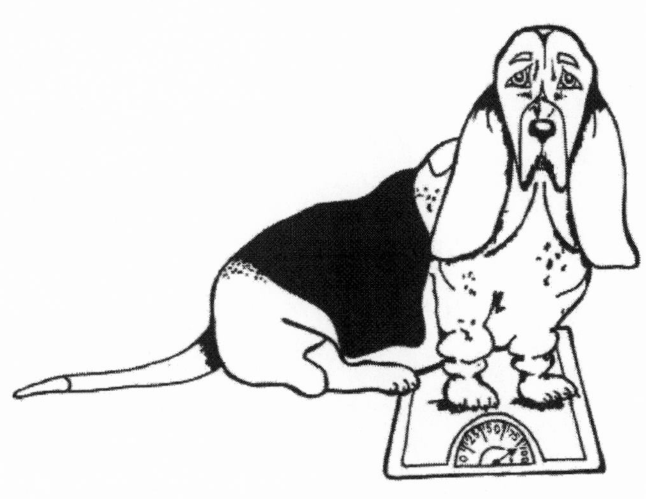

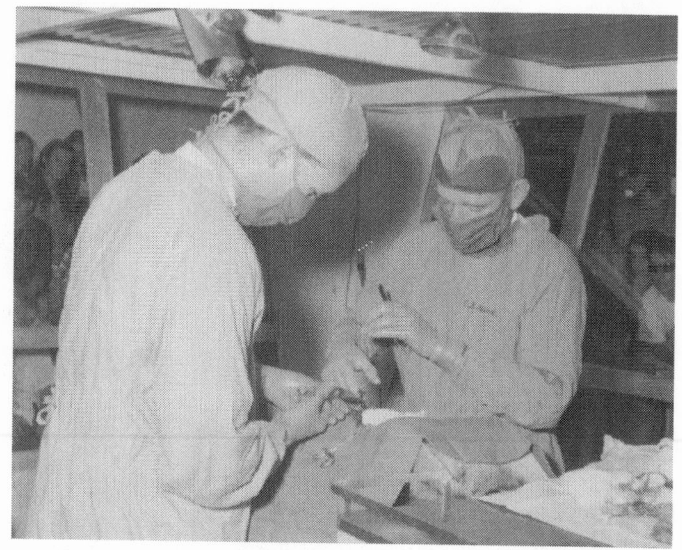

Author with Dr. North at New Jersey State Fair

6

Snoopy

Time is of the essence.
A Saying

Even having almost two years of veterinary practice *under my belt*, I was still not sure how to proceed with this particular case. I was faced with a major dilemma. There was no helpful green light for *Go*, only a yellow light indicating *Proceed with Caution*. Nor was there the following warning label, *This case may be hazardous to your health.*

Ultimately the question for me was basically two-fold. First, am I still a student or intern after two years of practice or not?

Answer: *Yes* and *No*.

Yes, because throughout my career there will always be something new in medicine to learn or experience.

But *No*, I was no longer doing classwork, being graded, and told what to do. It was the real world that I had heard so much about.

The second part of the question and the key to the dilemma was more problematic. What do I do when confronted with a difficult client, who happens to have a great deal of medical expertise, is well respected in the community, holds a position of authority and insists on one thing? And I disagree!

Let me tell you this sad tale.

* * *

The flowers seemed to have all burst open at once producing a brilliant display of colors and fragrant aromas. After a very cool, wet spring, it was a welcome relief to have a sunny, warm, mid-seventies Sunday in May of 1970. A refreshing light breeze rustled the leaves on the trees which were almost all in full bloom. The breeze swirled and disseminated this year's abundant crop of pollen. Having a particular attraction and fondness for my nasal passages and eyes, the pollen settled into its new home. My tissues, eye-drops and nasal spray would be my constant companions for the next few weeks.

The pollen and the fact that I was on emergency duty was not going to stop our little family from enjoying this splendid afternoon. Tina was preparing a picnic lunch to be had on our tiny deck which was just outside the front door of our second floor apartment. The picnic area extended out over the noisy dog runs, but this wouldn't deter us from having our picnic.

While waiting for the feast, Eddie, my two-year-old son, and I ventured out to the hospital's empty parking lot.

Holding his favorite truck in one hand and picking up a handful of stones to throw with the other, we had our little father-son bonding time. Eddie was fascinated with trucks, and we certainly had a plethora of them on the busy four lane highway in front of the hospital. Trucks of all sizes, shapes and colors constantly whizzed by, eliciting from my finger-pointing son, "Da-da, fruck!"

"Yes, yes, big one!" I agreed wearing a proud smile.

Our newest family member, the ten-month-old Theresa, stayed with mom while she made the potato salad. Terri, as we called her, was a beautiful, inquisitive baby with dark brown eyes and a happy smile. Tina dressed her in assorted, mostly pink dresses to emphasize her femaleness.

Soon it was picnic time, and we sat on our folded blanket and gobbled the banquet that Tina lovingly prepared. Half-way through the picnic, the phone rang.

"Aw nuts!" mumbling to myself, I entered the apartment to answer the telephone.

Answering with a simple, "Dr. Dionne," I also heard a sniffle while waiting for a response.

"Dr. Dionne, sorry to bother you. This is Angel from the answering service."

"Angel, are you crying? What's the matter?"

"I received a call from Dr. Charles Brown. He said that he was a good friend of Dr. North. They play golf together, and Dr. North takes care of his dog, Snoopy. Dr. Brown wanted, actually demanded to know, 'Where's Art?' He has been trying to reach him at his home for the last hour with no answer. Snoopy has had three epileptic seizures and is very sick."

"Oh boy," I said.

Angel continued, "So I told him that I had no idea where Dr. North was, and that you were on emergency call for the hospital. While swearing a few profanities, Dr. Brown said that he didn't believe me and furthermore would not want to see some *intern*. And then he hung up."

"Angel, I don't believe what I'm hearing."

"It gets worse. Ten minutes later, Dr. Brown called back and wanted to speak with my supervisor and threatened to have me fired if I didn't call Dr. North right now!"

"You're right, it is getting worse!"

"I tried to explain that I have been here for eight years and do not need a supervisor which only made him more angry and upset. Finally, he said to have you call him immediately!"

"Angel, you do a terrific job and don't worry, I'll handle Dr. Brown," I hoped.

Quickly dialing the irate doctor, I was greeted with, "Where's Arthur?"

"Well, right now he's somewhere in the Bahamas on vacation. Can I help you?" I suggested.

SILENCE...

Finally Dr. Brown answered, "Do you know how to treat a grand mal, epileptic seizure? Because my dog, Snoopy, just had his fourth one,"

I then made the major mistake of asking, "Are you sure it is an epileptic seizure? Describe it to me."

Dr. Brown gave the following curt answer, "I have been a very important member of the hospital staff and have been practicing medicine before you were even born, *sonny*. I know an epileptic seizure when I see one!"

"Okay, I'm at the hospital now, so bring him right over."

CLICK...... No good-bye, no thanks.

Oh boy, this is going to be a tough one, I thought while wishing to be in the Bahamas with Arthur.

After telling Tina what had just transpired, she sighed and with some disappointment said, "Okay".

Giving the kids a hug and a kiss, I told them, "Daddy's got to go to work right now, but I"ll be back soon."

Eddie tearfully said, "No work da-da."

My ten-month-old Terri simply burped and smiled.

Racing down the steps from our apartment to the office, I pulled Snoopy's record and read that he was a two-year-old male, tri-colored beagle. All his vaccinations were current, and there was no history of any previous illness or head trauma.

While turning on the office lights and unlocking the front door, I couldn't help but ponder the question, *Why couldn't I have chosen to be a baker instead of a vet? Everyone likes a baker, all you have to do is put lots of chocolate chips in your cookies. There are no emergencies for sick muffins or lethargic cupcakes. Oh well.*

* * *

Then Dr. Charles Brown arrived carrying his very sick Snoopy. He was not exactly what I had envisioned him to be over the phone. Guessing that he was in his late fifties, Dr. Brown was a large imposing man probably five foot eleven inches, and tipped the scales at over two hundred pounds. He had thinning gray hair, a well-kept mustache, ruddy complexion, blue eyes with slightly puffy eyelids and pronounced sagging jowls.

He was dressed like he had been doing yard work or gardening. Wearing just an old, red Rutgers tee-shirt, a pair of blue, dirt-stained Bermuda shorts, white socks and old worn out tennis sneakers with a hole in each toe, he didn't appear as gruff as he sounded.

Without much of a greeting, I went to work examining his pet. Snoopy was conscious but unable to move or rise up. His heart rate was faster than normal and weak, breathing was shallow, mucus membranes were slightly cyanotic (blue), indicating that he was not getting enough oxygen into his system. All four legs were rigid and extending straight out from his body. In addition, Snoopy's temperature was slightly elevated.

Not wanting to move him too much, I again asked, "Dr. Brown, please describe the seizure and how it happened."

Being more cooperative, he said, "I spent the entire morning doing projects around the yard, and Snoopy just played like he normally does when we're outside together. Suddenly, he whimpered and had trouble walking. And just like that he fell over onto his side and the seizures began."

"When was the first seizure?"

"About two hours ago and they have been getting longer and more intense. He had a real bad one on the ride over here."

"Did his legs thrash about or were they rigid as they are now?" I asked delicately.

"No, he just gets real rigid like now and his whole body shakes."

Continuing to quickly take a history, I asked, "Did Snoopy lose control of his bowels or urine during these attacks?"

"No!" as Dr. Brown inadvertently bumped the exam table, which sent poor Snoopy into another seizure which lasted almost two minutes.

Having witnessed the seizure, I now knew what I had suspected all along.

I informed Dr. Brown, "These are not epileptic seizures, and I strongly suspect that your dog was poisoned."

Noticing that the good doctor's face was now crimson, I fully expected at any moment to see whiffs of smoke escaping from both ears and nose, ending in a Mount Vesuvius-like eruption.

I explained further, "We have no time to debate my diagnosis. You have to go home, search the yard, garage and anywhere else Snoopy had been today for anything that might be poisonous."

"Are you serious?"

"Yes, and I'm taking him in for treatment right now!"

As his anger continued to smolder, he said loudly, "We don't have any poisons at our home, young man."

The outburst precipitated another seizure, a very bad one.

Exasperated, I scooped Snoopy up and ordered Dr. Brown, "Just go home and look!"

Hurrying up the steps to our surgery and treatment room, I said aloud, "Ed, you'd better be right. If not, expect a major malpractice suit, plus a complaint to the New Jersey Veterinary Ethics Board with a possible loss of my precious license."

Contemplating the worst, my mind was out of control. I muttered again, "Two years out of veterinary school and probably after today the only place I would be able to practice is in Greenland. But, maybe I could open up a walrus practice. Hey, Wally, ever think about braces for those tusks of yours?"

* * *

Forcing myself to snap out of it and think about my sick patient, I mentally ran down all the more commonly used poisons:

Warfarin-- No--primarily just has bleeding symptoms

Thallium-- No--saw two cases at vet school and not the same

Lead-- No-- more chronic type of poisoning, G.I. symptoms, then seizures

Arsenic-- No-- vomiting, no seizures

Organophosphates and chlorinated hydrocarbons-- No-- vomiting, salivation, constricted pupils, and thrashing type of seizures, not rigidity

Strychnine-- YES!-- exactly Snoopy's symptoms-- muscle rigidity, attacks brought on by loud sounds and noises, poison rapidly absorbed, progresses quickly to death usually within 1-2 hours, death from asphyxia and patient unable to breath during these attacks.

* * *

The initial treatment would have been to induce vomiting with apomorphine, but it was too late for that now. Snoopy was not able to vomit without inhaling the vomitus. I hooked up an intravenous drip into his rigid right front leg. Then, I gave him some

Pentothal to quiet his nervous system from sound. Inserting an endotracheal tube to administer oxygen, I was now prepared to assist his breathing.

My next step was to pass a stomach tube to flush out any poison that might still be in his stomach. Knowing that the fluids would eventually flush the strychnine out through his kidneys, I hoped it wasn't too late.

Despite working feverishly, it was all to no avail.

Snoopy's heart just gave out, and he died on the table.

I felt sick.

He could have possibly been saved if only he had come in an hour or so sooner.

Leaning against the surgery wall, I slowly slid down and sat on the floor. Holding my head in my hands, I tied to compose myself and call Dr. Brown.

Just then our hospital direct line rang. I knew full well who it was because I had given Dr. Brown this number to call me directly.

Picking the phone up I said, "Hello." This time it wasn't Angel crying, but Dr. Brown himself.

"Dr. Dionne, I know what happened to Snoopy, he was poisoned!"

"Yes, I know, with strychnine," I said.

More crying, "*AND I DID IT!*"

Between sobs, the distraught doctor composed himself and explained, "This morning, I was digging holes all around the yard and putting pellets into each hole to kill moles. I didn't notice that Snoopy went around and dug up each pellet and ate them. I purchased the pellets at the hardware store and never looked to see that the main ingredient was strychnine."

Dr. Brown seemed to expect the bad news when I told him about his pet. Now I could hear the whole family crying in the background. Mom and the kids realized what had happened by seeing their father in tears.

His last words were, "Thank you for trying, Dr. Dionne. We will pick up his body tomorrow and bury him in our back yard."

After removing the intravenous drip, endotracheal tube, and turning off the oxygen and anesthesia machine, I wrapped Snoopy's body for burial.

Walking into our apartment, Tina could tell by the weary, unhappy look on my face that things didn't go very well.

The kids were already asleep, and the fatherless picnic was long over. Managing to eat some potato salad and two chocolate chip cookies, I realized that life and death happen, and tomorrow is another day.

* * *

A few weeks later my appointment sheet read: *9:00 a.m.-- New Account-- Brown--puppy-- checkup and shots.*

It was my first appointment of the morning, and my clients, Dr. and Mrs. Brown were already in the room with their new beagle puppy. They were both smiling-- a good sign.

Extending his hand to shake mine, he said, "I want you to meet my wife, Patty. She will be bringing in our new pup to see you for all his visits. Please accept my apologies for not trusting you and worse yet for belittling you. I'm nothing more than a pompous fool, and it will never happen again to you or anyone else! I promise."

Being totally flabbergasted, I replied, "Under stress, people often say and do things that they regret later on. It's okay."

"No, no. Thank you for saying that, but I have acted like an obnoxious idiot for a long time, but no more."

Patty was nodding her head in complete agreement.

Changing the subject, "Well, Dr. Brown, what's your new puppy's name?"

"Hold on there, Dr. Dionne. Please call me Charlie, and this little guy we call Snoopy 2."

"Okay, then it will be Charlie Brown and Snoopy 2," I said as the curious puppy was now chewing on my shoe laces.

We all had a good laugh and became friends for many years.

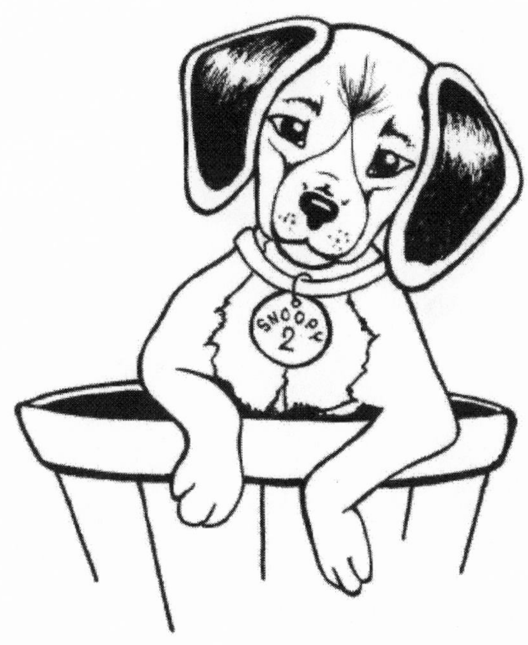

Author with family and Enu the dog

7

Andy

My goal in life is to be as good of a person as my dog already thinks I am.

Unknown

Life has often been described as a journey with numerous crossroads and choices to be made. Should I go left, right, or straight ahead? Each decision, even small ones, can have a markedly significant impact on not only your life but others as well. And life is like a story, with a beginning, middle and end. This is the beginning story of Andy, an English bulldog, who decided one day to go swimming.

* * *

In 1961, three recent graduates from Binghamton Central High School in upstate New York enrolled in the Pennsylvania State University, or simply *Penn State* as it is more commonly referred to by most people and alumni. Two of these graduates were in the College of Agriculture - Barbara Sanderson and me. During our first semester, Barbara and I had one class together, *Introduction to Botany.*

Each week, I eagerly looked forward to botany class, and not because botany lectures were so stimulating. They were not, but coed Sanderson certainly was. Always sitting near the back of the lecture hall, Barbara and I took a few notes and chatted quietly to each other. While the professor droned on and on, we secretly passed humorous messages back and forth about stamens and pistils.

At this time, the ratio of males to females at Penn State was an unfair 3:1. Most of the freshmen guys in my dormitory were both *love-starved and date-less*. Considering myself lucky, I tried to make the most out of our *dates* in botany class.

Barbara was certainly no longer the girl I knew in high school-- the tall, slender string bean with the thick, heavy braces on her teeth. Fortunately, using the words of my botany professor, Barbara had *blossomed* into a young woman; discarded braces and rubber bands were replaced with more appealing and gentle female curves. At five foot ten inches, blond hair, deep blue eyes, a slightly upturned nose, flawless complexion and a warm smile, she was eye-catching. After our first semester, Barbara was soon snatched up by a frat boy, and our lives went off in different directions.

That is, until twelve years later, in July of 1973. The note in my office mailbox read,
Dr. Dionne, please call Barbara Capulet, an old friend from high school. The name was not one that I could recall.

Returning the telephone call, I heard a vaguely familiar voice, "Hi Ed, this is Barbara!"

"Uh..." I hesitated.

"Sorry, it's Barbara Sanderson."

"Oh! Hi, how are you?" I asked.

"I'm fine. My married name is Capulet, and we just moved to Martinsville with my two children and our dog. I was looking through the yellow pages for a vet and saw your name. I couldn't believe it!"

We reminisced about high school and Penn State for the next few minutes before I had to go to my next appointment. Barbara promised to bring her dog in for a checkup as soon as she was settled into her new home.

On a hot Wednesday afternoon, not more than one week later, a flustered Rosalee, our secretary, rushed into the doctors' lounge and loudly announced, "Dr. Dionne, your friend is coming in!"

In the midst of concentrating on writing up my patient records, I looked up with some irritation and said, "Rosalee, what are you so excited about? What friend?"

"You know, Barbara, your high school friend, her dog just fell into their swimming pool and almost drowned! She's on the way in right now!"

Waiting by the exam room window, I saw Barbara, driving a blue station wagon, come to a screeching halt in front of the hospital. Rushing out to help, I carried in her limp, very wet English bulldog. Barbara and her two crying children were also soaking wet as well. My white doctor's uniform acting like a sponge, became quite damp from carrying in her dog.

Entering Exam Room 2, I placed her on the table and dried her off with a kennel towel.

The barefoot children, Taylor, seven years old, and Sam, six years old, were still in their bathing suits and appeared worried and anxious. Mom had on flip-flops and gray shorts pulled up over her one piece, black bathing suit. Even having no makeup on and wet, straggly blond hair, Barbara still looked great.

Before starting the exam, I asked, "What's your dog's name and how old is she?"

"Andy is two years old," answered the helpful Taylor.

Just knowing the age is often important for making an overall clinical evaluation and prognosis. Listening intently with my stethoscope, I had found her lungs to be clear and her heart strong.

After the exam, I was pleased to tell Barb and the kids that their dog would be just fine. The awake Andy was now sitting up-- a good sign. She was busy coughing and spitting out little drops of pool water onto the exam table.

"Barb, it's good to see you again."

"You too, Ed."

"Okay Barb, let's make a patient record for Andy."

"Her real name is Princess Andrea of Stratford upon Avon," proclaimed the precocious Taylor, who, I noted, had a striking resemblance to her mother.

Adding this information to the patient record, I also jotted down that the *Princess* was two years old, spayed, forty-two pounds, and brindle in color (brindle is basically brown or tan with black streaks).

* * *

The English bulldog has a smooth, short coat and can also be white, red or fawn in color. The male bulldogs are somewhat larger than the females and weigh around 50-55 lbs. Both sexes have wide shoulders, sturdy legs, very muscular bodies and short tails. Their paws are disproportionately large as compared to their overall body size. Bulldogs have turned-out elbows resulting in a shuffling kind of gait when they walk.

The most distinctive physical features are certainly their rather large head and *pushed-in nose*. Many bulldogs also have a pronounced under-bite, so much so, that the lower canine and incisor teeth are always visible.

Their large tongue often flops around both inside and outside the short mouth producing an abundance of sticky saliva and flying spitballs. The eyes are widely spaced, round and dark in color. There are many skin folds and wrinkles on the brow, over the nose, and hanging under the neck. With drooping lower lips, this gives the English bulldog their unique, lovable appearance. Bulldogs look like they just woke up from sleeping or conversely are in dire need of a nap.

* * *

After the exam, the relieved Capulet family gathered their precious Princess and started for home.

"Barbara, call me if there are any problems," I yelled out the door.

"Don't worry, I will!" She smiled, waved and drove off with her soggy crew.

Two weeks later, Barbara did telephone about the continuing canine pool problem. Andy had not learned her lesson.

"Ed," she said, "Andy will not stay out of the

pool. She sees Taylor and Sam go off the diving board, and she jumps right off the side and into the water with a splash. I thought all dogs knew how to *doggy paddle*. Not her. Andy takes two strokes and sinks like a rock. Fortunately, I have been in the pool each time to pull her out."

"What if you keep her in the house when you use the pool?" I asked.

"I've tried that. But, she will bark and carry on so much that I'm afraid that she will have a heart attack."

"Oh, that wouldn't be good," I said.

"So Jim, my sweet, engineer husband, designed a special life jacket just for Andy. A friend of ours at the shore owns a boat supply business. He took Jim's design and was able to make a life jacket for Andy. The grand unveiling is tomorrow at noon. Can you and Tina come?"

"We'll most definitely be there. I'll bring some emergency medical supplies, just in case."

"Great! We are planning a picnic afterwards, plus a reporter from the newspaper wants to do a human interest article on Andy. He said that he would bring along a photographer to take pictures of Andy wearing her life jacket in the pool."

"Okay, sounds good. See you tomorrow," I said and hung up.

Tina and I arrived at the designated time, noon, and as promised, the picnic was already prepared. Two picnic tables were covered with bright tablecloths and placed next to the pool. Each table had several bowls of tasty salads, bread and other luncheon items. Hot dogs and hamburgers were being cooked on the barbecue grill.

The newspaper reporter and photographer had also arrived, plus a handful of curious friends. After introductions, we waited a few moments for the star performer to make her appearance. With a drum-roll and much fanfare, Princess Andrea of Stratford upon Avon, wearing her *royal* life jacket, walked out to the adoring public.

The life jacket was a shockingly bright, fluorescent pink in color with holes for her short, bowed front legs. The jacket covered all of her chest and part of her abdomen with three straps to keep it secured to her wide body. An inflated portion circled her short thick neck and stuck out like an Elizabethan collar.

With music playing, the children, Taylor and Sam. marched to the diving board and climbed the steps. With a loud whoop and holler, the kids, one by one, sprinted to the end of the board and dove non-gracefully into the pool.

Andy just watched.

The kids and the crowd were encouraging, "Come on Andy, you can do it!"

Barbara walked Andy over to the diving board and had her climb the ramp that Jim had also built for her. Once on the board, the Princess took her time and posed for the cameras. A knowing and excited expression seemed to appear on her face.

At last, she *ran*, well not exactly, but as fast as an English bulldog can run with a pink life jacket on, can run. Upon reaching the end of the board, Andy did not hesitate and leaped off the diving board.

Entering the water with a monumental bulldog cannonball, she disappeared under the water for a few anxious seconds, then came bobbing up to the surface.

The life jacket worked! The crowd cheered.

Andy needed some help getting out of the pool, but returned to the diving board again and again throughout the day. The picnic and life jacket were a great success.

That Sunday, on the front page of the Life Styles section of the newspaper, Tina and I admired the picture of Andy standing on the diving board. The details were reported in a lengthy article.

However, this was just the *beginning* of Andy's remarkable story.

To be continued...

8

Amos

The purity of a person's heart can be quickly measured by how they regard animals.
Anonymous

Upon hearing or even reading the word *imperfect*, I immediately associate it with something that has a significant flaw or obvious blemish. Imperfect would certainly be an appropriate label when discussing a piece of artwork where a mistake was made-- the wrong mix of colors, a scratch on the canvas or a noticeable chip in the sculpture. Imperfections of all sorts are found in our more mundane possessions as well-- a crack in the favorite teacup, or the marred, but comfortable sofa.

But, all too often, imperfect or other similar, demeaning adjectives are used to describe and mock another person or in this case an animal. This is the *beginning* story of my association with Amos and his wonderful imperfections. Let me explain.

* * *

The summer of 1973 moved onward, passing slowly from a sweltering July into a blistering, record breaking August. Clients and their pets seemed to enjoy lingering in the cool waiting room and the slightly warmer, but still comfortable, exam rooms. Each time the two office doors opened for entering or exiting, a blast of hot air blew in creating an unwelcome sauna. The sauna-like conditions briefly tormented the clients, the pets and me. Not quite reaching the meltdown point, the air conditioning system rallied each time with a cough and a sputter to save the day.

Dr. North, oblivious to the weather conditions, carried on at his normal whirlwind pace. The pharmacy was the usual meeting area for those of us with afternoon appointments. While counting out pills or gathering ointments, shampoos, flea sprays and the like, we were able to hold brief conversations.

This afternoon in the pharmacy, Dr. North said, "Ed, I need you to do me a favor."

Realizing that it wasn't a question, I said, "Sure."

"I have an unexpected meeting tomorrow afternoon, so I would like you to make my house call to Shakespeare Kennels for me. Mike will fill you in on the details."

"Okay, no problem," I replied.

Then, having gathered his patient's medicines, Dr. North scurried back to his exam room and client. And, that was the extent of the conversation.

The kennel call would be a nice change of pace, I thought.

But, I couldn't help but wonder what those unmentioned *details* might be-- not knowing at this time, that the visit would lead to a chain of events that would be quite remarkable and memorable. I gathered up my patient's medicines and made a note to see Mike about tomorrow.

* * *

Later, just catching Mike before he left for home, I asked, "Mike, what's up with the kennel visit tomorrow?"

With a laugh, he replied, "Well Doc, you are in for a real treat. Have you ever met Joe Montague, the owner of Shakespeare Kennels?"

"No, I've said hello to him in passing, that's it."

"Okay, so you already know that he raises English bulldogs, and Dr. North has been his veterinarian for the past twenty years or so. Joe was born in Italy and immigrated to the U.S. just before World War II. That's when he met Dr. North, and they have been buddies ever since. He remains very Italian and will probably talk your ear off. Joe loves food, wine and English bulldogs."

"Does he know that Dr. North is not coming, and it will be me instead of him?"

"Yes, he does. I called him this afternoon. So here are the directions, and a list of what he wants done. By the way, since it's your day off on Thursday, take your time. You don't have to come back to the hospital and work after the kennel visit."

"Thanks." Then glancing at the list, I thought, *Wow, this is going to be a snap.*

Wednesday morning arrived, and I was looking forward to meeting with Joe Montague and his English bulldogs. Double checking my *To Do* list,

I certainly did not want to *screw up* and forget something important. I wouldn't want a bad report coming back to Dr. North.

* * *

I made notations on the *To Do* list of the supplies that would be needed:

A. six puppies-- first shots and checkups-- need six vaccines, six syringes, cooler, ice pack, cotton, alcohol and six vaccine and health certificates
B. Hamlet-- ear infection-- need q-tips, otoscope and ear ointment
C. Caesar and Macbeth-- check hearts-- need refill of heart pills (digoxin) for both
D. Othello-- check for possible cataracts-- need opthalmoscope
E. Queen Mab-- pregnancy check
F. Amos-- pre-surgery check for Thursday with Dr. North
G. fecal samples on all dogs-- check for worms-- need microscope, fecal solution, glass slides, cover slips, cups, gauze and worm medicine

I was ready!

* * *

On the way, I drove right past Barbara Capulet's house and wondered if Andy was still diving into the pool with the kids. I was also surprised to find out that Joe lived less than one mile from Barbara. Spotting the white sign with bold black letters announcing Shakespeare Kennels, I made a quick right turn and drove up the tree-lined driveway.

A modest white, one story house with

numerous black shuttered windows was off to my left. The house was surrounded by beautifully manicured shrubs and plants. Despite the summer heat, most of the well-watered flowers were still in full bloom. The numerous flower beds were strategically placed providing a visual display of vibrant colors.

I recognized the red and pink geraniums, the tall purple and white phlox, the majestic tall red lilies, the multicolored mix of marigolds, and the white daisies. Most of the others, I couldn't recognize by name.

I parked in front of the impressive, white kennel building with black trim. Everything was meticulously cared for, including the trestle of grape vines and large vegetable garden that I could just see behind the house. Getting out of the car, I said to myself, "I wonder if this is what a country home in Italy is like?"

A smiling Joe Montague walked out of his kennel and said, "*Ciao*, Dr. DeOni, *buena sera*. Welcome to my home!"

Letting the mispronunciation of my name slide, I stepped forward to shake his hand.

Joe was quite smartly dressed considering the fact we were about to handle quite a few of his dogs. He wore white and black colors matching his house and kennel. His shirt was white and short- sleeved. The two top buttons were open exposing a manly crucifix. The neatly pressed slacks, loafers and socks were all black. A gold watch, a large diamond ring and wedding band completed his ensemble.

I guessed that he was about five-foot-eight inches tall, 165 lbs. or so, and in his middle fifties. He had an abundant supply of salt and pepper hair, combed straight back over his head. His muscular build was comparable to a sturdy bulldog.

His complexion was naturally tanned, presumably from years spent outside. Numerous laugh lines spread out from his dark brown eyes and mouth. Joe appeared to be a very pleasant, and obviously, quite a handsome man.

While shaking his hand, I said, "You have a beautiful home and yard here."

"*Grazie, grazie,*" he proudly smiled.

"I'll just get my supplies from the car. Should I bring them into the kennel?"

"*Si*, butta let me help you, no?"

Practicing my Italian, I said, "*Si*, okay."

The kennel was comfortably air conditioned and like the outside spotlessly clean. It was a far cry from some of the other kennels that I had visited. The kitchen area had a refrigerator, a sink for washing dog bowls, and two banks of cabinets for handy storage of food, bowls, dishes, medicines and miscellaneous items. There was also ample counter space. An American flag and an Italian flag hung side by side, decorating one of the walls.

In a separate area of the kennel, a raised bath-tub and grooming table were in place for keeping his *flock* neat and clean. A separate room was built for whelping (giving birth), and for raising inquisitive puppies.

Each of his twenty bulldogs had their own spacious cage. And each cage had a two-way door allowing them free access to an enclosed exercise run outside. Soothing music floated through the kennel area throughout the day. In my opinion this was a luxurious five star kennel!

Getting out my *To Do* list, I said, "Well Joe, ready to get started?"

"*Si*, of course."

"Let's start with the six puppies," I suggested.

Joe brought them out one at a time, kissed each one, and placed them on the grooming table. The four male and two female puppies were nine weeks old. No two puppies looked alike; each had different markings and colors. They did, however, all act alike-- friendly, wiggly and roly-poly. Joe had named them some rather unique names-- Benvolio, Mercurio II, Rosaline, Tybalt, Juliet and Escalus.

"Joe, how did you choose these names for the puppies?"

"My *bambinos* are named for characters in *Romeo and Juliet*. You no read?" he asked, while looking at me like I was from another planet.

"Of course, I read *Romeo and Juliet* in high school but that was several years ago."

"You read again. *Si*?"

"Sure, *si*, I will," I stammered.

"Doctor DeOni, you know where *Romeo and Juliet* takesa place?"

"Yes, uh...Italy," I knowingly smiled.

"*Si*, in Verona. That's where my *famiglia* is from and where I was born!" Joe said with obvious pride. "Thatsa why I named my kennel after William Shakespeare!"

"Well, that is very interesting and after today, I will read *Romeo and Juliet* again," I promised for the second time.

Moving on with the list, we treated Hamlet's ear infection. Caesar and MacBeth's hearts were doing quite well. Othello did not have cataracts, just a normal bluing change in the lenses, typical of dogs over eight years old. Queen Mab was about four weeks pregnant which made Joe quite happy. The stool samples were all negative for worms except for a light case of roundworms in the puppies.

* * *

Then it was Amos's turn for his pre-surgery check up.

Joe took Amos out of his cage, snapped on a leash and walked toward the grooming table. The bulldog obediently shuffled along slowly behind his master. He seemed to be a little larger than the other males and looked a bit different than the rest. As Amos got closer, I could then see several physical flaws or imperfections. Joe saw the surprised look on my face.

With some embarrassment, he said, "Dr. De-Oni, I know my Amos is ugly. I had great hope for him when he was a little *bambino*. He gots too big. His mouth has a bigga under-bite, you see his bottom teeth stick way out?"

I nodded sadly and Amos lowered his head like he was ashamed as well.

Joe continued on, "His eyelids droop, the ears are set back too far and are crooked." Then grabbing Amos's lower lips, he pointed out, "Look, the lips are too loose, they sag, and how you say, the saliva drips out. His back is not straight, it's ..uh, uh...sway back."

"Yes, I can see all of that," I said.

"But worst of all, his nose is pinched almost shut! How you like that? He has to breath through his mouth all the time so he snorts and slobbers all over the place."

Lifting Amos onto the grooming table, I

examined him, and everything that Joe said was true. However, despite these inherited breeding imperfections, he was not in bad physical shape except for the stenotic nares. The opening to each nostril was too small or as Joe said, *pinched shut*. Dr. North was going to neuter Amos tomorrow and also try to correct his nasal opening.

Joe went on to say, "I hope somebody will take Amos. I try and find him a nice home. Maybe you help me, *si*?"

"I'll try my best, Joe," I said, which was now my third promise of the afternoon. I glanced at my watch and it was almost 5 o'clock. Time to go.

"Okay, now we eat and have some vino!" Joe excitedly announced.

"What? Listen Joe, you don't have to feed me. Just because....."

Raising both hands, Joe stopped me in mid-sentence, and said, "Dr. DeOni, you come to my home, look at my *bambinos*, now we talk, drink and *mangia* some good Italian food. *Capisce?*"

Not wanting to insult my host, I said, "Yes, I would like that, but first I'll need to call my wife and explain."

"There's a phone right there in the kitchen, call her. Here's Amos's leash, he keep you company while me and my Marie set the table. Oh! Marie is my beautiful wife for twenty-eight years. You meet her soon." Then Joe hurried out of the kennel.

I called Tina and told her of my predicament; she understood and said, "Ed, it's best to stay, just relax and have a good time."

After saying good-bye and hanging up the phone, I looked down at Amos. He was mostly white with small spots of tan on both ears and two larger patches of tan on each side of his chest. Amos's white fur was very fine, so much so, that in some areas you could see his pink skin and numerous black skin spots below the fur. His eyes were dark brown with black eyelids, nose and lips. He was seated obediently by my feet with his mouth open, tongue hanging out a few inches and breathing somewhat loudly.

Squatting down to his level, I said, "Amos, you are not ugly, I think you're very handsome!"

Amos stared into my eyes and responded telepathically, *Thanks for saying that Doc, I sure hope that you guys can fix me up. All my bulldog kennel mates call me names because I snort and slobber so much.*

"Don't worry, we'll do our best. Now let's go find Joe."

* * *

Amos and I shuffled slowly from the kennel and up the stone walkway to their home. On the way we stopped twice, so my new bulldog friend could *water* the plants. Adjacent to the house, a circular table, with a red-checkered tablecloth, was being set for dinner.

Marie was busy placing the plates and silverware on the table as Amos and I finally arrived. Joe was uncorking a bottle of vino, and said, "Dr. DeOni, this is my wife, Marie. She's beautiful, no?"

"Yes, yes," I said and added, "please call me Ed. Okay?"

"*Si, si*, Dr. DeOni, we will," replied Joe.

Marie was quite beautiful, I noted. She looked younger than her husband by four or five years, I guessed, and maybe two inches shorter as well. It was hard to tell accurately because Marie was in constant motion, flitting back and forth to the kitchen. She, like Joe, had thick black hair streaked with gray, dark brown eyes and an olive complexion. Marie wore a tomato-stained, chef's apron over a pink dress with white flowers.

Sitting down into a comfortable cushioned chair with Amos laying by my side, I watched Joe light the candles and pour us a glass of red wine-- *il vino rosso*. After the proper salute, Marie started with the ante-pasta-- a plate of assorted cheeses, Genoa salami, large black and green olives, and bruschetta with a bowl of olive oil with herbs for dipping.

Picking up a slice of cheese and bread, Joe said, "*Buon appetito*," and pointed at me. "*Mangia!* Eat my friend."

I did.

Marie came out of the kitchen carrying a large bowl of *insalata mista*--a mixed salad of fresh vegetables and lettuce from their own garden. She refilled our wine glasses, cleared the used plates and disappeared back into the kitchen.

While waiting for the main course, Joe asked, "Do you know how bulldogs gots their name?"

"No, not really."

"Bulldogs originated somewhere in the British Isles. England, maybe Scotland, who knows!" he shrugged.

"They were bred to be, how you say, *tough as nails*. They helped the farmers control their bulls. Bulldogs were very aggressive so sometimes they be put in a ring to fight each other. Also, there was *bull-baiting*. Thatsa where they tie up a big bull with a strong rope around his neck. Then each farmer puts in his best bulldog to fight the bull."

"Gee, I didn't know that."

"The bravest bulldog would bite the bull on the nose and hold on. The bull would try to shake him off, kick him, bang him on the ground. Anything he could do. But that bulldog hold on so tight and notta let go. The bull would be bleeding badly from his nose and blood run down onto the bulldog's face, but still he hold on."

"It sounds quite gruesome."

"Yes, it was. Eventually, the bull would tire because that bulldog is so heavy, and he loses so much blood, and he can't breathe so good. Then boom, the bull falls down and that bulldog is the winner. In 1835, England outlawed this bull-baiting and dog-fighting because it was so cruel and so many bulldogs and bulls were killed in the ring. So then breeders like me started to breed only bulldogs with nice temperaments like my Amos."

On hearing his name, Amos stood up and tried to wag his short stubby tail. I gave him a gentle pat on the head and told him, "Good boy."

Marie walked out with a steaming serving dish of lasagna, smothered with her homemade tomato sauce. She lovingly scooped out a generous portion, refilled our wine glasses again and cleared the salad plates.

Joe lifted his red linen napkin and stuffed it into his shirt collar. "We gonna need this Doc."

I followed Joe's example. After two servings of Marie's lasagna, I was getting quite full. Joe was busy uncorking another bottle of vino.

"That's enough for me. I have to drive home," I wisely stated.

Since Joe was already home, he kept refilling

his own glass as needed. After dessert of cheesecake covered with freshly picked blueberries, we sat and talked some more.

Actually, Joe talked, I listened. My now tipsy host was getting louder and laughing harder at his own jokes.

"Hey Doc, do you know how you look and act like a bulldog?"

"No." I smiled waiting for the answer.

"Well, you run into brick wall a few times, flatten you face. Then put clothes pin on you nose so only breath out mouth. Then, get down on hands and knees, pull you tongue out a few inches, put hot pepper on tongue so drool runs out of mouth and turn elbows out to side. Then you fart every thirty seconds. Presto, you a bulldog." Joe laughed so hard that he almost fell out of his seat.

I controlled myself for Amos's sake.

Marie came out and scolded, "Joe Montague, that's enough of those jokes." The boss had spoken and Joe obeyed. It was also a good time for me to leave.

I thanked Joe and Marie for dinner and their hospitality.

"Oh, don't forget, do not feed Amos any food for the rest of the evening and pick up his water bowl when you go to bed tonight. Tomorrow is my day off, but I will see you for Amos's surgery in the morning."

I knew Joe would be there at the surgery, because Dr. North often allowed certain friends to sit in and observe.

After hugging both, I said, "*Arrivederci* and *grazie*."

"See, you going to be *Italiano* soon. And wait, I have something for you." Joe ran into the house and returned with a small book.

"For you, *amico mio (my friend)*."

"Thank you," I said. Turning the well-used book over to see the title, it read, *Romeo and Juliet* by William Shakespeare.

"But..." I said with utter surprise.

Marie chimed in and said, "You take it, we have at least two more."

Thanking them again, I drove home happy and stuffed. Now I knew what Mike meant when he said, "You'll be in for a real treat."

To be continued...

9

Amos - The Surgery

Animals adapt, we complain.
Author

Thursday morning, awakening with a slight vino headache and pleasant memories, I crawled out of bed. It was my day off! It was errand, food shopping and spend quality time with the kids day. Last night, I had explained to Tina, in detail, the events of the kennel visit and the Italian dinner. Feeling a bit guilty, I decided to wait until today to tell her about watching Amos's surgery on *our* day off. She was still sleeping peacefully, so I went to entertain and quiet the kids who were playing in their bedroom.

Eddie was still in bed reading one of his many dinosaur books. Our son, now six years old, had become fascinated with dinosaurs from about the age of three. His half of the bedroom and much of the bed was littered with everything to do with his favorite extinct animals. Posters, books and plastic replicas were everywhere. T. Rex, Bronto., Stega., and all the rest of their *Saurus* cousins were set up in some imagined play world.

Terri, my precocious five-year-old daughter was out of bed and singing softly. She twirled and danced gracefully across the bedroom floor. Terri was wearing her favorite pink tee-shirt, black leotard and blue tutu. She was busy rehearsing a dance routine and concert for her parents and brother.

"Hi kids," I happily said.

A simultaneous, "Dad," resounded from the bedroom, "we missed you last night!"

"Shh," I whispered, "you'll wake mom and the baby." Our six-week-old Michelle, was still asleep much to Tina's joy.

After moving a few Barbie dolls, I hopped onto Terri's bed and said, "Come here kids, let me tell you about a bulldog that I met last night."

"Yeah, a story!" they shouted and snuggled up beside me.

"Okay, once upon a time, there was a bulldog named Amos who lived in a kennel with other bulldogs. But, Amos was different from the rest, and they called him ugly and other not very nice names. They wouldn't play with him because he was always snorting and slobbering. Amos was very sad and lonely."

"Dad, this story makes me want to cry, tell us a happy story!" said my sensitive daughter.

"Yah, come on dad. This is no fun," echoed my son.

"Listen, it's going to get better because today Amos is going to have surgery to fix his nose and other things." I didn't want to explain the neutering part of the surgery. "And guess what?"

"What?"

"Daddy is going to help! Then Amos can get a new home with nice kids like you and live happily ever after."

Suddenly a voice from the doorway said, "Ed, are you trying to tell us something about today?"

Glancing up sheepishly, I saw Tina standing there with both hands on her hips giving me the *look.*

"Today is your day off to be with your family. Remember?"

"Listen honey, I promised that I would go in this morning for maybe an hour at the most. Then we will have the rest of the afternoon and evening to ourselves."

"We'll see, come on kids, let's have breakfast."

I was abandoned for orange juice and scrambled eggs except for the Barbie that remained on my lap and T. Rex that was currently under my butt.

At 10 a.m., the phone rang. It was Sandy, our surgery technician. "Hi, Dr. Dionne, the surgery will be starting in about fifteen minutes."

"Thanks, I'm leaving now."

Grabbing a banana and a piece of toast, I said, "Good-bye kids, I'll be home right after we fix up Amos. It won't be long."

Then turning to my wife I said, "Okay honey?"

She was still a little frosted, but I knew she would melt once I was back home. Grabbing my car keys, I ran out the door and down the steps to our well-used, green station wagon. We were seven miles from the hospital, and by now I could probably drive blindfolded from our home in Pluckemin, down Route 202, to the hospital in Somerville. Driving a little faster than normal, there were a few reasons not to be late.

First, I wanted to see my new friend, Joe Montague, so that I could thank him again for the book and dinner. And there was Amos; I was already attached to this lovable outcast.

Second, there was the nasal surgery that I had only read about in veterinary journals but had never done one myself.

Somehow, I erroneously felt that if I drove in faster, I would then be back home to my family that much sooner. The wine may have still been clouding my thought processes.

Parking my car in the rear of the kennel, I then hustled and entered the side door to the hospital. I did not want to be seen by Mike or any regular clients of mine.

Especially if they had a few questions like, "Oh, Dr. Dionne, since you are here today could you take a *quick peek* at Zelda's ear?" There is no such thing as a simple quick peek; most last about fifteen minutes or so.

Navigating safely through the pharmacy and kennel areas, I climbed the surgery stairs, two steps at a time. On seeing me enter the surgery room, Joe said, "Dr. DeOni, good to see you!"

After an abbreviated Italian hug, I said, "How's everything going so far?"

"*Bello*, great!"

But, Dr. North was a little more concerned

and said, “Amos has a very elongated soft palate and his laryngeal opening is quite small. We had a little trouble inserting the endotracheal tube into his trachea (windpipe). He seems fine now that he is connected to the anesthesia machine. I’m just finishing the neutering, and then we’ll start his nose.”

The elongated soft palate is seen in mainly short-nosed breeds and can cause difficulty with breathing just like Amos’s pinched nose.

Sandy, the well-trained surgery tech., was monitoring the anesthesia, oxygen and intravenous fluid drip. Joe was unusually quiet, not wanting to disturb his friend, Arthur.

I paid particular attention now that the nasal surgery had started. I admired the skill and dexterity with which Dr. North’s hands moved from one instrument to another. He certainly was an artist with a scalpel.

After removing the excess nasal tissue from each nostril, Dr. North placed very fine cosmetic sutures in each incision, and was finished in less than thirty minutes.

Sandy shut off the gas anesthesia and just kept Amos on oxygen. The endotracheal tube is kept in place as the patient wakes up. Once the gag-reflex returns, then it is safe to pull the endotracheal tube out. This usually only takes a few minutes, and Amos was no exception. Sandy deflated the cuff that holds the tube in place in the trachea and removed it from the patient.

Then the problems started.

Amos was awake but couldn’t breathe and was choking. I stepped forward from being an observer to help. Amos’s gums and tongue were turning *blue*. I grabbed the *Pentothal* and injected the liquid anesthetic into the intravenous drip. Amos was induced back into an anesthetic state.

Dr. North grabbed the laryngoscope so that he could see into the back of his patient's mouth. Sandy handed Dr. North another endotracheal tube so that he could reinsert it. With much difficulty, he managed to get it back into the trachea.

Turning the oxygen and anesthesia machine back on, I squeezed the rubber re-breathing bag three times. This positive pressure ventilation forced oxygen back into Amos's lungs, and his membranes and tongue were now pink again. Our patient was back under light anesthesia and breathing comfortably on his own.

The four of us collectively breathed a sigh of relief as we all looked at each other. A very close call, but now what?

Dr. North explained to Joe and to us, "When we pulled the tube out, the larynx which sits at the top of the trachea essentially collapsed inward creating an even smaller opening. And, to make matters worse, the elongated soft palate also flopped into the opening so Amos couldn't breath."

An emotional Joe asked, "What are we gonna do now?"

A worried Arthur replied, "That's a good question. I'm afraid that if we turn off the anesthesia and oxygen, Amos will wake up, and the same thing will happen all over again. He will choke, turn blue and might die this time."

"I don't want my Amos to suffer. Do we have to put him to sleep?" asked Joe whose tears were now streaming down his cheeks.

Silence.....

Sandy turned away, and it was the first time that I saw my boss at a loss for words.

Thinking for a moment, an idea popped into my mind, "What if we do a tracheotomy and make an opening in his trachea? This will bypass the collapsed larynx and soft palate. We can wake him up and safely remove the endotracheal tube."

Dr. North agreed, "However, this will have to be a permanent opening, and we will need a special tracheotomy tube. And we don't have one!"

Undaunted, I suggested, "Why don't I call Dr. Brown, Snoopy's owner, at the hospital? I bet he would give us one."

Dr. North looked at his friend, "What do you think, Joe?"

"I'm confused with all these uh... tubes and things. You explain it to me more simple, please."

I obliged as best that I could, "Joe, you have two choices-- put Amos to sleep right now with an overdose of anesthetic while he's still asleep. Or two, we do a surgical procedure where he will have a permanent hole in his neck which will require daily care at home for the rest of his life."

Holding his head with both hands, Joe started to pace and speak to himself in Italian.

Finally he said, "If I putta him to sleep, maybe that's the best thing. But I can't! If you do the surgery and make the breathing hole, he will look more ugly, and no one will adopt him."

Silence..... More tears.

"Marie and I have to make him a house dog."

Joe weighed his options for another couple of minutes. Then he said, "My Amos make a fine house dog. Please get those breathing tubes!"

That's all we needed to hear, and the team sprang into action.

"Sandy, you clip the fur on his neck from his chin down to his chest, scrub it well and spray it with the iodine solution," said the revived surgeon.
Sandy picked up the clipper and started right in with the shaving.

Arthur continued on, "I'll get a clean set of sterile instruments, drapes and suture material."

Knowing what my job would entail, I said, "While you are doing that, I'll call Dr. Brown and hopefully get Amos a tracheotomy tube."

"Okay, time is of the essence," Dr. North said. "Let's get to work."

I ran out of surgery and down the stairs. Slipping near the bottom step, I grabbed onto the railing to keep from taking a tumble. Righting myself, I proceeded to the office. Pushing the door open with a thud, I burst into the busy room.

Mike was seated at his desk with his back towards me. Upon hearing the commotion, he said, "That sounds like Dr. Dionne has arrived." Turning around in his chair, he asked, "What are you doing here on your day off?"

Not bothering to answer the question, I said, "Mike, we have a big problem up in surgery with the Montague dog. I need the Dr. Brown-- Snoopy record right away!"

Rosalee jumped up, "I'll get it," and deftly pulled the record from the filing cabinet.

"Thanks, and one more thing, could someone call Tina and tell her I'll be a little late because of the emergency with Amos?"

Doris volunteered and started dialing.

"Oh Doris, tell Tina that I'm sorry, and I'll sign the divorce papers when I get home."

Doris laughed, and I left with the Brown record. Stopping next in the doctors' lounge, I dialed Dr. Brown's hospital number that was in the record. Hoping to get him directly, I was disappointed when his protective secretary answered the phone.

"Good morning, Dr. Brown's office, may I help you?"

"Yes, this is an urgent situation and I need to speak with Dr. Brown right away!"

"Well, he's busy at the moment. Can I take a message and have him call you back?"

Trying to control myself from exploding, I gave it another try, "Tell Dr. Brown that Dr. Dionne is calling for his friend, Arthur North, who has an emergency with a patient."

The secretary then asked, "Do you mean Dr. North the veterinarian?"

"Yes."

"Why he's my vet, we take our cats to him. I'll get him right away."

Thinking out loud, "Is there anyone around here that doesn't know Arthur?"

A few seconds later, Dr. Brown picked up the phone, "What can I do for you, Ed?"

I briefly explained our predicament and asked about the tracheotomy tube.

Dr. Brown replied, "I'll have three sterilized *trach* tubes of different sizes waiting for you at the reception desk in the main entrance to the hospital. Take all three and use the one that fits best."

"Thanks, Charlie. I'll be right over."

* * *

In a flash, I was out the door and into my trusty green station wagon. The hospital was no more than three miles from here, but there was a formidable obstacle in the way-- the four lane Route 22. The traffic in both directions, east and west bound, was like the ocean waves, never ceasing. Making a right hand turn out of the parking lot, I *revved* the car engine and *dove* across the two eastbound lanes to the safe u-turn lane. A pair of truck drivers honked their disapproval as they hit the brakes on their big rigs.

Next, I had to turn left and enter the westbound lane. Good fortune smiled, there was no one coming at this time. Peeling out, I accelerated my green *aircraft* up to 70 m.p.h. The third and last turn was only one-half mile ahead. Making another left to cross over the eastbound lane again, I *flew* onto the road that led to the hospital. A few motorists seemed to be miffed at my low flying, green aircraft crossing in front of them. They saluted with a long horn-blowing and one or two shook their fists at me.

The hospital was just up the road, so I slowed the craft and made preparations for landing. Finally, I taxied up to the hospital's main entrance, opened the door, and ejected myself from the cockpit. Leaving the engine running, I then jogged through the open sliding glass hospital doors.

Dodging and side-stepping two wheelchair patients who were being discharged, I arrived at the reception desk. I was sweating, disheveled and out of breath.

The receptionist asked pleasantly, "Sir, may I help you?"

Trying to speak was difficult, "Do you... do you have three tracheotomy tubes for me?"

She answered, "Sir, I'm afraid I don't know what you are talking about. Are you okay? Shall I call for an orderly?"

"No!" I stammered loudly, "Dr. Brown said he would have them here for me!"

"Sir, why don't you take a seat right over there, and I'll get some help."

Just seconds before having a nervous breakdown or possibly a major stroke, I was saved by a loud, "Hey Ed!" Dr. Brown had stepped out of the elevator carrying three sterilized tracheotomy tubes. "How did you get here so fast?" Charlie asked.

"Private jet," I responded with a relieved smile.

After handing me the packages, I thanked him again and said, "Charlie, I gotta run, give my regards to Snoopy 2."

Then I sprinted out the glass entrance doors, hopped into the station wagon and headed back. The return trip was easy, just one right hand turn, then pull into the *safe* veterinary parking lot.

"Made it," I said aloud while turning off the car's engine.

* * *

Running into the kennel entrance, then up the surgery stairs, I misjudged the steps once again. Slipping and about to fall on my face, my left hand shot out and saved me by grabbing the step. My right hand managed to hold on tightly to the precious trach tubes. I picked myself up and muttered, "What the heck!"

Entering the surgery room, I saw that Dr. North had started the operation. Looking up, and speaking through his mask, "You got them I see. Any problems?"

"No, nothing major," I answered, "unless if you call two or three near death experiences a problem."

"I'm at a point where you would be a big help with the surgery," Arthur stated.

I was flattered and handed the sterilized packs to Sandy to open and place carefully on the instrument tray. After quickly donning a cap and mask and scrubbing up, I slipped on a pair of size 7, sterile latex surgery gloves.

Stepping up to the opposite side of the operating table from Dr. North, I surveyed the scene. The trachea was fully exposed. On the left and right side were the large bluish jugular veins, pulsating carotid arteries and whitish vagus nerves running parallel to the trachea. Each set of three laid in their respective jugular groove.

Dr. North said, "Well Ed, since this was your idea, what do you think we should do from here?"

Flattered for a second time, I answered, "Let's make sure we identify all the thyroid tissue and tiny parathyroid glands so we can avoid them."

The next step was to decide where to open the trachea. Several evenly spaced rings of cartilage hold the windpipe open like a flexible tube. This allows air to pass unimpeded into the lungs. We didn't want to make too big an opening, or too little for that matter.

Having picked a suitable spot, Arthur, using a scalpel, opened up the trachea. We could now see Amos's endotracheal tube sitting comfortably inside.

"Okay, what's next?" he asked.

Selecting the best sized trach tube, I answered, "We have to be quick about this. Sandy, you will deflate Amos's endotracheal tube and pull it out of his mouth. I will stick this trach tube into the wind pipe through the opening we just made. Dr. North, you will hold it, while Sandy re-connects the anesthesia machine to the trach tube."

Everyone nodded in agreement.

"Sandy, make sure you hold the non-sterile anesthesia hoses up and away from our surgery site. Dr. North, you can suture the trach tube in place. After that, you can also close the top half of the incision, and I will close the bottom half."

We did everything smoothly and perfectly. Shutting off the anesthesia, then the oxygen, we disconnected everything from Amos. Stepping back, but ready to start again if necessary, we waited nervously for Amos to wake up.

Joe paced, chewed his nails and said a few *Hail Marys* in Italian for all of us and Amos.

A few anxious minutes later, Amos opened his eyes. I tested the new *breathing hole* with my hand to feel for exhaled air.

"It's working!" I exclaimed.

Dr. North said, "And, I can hear air flowing into his lungs with my stethoscope."

Joe was crying tears of happiness, "*Grazie*, *grazie*, thatsa all I can say."

As soon as Amos was fully awake, Sandy and I put on a sterile dressing and bandaged his neck. The trach tube was supported by the bandage and only protruded slightly. Arthur suggested that we leave Amos in the surgery prep room for the night. We placed him gently in the padded recovery cage.

Dr. North also said, "I will be here until 7 p.m. to watch him."

Sandy chimed in, "I can check him after 11 p.m. as needed."

Not wanting to be left out, I volunteered for a 9 p.m. check and first thing in the morning at 7 a.m.

"But it's your day off," said Sandy.

"It is?" And we all had a good laugh.

Saying good-bye, I walked slowly and carefully down the *treacherous* surgery stairs and hopped into my green, ex-airplane and drove home. Pulling in the driveway to our home at 2:45 p.m., I was about to rejoin my wife and kids once again. All of them were at the beach area of the small Sunset Lake within view from our house.

Michelle was asleep in her playpen; Tina was seated in a beach chair watching Eddie and Terri splash around in the water on this beautiful sunny day. Walking down to the beach, I sat in the empty chair next to my wife.

"Hi, is this chair saved for me or someone else?"

"For you silly, and I don't have any divorce papers either!" she smiled. "How's Amos?"

"He's fine."

My wet children ran from the water and wrapped themselves in their beach towels.

"Dad, tell us about Amos."

On hearing most of the story, everyone was relieved and glad to know that he was okay so far.

After dinner that evening, I suggested that we all go into Somerville for an ice cream treat at our favorite restaurant.

They unanimously answered with, "Yeah dad, let's go!"

We all indulged ourselves with hot fudge sundaes except for baby Michelle who was quite happy looking at the ceiling fan. I was a hero again in their eyes.

Before going home, I asked hopefully, "Would you like to meet Amos? We can stop at the hospital and see how he's doing."

"Yes!" the ice cream-loaded kids yelled.

Tina gave me another *look* and said with a grin, "You planned this all along, didn't you?"

"Sort of," I smiled.

After parking, we quietly entered the surgery and turned on the lights. I introduced everyone to our sleepy patient.

Tina and the kids all loved Amos as I knew they would. Rising up slowly to a standing position and still breathing well, Amos attempted to wag his tail but lost his balance and plopped back down. Seeing their worried looks, I reassured them that he was all right, and that they could pet him gently on the head.

They did, and after a few pleasant minutes we said good-bye and left for home quite a happy lot.

To be continued...

Eddie with sister, Terri

10

Amos and Andy - A Love Story

And ever has it been known that love knows not its own depth until the hour of separation.
Kahlil Gibran

According to the latest edition of *Webster's Dictionary: Love-- an intense feeling of positive emotion toward somebody or something, especially a romantic or sexual feeling toward the opposite sex.*

Wise old Daniel seems to have left open quite a few possibilities when he describes love. There is no mention that love is the sole realm of we humans. On the contrary, love can be found everywhere. One only needs to look closely. This narrative is based on such an observation.

* * *

At precisely 6 a.m., the alarm clock went off with a brain-rattling clamor. After yesterday's complications with Amos's surgery, my body yearned for one more hour in bed.

I asked my pillow, "Just who was that who volunteered to check Amos at 7 a.m.?"

"I think it was you, Ed," mumbled the sleepy woman that I married.

Feeling a prodding female foot in the small of my back, I threw aside the covers and rolled out of bed. It was another work day.

Driving at the posted speed limit for a change, I arrived safely and calmly at our vet hospital. The three kennel employees had arrived a few minutes before me. They were busy leading the dogs out of the cages and into their designated outdoor exercise runs. Each cage would then be thoroughly cleaned before bringing them all back in for breakfast. The cats, and those dogs unable to go out for medical reasons, would be moved to temporary quarters while their cages could be tidied up as well.

"Hey Doc, what are you doing here so early? Got an emergency?" inquired Rocky, one of the kennel workers.

"No, I'm just checking on the Montague dog. He's still up in the surgery recovery cage."

"Do you want us to feed him?"

"Hold off on that until I check him and see what Dr. North thinks. One of us will let you know."

Climbing the surgery stairs, quietly opening the door and turning on the lights, I hoped that Amos was all right. You never know with a surgery like this. It would be absolutely dreadful to find that your patient, whom you had worked so hard on, had died.

This would not be the case with Amos. He was sitting up as I entered.

"Good morning, how would you like to go for a walk?" I suggested.

The message that I received was, *Sure, let's go!*

Sandy had also left me a note saying that Amos seemed to be fine every time she checked on him throughout the night. Good news indeed.

Carrying Amos carefully down the stairs and outside, I placed him gently on the driveway. Slipping a leash behind his front legs and around his big chest instead of his bandaged neck, we began a slow walk to the grassy area behind the hospital. Stopping in the first shady area, I bent over to check the status of his tracheotomy tube. It was open and very clean; I surmised that Sandy probably did a little swabbing out earlier this morning.

Staring into Amos's dark brown eyes, I asked, "How are you feeling today, buddy?"

Like crap, came the reply.

"That's kind of to be expected."

No, it's more than that Doc. What happened yesterday? I woke up and have this hose in my neck. I tried to bark last night and nothing came out! No one could hear or come and help me. I was afraid.

He then started to ask, *Where's you know... uh...*, while looking back at his hindquarters where the neutering had been done.

* * *

Starting from the beginning, I explained in detail what had happened, the complications, and how he almost died.

I'm depressed, said Amos. *Now I'm uglier than ever!*

"Hey, don't talk that way. You'll see, things are going to work out," I encouraged with a modest degree of conviction.

When I get back to Shakespeare Kennels, those mutts are going to be really mean to me now. And Rosa, the beautiful one that I have a crush on, will surely find someone else to flirt with like that no-good Mercurio.

"Just hold on a minute. Joe told me that you will now be his number one bulldog. Furthermore, your kennel days are over pal. You will be moving into the house as soon as you get home. If you play your cards right, Marie will feed you plenty of delicious Italian food and spoil you rotten. We'll be calling you King Amos from now on."

Walking back to the kennel, Amos's spirits picked up and he looked forward to going home.

* * *

Two days later, Dr. North released him to Joe and Marie with his list of home-care instructions. They were to return in ten days to have his stitches removed. Sometime in the future, we would remove his trach tube as well. A careful watch would then be required on the new breathing hole to prevent it from healing over with scar tissue.

My wife, Tina, has always espoused the belief that there are *no coincidences* and *everything happens for a reason*. Over time I became an ardent believer as well. Therefore, by some act of fate or destiny, an example occurred on this very afternoon.

Joe and Amos were scheduled for a checkup

with Dr. North at 2:15 p.m. Barbara Capulet and Andy were scheduled with me at almost the same time, 2:45 p.m. Andy needed her annual physical exam and booster vaccinations.

Entering Exam Room 3 with a smile, I said, “Hi kids! Hi Barbara! You’re all looking nice and dry today.”

They all laughed remembering the almost-drowning incident two weeks ago. Bending over to help pick up Andy, Barb and I placed her on the exam table.

“I saw your picture in the newspaper, Andy. Maybe I could get your autograph?” I teased.

She countered with a slobbery tongue wipe before I could get out of the way. The long wet kiss started at my mouth and swept up across my nose.

Taylor and Sam squealed with laughter.

Wiping off my face with a paper towel, I said, “Guess I better stick to business. So how’s she been feeling? Any problems?”

“No, she’s fine, except we had to put her on a diet,” said Barb.

“Yah, she’s too fat!” added Sam.

Sticking up for Andy, “Well, I don’t think she’s too bad, maybe just a tad too heavy. But, it’s always best to reduce the amount of dog food in the summer anyway, because she’s probably not exercising as much in this hot weather.”

“Andy likes to swim with the kids, but other than that the heat does bother her a great deal as you say. So she just stays in the house and sleeps,” added Barbara.

Turning my attention now to the checkup, I found her to be a very healthy two year old. After her *shots*, cleaning her ears and a toenail trimming, I said, keeping a safe distance, "You're done, cutie."

I lifted her off the table and back to the floor. "Let me walk you guys out, I need the exercise!" I chuckled.

"Okay, let's go kids," Barb said smiling.

Escorting everyone to the exit door, we *non-coincidently*, bumped into Joe and Amos as they were about to leave as well. Stepping outside, I introduced the two bulldog owners.

"Joe Montague, this is Barbara Capulet, an old friend of mine from high school."

Joe bowed slightly, and said, "*Ciao, buena sera*, pleased to meet you. Eh, are you Italiano?"

"I'm not but my husband is. He has a lot of relatives that still live in Italy."

"Could it be in Verona?" Joe asked.

"Maybe, I'm not really sure."

"In the old days, the Capulet *famiglia* and Montague *famiglia* no getta long. Sometimes they even fight! This ah no good, but now little by little they, what you say, bury the hatchet, and become friends."

"Uh, excuse me, but did you guys know that you both live about one mile from each other in Martinsville?" I asked.

"Really!" exclaimed Barbara. "So you must be the owner of Shakespeare Kennels?"

"Thatsa right, and we breed and raise only the best English bulldogs, like your nice dog here. You and children must come and visit me and my Marie sometime, no?"

"We will. That's a promise." Barbara smiled. She then reached out and warmly shook Joe's hand.

Meanwhile, Amos's heart gave a mighty leap on seeing Andy. For the next few minutes, he stood transfixed by her beauty. Standing only inches from each other, Amos was somewhat tongue-tied. Summoning up all the courage he could muster, the captivated bulldog managed a weak, *Hello, I'm Amos*.

Responding with a feminine, *Hi, nice to meet you. I'm Andy*.

Before leaving for home Andy eyed him coyly and flirted as only a bulldog can do. By this time, Cupid's arrow had dug deep into Amos.

I had to get back to work and stepped away from the conversation after saying good-bye. Taylor and Sam were bored and getting hungry. Barbara and Joe said their farewells.

Amos finally asked hopefully, *Andy, may I come see you?*

She answered with an affirmative nod of her head and said, *Of course, that would be nice*. Then with a wink and a seductive smile, Andy left with the rest of the Capulets.

Joe had to pick up his un-moving, thunderstruck bulldog, who was by now totally and hopelessly in love. Amos sat in the front seat listening to Joe sing from his favorite opera, *The Marriage of Figaro*. Just before reaching Shakespeare Kennels and home, Joe pointed out the window, "Hey, thatsa where your new girlfriend lives. She's *bella*, *bella*, no?"

With his eyes widened, tongue hanging out a few inches and heart racing, Amos had to control himself from jumping out the window. Now that he knew where Andy and the Capulets lived, Amos had the beginnings of a plan.

* * *

By the next morning, he had all the details worked out. The usual morning routine was after breakfast, Joe would go to the kennel to work with the *mutts*, and Marie would tend the garden and water the flower beds. Amos would either follow Marie and watch, or simply take a nap.

But today would be totally different. After they had both left, Amos easily pushed the screen door open and headed east toward the Capulet household. Even though his destination was less than a mile away, it was not an easy task for a bulldog with a trach tube still in his neck.

Navigating his way first through the woods, then a thicket of heavy brambles and blackberry bushes with their prickly thorns, Amos pushed on. Oblivious to the painful scratches received in the bushes, he would not stop to rest. A small but wide stream now presented a major obstacle.

While looking for a suitable place to cross this meandering stream, Amos had random thoughts, *Don't fall in. I can't swim. Don't get water in the breathing hole. Wow, it's hot out. I gotta see my Andy!*

A short distance away at a bend in the stream, Amos found what he was looking for. A shallower area where fairly flat rocks jutted up from the streambed, inviting this short-legged bulldog to step across. He accepted the invitation and made it safely to the other side.

Now only a cornfield stood between him and his love. The anxious Amos decided to pick up the pace.

Bulldogs are built low to the ground and with turned out elbows. This results in difficulty walking in a straight line, so they zig-zag a little with each forward step. This proved hazardous to several immobile corn stalks that were plowed over in the wake of the starry-eyed lover.

Arriving at the edge of the field, the Capulet house was now in sight. *Boy, am I hot. I could really use a drink of water. Maybe I should go back to the stream. Don't be silly, Andy is just ahead. They will have water.*

Ignoring the early signs of dehydration and heat prostration, Amos continued to push onward, but as he neared the house his pace slowed. His zig-zag gait became more unsteady and his tongue hung out further, almost to the ground.

Climbing the two steps to the low back porch, he stared through the glass door to the kitchen. It was useless to try and bark. The tracheotomy made it impossible for that. Putting his paw on the door, he scratched several times before he got dizzy and fell down in a heap.

Taylor and Sam were having a late breakfast when they heard the scratching followed by the thud.

Rushing to the door, Taylor shouted, "Mom, there's a dog on our porch!"

Sam followed with, "It's a bulldog!"

Realizing who it was, they both shouted, "It's Amos, and he can't get up!"

Barbara left the dishes in the sink and hurried to the door. Andy slid off the couch to see what the ruckus was all about.

Amos's slumped body prevented the door from opening easily. Mom was able to gently push open the door just enough to squeeze out.

After moving Amos a little, she said, "Wow, he feels really hot! And look at all those scratches."

The three of them managed to pull him inside out of the blistering sun. Taylor ran to get her portable fan to cool his body. Andy stood near Amos and licked his face. Not having Joe's number, Barbara called me at work. On hearing what had happened, I knew it was probably a heat stroke so time was very important.

"Cover him with cold wet towels, be careful so water doesn't get in the breathing hole, and take ice cubes and rub them on his head, ears, paws and groin," I instructed.

"Do you have a rectal thermometer?" I asked.

"Ed, don't even go there!" she answered.

"Okay, don't worry about it . I'll call Joe and send him over. He knows what to do."

Hanging up, I rushed into the office and pushed opened the door resulting in the usual noisy bang.

Mike calmly said, without turning around first to see who it was, "Hi, Dr. D., what is it now?"

"Rosalee, I need the Shakespeare Kennels' telephone number and Joe's home number quickly."

"What's the problem?" Mike asked.

"His dog, Amos, got loose and now he has a possible heat prostration over at the neighbor's house."

Handing me the telephone numbers and pointing to her own neck, the worried Rosalee asked, "Isn't he the one with the....."

"Yes, yes, that's the one," as I rushed out to call Joe.

Figuring that Joe would be in the kennel, I

called there first and was relieved when he answered the phone.

"*Ciao*, Shakespeare Kennels."

"Joe, this is Dr. Dionne."

"Hey, Dr. DeOni. How are you?"

I rapidly explained where Amos was, and that I believed he has heat prostration.

"Oh no, Holy Mother of God, I go right over!"

"Joe, take a thermometer and call me with his temperature reading."

"Yes of course, now I go!"

* * *

Hanging up and waiting was nerve-wracking, so I started to pace. Heat prostration is not rare in dogs and is much more common in the short-nosed breeds like boxers, Boston terriers, pugs and of course English bulldogs.

Dogs cannot cool themselves off by sweating as we're able to do. The only place where there are functional sweat glands is between the pads on their feet, and they are so few in number to do much good. So the dog has to pant and blow off excess body heat mainly through the exhaled breath. In hot, humid weather like now, this process is not very effective at cooling either. Dogs kept in automobiles on a hot day with the window cracked open only slightly, will rapidly get heat stroke. Their body temperature will rise from a normal of 101-102 degrees to 106-108 degrees. Staying at this level, for even a relatively short time, is life threatening.

* * *

Finally the phone rang on our inside number. I picked it up and asked, "Yes, how's he doing?"

"He's doing okay, Dr. DeOni. Barbara and the *bambinos* got him cooled down very good. His temperature is 103 point a 2 degrees. That's good, no? Amos is even standing up when his girlfriend started kissing him."

"That's great Joe, take him home, give him water a little at a time, keep him cool, and if his temperature goes back up bring him in."

"Okay, I take him home now. *Ciao*."

Hanging up and mumbling, "I swear that bulldog is going to be the death of me yet!"

Amos went home and regained his strength over the next few days with the help of Marie's favorite pasta and meatballs. He was also being *grounded* slightly for running away. Joe put a harness around his chest, and Amos could only go out on a leash.

Amos would also have no reading of Shakespeare's plays to him in the evening for one week! Such harsh punishment!

Slowly the heat wave had finally ended with two days of heavy non-stop rain.

All Amos could do was look out the now locked screen door and wonder, *I bet Andy misses me. It was her kisses that saved me. I should go see her and thank her again.*

A new plan developed in his little bulldog brain.

* * *

The next day the rain had stopped, the sun was out, but a refreshing cold front had passed through. The air was crisp, almost fall-like. Joe went off to work in the kennel.

Marie took Amos out on his leash. She tied the leash securely to a sturdy rope near her garden and under a shade tree.

With hands on her broad hips, Marie warned Amos, "You be a good boy, no runnin' away!"
Amos put his head down and looked up with the saddest face that he could muster.

Sure, you bet, he thought to himself.

About thirty minutes later the phone rang and Marie ran into the house to answer it. This was the chance that Amos was waiting for. Marie was quite the talker. Once on the phone, she could be there for an hour or more.

Turning around, Amos grabbed the rope in his powerful jaws. He chomped and chomped until the rope was severed. The prisoner was free once again.

Amos had to pass by the kennel building in order to reach the woods. So with the stealth of a ninja warrior, he darted from one bush to another to stay hidden from Marie and Joe. Cautiously tip-toeing past the kennel building, followed by an all-out sprint, Amos reached the woods unseen.

He lingered for just a moment to catch his breath. Amos then followed the same trail that he had blazed last week.

Upon reaching the stream, he was shocked to see that the water had risen significantly higher due to the two days of heavy rain. His stepping stones were now slightly submerged.

Thinking to himself, he said, *Amos, you can do this. Just go slow and easy.*

Like a circus performer on the high wire, he took one careful step after another. Resting on the very last stone, he prepared himself to leap onto the dry bank. Counting in Italian, *Uno, due, tre*, Amos leaped. *Ouch!* he cried as his right rear foot slid off the slippery rock.

Scrambling out of the water, he looked down at his injured paw. He had a deep cut in the main pad, and it was bleeding.

Aw, cat crap, he said.

After giving his paw a couple of good licks, he continued on with a noticeable limp. Each step with the injured paw left a long trail of ruby-red polka dots headed in a straight line for the Capulet's house.

Meanwhile, posing and flexing his muscles for his non-interested sister, Sam was preparing to spring off the diving board into the somewhat chilly pool. The abrupt change in the weather didn't seem to faze this aquatic loving lad.

From his vantage point on top of the board, Sam spotted Amos charging and limping across the adjacent field. Sam yelled to his non-swimming sister, who was busily polishing her toe nails and trying to ignore her little brother's diving exhibition,

"Taylor, look who's coming!"

Standing up, she peered over the swimming pool's fence, "Oh my God, it's Amos! Mom, come quick!" she cried.

Such a cry sent a momentary chill down Barbara's spine. Putting down her newspaper, she hurried through the kitchen door and out onto the porch. She was relieved to see that the children were both okay.

Before she could even ask, the kids pointed and said, "Look!"

By now Amos had reached the low porch once again. This time there would be no fainting from heat stroke. He stood at Barbara's feet and looked up proudly. Standing on his three good legs, Amos held the injured limb up.

Periodically, like a leaky faucet, his cut pad produced a red drip which plopped and splattered upon the wooden floor.

"Now what have you done?" Barbara asked. "And what are you doing here again, mister?"

Amos shook his head in disbelief and thought to himself, *Such a foolish question. Where's my Andy?*

Barbara reached down and grasped the frayed end of the chewed rope, still attached to the leash and harness. Lifting up his paw, she could see the cut pad.

The curious Taylor grimaced and turned her head, "Yuk, that's gross!"

Sam also opened the kitchen door to let out the frantic, barking Andy, who immediately ran over to comfort her wounded hero.

As Andy and Amos relished their reunion with lavish kisses, Barbara headed back into the house for the telephone. The first call was to Shakespeare Kennels. The next was to me.

My first reaction was, "Barbara, you have to be kidding! Right?"

"No, I'm not! I called Joe and he should be here any minute now. What should I do for his bleeding foot?"

"Pour a little hydrogen peroxide on the cut, then put a gauze pad over the wound and wrap a piece of tape over the gauze using a little pressure to hold it in place. This should also stop the bleeding. Then slip one of the kid's white socks over the whole paw and bandage. Tell Joe to bring him right over, and I'll see if it needs stitches."

"Okay, bye."

Barbara just finished the first aid measures as Joe came roaring up the driveway in his white van.

Jumping out, he immediately started scolding Amos, "Whatsa matter for you. Runnin' away like this two times already. I should lock you up!"

On hearing this, Andy let out a low warning growl and stepped between Joe and her injured boyfriend.

Amos quickly intervened, *Honey, he doesn't mean it. Sometimes Joe is just a big Italian meatball!*

Andy backed away a few steps, and Joe scooped up his dog, put him in the van, thanked Barbara and zoomed back to our vet hospital once again.

* * *

It was now my lunch break, and I waited patiently for Amos's arrival. Joe carried him in, and Rosalee put them in Exam Room 3. Leaving my half-eaten tuna fish sandwich, I followed them in. After removing the sock and bandage, I could see that the main foot pad had a deep laceration about one inch in length. It needed suturing.

"Well Joe, here we go again," I said.

He was worried, "What about his tube, Dr. DeOni?"

"It won't be a problem. First, we will sedate him, then inject a local anesthetic around the cut. Then, he won't feel any pain and finally I'll stitch him up."

"Whew, I like what you say, thatsa good."

Finishing up with no difficulties, I put on a better bandage, gave him an injection of amoxicillin and some pills for home.

"Keep the bandage dry, and we'll take the stitches out in ten days."

"*Grazie, grazie*."

The glassy-eyed Amos was still in *la-la* land from the sedative. Joe picked him up and carried his limp body out to the van, still scolding him gently in Italian. As I watched them leave, Rosalee announced that my first patient of the afternoon was here. My half-eaten tuna fish sandwich and banana would just have to wait awhile longer.

* * *

Joe kept his misbehaving runaway in the house that evening to sleep off the sedative. In the morning, Amos was now fully awake and able to walk.

Seeing that, Joe laid down the law, "I'm sorry my Amos, but you a bad boy. You going back to live in the kennel. No more runnin' away. Thatsa that."

Marie, with tears welling up in both eyes, nodded her head in agreement.

Walking into the kennel, Joe led the forlorn bulldog back to his old cage in the rear of the building.

MacBeth saw Amos first and shouted, *Dead dog walking!*

This aroused the rest of the *mutts*, and they all gathered at the front of their cages to see who it was.

It's Amos, said a surprised Queen Mab. *What are you doing back here?*

Amos refused to answer and just trudged on with head held low. The other bulldogs took offense to his lack of respect. A deluge of insults could be heard as a thunderous roar of barking ensued.

What's the matter, too good for us?

What's that on your foot, a baby booty? resulting in more commotion.

Finally, Othello noticed the tracheotomy tube. *Man, look at that will ya, there's something coming out of his neck. What is that?*

You're sure one ugly looking English bulldog.

More barking. *Say something Amos, does the cat have your tongue?*

By the time Joe and Amos reached his old home, the *mutts* were having a field day with all their insults. Each one trying to outdo the other.

Amos walked into the cage, and Joe took off his leash and harness. Amos slowly sat down, then laid down with a sigh.

Joe closed the cage door and said, "I'm goin' back to the house, I be back later to feed everyone some good food, no?"

Amos didn't bother to even look up, he remembered the routine. *Who can eat*, he thought, *I'll never see Andy again!*

With a heavy heart, a small tear trickled down one of his many wrinkles.

As promised, Joe was back in less than an hour. The *mutts* were still in an uproar and throwing insults back and forth.

"Shut up already," Joe yelled at the top of his voice. "You want to *mangia* or not? This ah noise givin' me ache in my head."

Things quieted down considerably; eating is a top priority for all English bulldogs.

Well, almost all.

Amos didn't bother to even look or sniff at his serving. The second day, then the third day, Amos refused all food and now even his water bowl remained untouched. After refusing Marie's pasta with meat sauce on the fourth day, I got a call at home. My day off!

I waited patiently for Joe to finish his detailed, minute by minute, account of the last three days in Amos's life,

Twenty minutes later, leaving no stone unturned, he finally finished.

I thought a simple, *Dr. DeOni, this is the fourth day Amos hasn't eaten, and now he has stopped drinking as well*, would have sufficed.

"Joe, I think I know what his problem is."

"What, I punish him too bad? Should I bring him back to the house?"

"No... no, that's not it. Amos is in love with Andy. Without her, life is not worth living. I'm afraid he'll get very sick and maybe die of a broken heart."

"But, whatta we gonna do?" said a frightened Joe.

"Let me call Barbara."

To be continued...

FOREVER
AMOS & ANDY

11

Amos and Andy - Together at Last

Where there is love, there is life.
Mahatma Gandhi

Swans, gibbons, turtle doves, black vultures, French angelfish, wolves, albatrosses, prairie voles, and bald eagles, all have one thing in common...

They all mate for life.

There is no divorce, most of the time, prenuptial agreements, or alimony payments. They simply go about their business each day and live in the present, the *here and now*.

* * *

After speaking with Joe, I called Barbara and said, "Hi, this is Ed, your favorite vet."

"Hi, what's up?" she asked.

"Well..." I stumbled. "How would you like another dog?"

SILENCE.

"He would be free. Good with kids. Friendly. House-trained. Well-behaved. Obedient (most of the time). Purebred. Neutered. Has all his shots."

Barbara interrupted and asked, "Ed, would this be an English bulldog, by any chance?"

"Yes...yes, very good guess."

"And would his name happen to be Amos?"

"Right again," I replied and proceeded to fill her in on the events of the last few days.

"Ed, you know darn well that I have a warm heart for a cold nose. Don't you?"

"Yes, you do Barb. Why not take him on a trial basis. You can always take him back," I said guiltily knowing full well that it would never happen.

"Uh.... oh, Ed!... Okay, tell Joe we'll be over this morning."

"Thanks, Barbara. I'll call Joe, and you can call me anytime if you have any problems."

"Don't worry, I will! You can count on it!"

Placing a quick call to Shakespeare Kennels, which actually is never quick, I told Joe the good news.

"Barbara and the family will probably be over pretty soon." The ecstatic Joseph Montague could hardly contain his delirious excitement.

"*Grazie, grazie*, Dr. DeOni. Tank you Father God. Tank you Blessed Virgin Mary."

Interrupting all the *tank yous*, "Joe...Joe, you

better get ready! They'll be there soon!"

"Okay, yes... *Ciao*."

* * *

Barbara, Taylor, Sam and of course Andy, arrived within the hour. Joe and Marie came out to greet them.

"Now, Mrs. Barbara, I want to tell you one thing, okay?"

Barbara smiled and nodded affirmatively.

"My Marie and I tank you from the bottom of our hearts. If Amos has any problems or expenses, we will pay. Like ah if he sick, needs medicine or God forbid surgery, then Shakespeare Kennels will pay. I have two big bags of dog food for you. And dog bowls, leashes, harness, I give them to you right now."

He then pointed to the big pile of supplies to be loaded into their station wagon. "Every month, I bring over more. Whatever you need, no?"

"Joe, I'm overwhelmed. I hope it works out."

"Yes, yes, you see Mrs. Barbara. It will. My Amos is very good boy." Joe seemed to forget how he was going to lock him up a few days ago.

"Now, follow me.... I show you beautiful Shakespeare Kennels, and we get you new dog." Joe led the way and expounded, non-stop about his lovely building. Visitors always brought a round of excitement that quickly spread through the cages.

All the *mutts*, as Amos would say, were lined up to say hello and evaluate each new person. Othello, being closest to the door, spotted Andy first. He was awe-struck by her beauty. Trying his best to wolf-whistle, he naturally failed. (F.Y.I.--since bulldogs have short noses and pushed in faces, it is impossible for them to whistle at all!)

Othello did manage to alert everyone else, *Hot babe coming in!* This led to an all-out spectacle. The noise was deafening, and each male bulldog tried to out-perform the other to impress this gorgeous female.

Andy remained very cool even though it was quite difficult. Each bulldog seemed to have his own preferred method of attracting her attention. Caesar opted to run to the rear of his cage, turn quickly and sprint back. He would then give a mighty leap onto the front of the cage and bounce off. It was very impressive for most of the ladies, but not this one.

King Lear displayed his skill and balance by chasing his tail in dizzying circles, first one way then the other. Andy didn't give him so much as a second look.

Figaro laid on his back and just wiggled. *Disgusting*, she thought.

Mercurio, the gigolo and Amos's nemesis, stood at the front of the cage. He winked, raised and lowered his eyebrows, and asked, *What are you doing tonight, honey?* Andy paid him no mind and looked straight ahead.

The female dogs were the worst. *Who does she think she is? Looks a little broad in the hips to me.* Ignoring everyone, she finally saw whom she was looking for..... Amos!

Joe opened his cage and said, "Hey wake up, you gotta company already!" Amos managed to open one eye even though he really didn't care. That was until he saw his dream girl. Like Lazarus risen from the dead, he was up and standing again.

Andy rushed in and licked his face and neck. Amos responded with attempted tail wags and face rubs. He was reborn.

The rest of the kennel went silent. *Well, look at that will ya*, said Othello.

I don't believe it, cried Mercurio. *He's so ugly.*

The Montague and Capulet family walked back out proudly. Amos was worried about walking past the mutts. *They are going to call me a freak in front of you.*

Amos, you are my perfection of imperfecticity, said Andy.

What! Is that good? asked a bewildered Amos.

Very good! she replied.

Amos and Andy strolled out side by side. As they walked by Mercurio's cage, Amos excused himself for a moment.

Walking over to his enemy he said, *This time I got the girl!*

The gigolo just turned and looked the other way. Amos quickly lifted his leg and *watered* all over Mercurio's backside.

Hey, if you ever come back here again, I'll get you for that.

Amos and Andy laughed and ran out of the kennel and caught up with his new owner.

"There you are," said Barbara. "We thought that maybe you two had decided to run away." Everyone laughed. Joe gave Barbara two traveling cages as going away gifts. He wanted the dogs to be safe as well as the passengers.

Marie handed Barbara one more present which was carefully wrapped in bright red gift paper. "Open this tonight when your husband gets home."

"Okay, I will. Thank you," Barbara said.

After each dog was placed in their cage, the Montagues waved good-bye, and the Capulets drove home.

"Mom, do you think daddy's going to be surprised to see Amos?" Sam asked.

"Oh yes, I do believe daddy's going to be just thrilled to see Amos."

Arriving home, Amos was fed and broke his fast. After wolfing down a huge meal, Andy gave him a tour of the house. Later in the day, Barbara's husband, Jim, came home.

His first words were, "Honey, am I seeing double or are there two bulldogs in our house?"

Barb answered, "Here, have a glass of wine and sit down. I have a long story to tell you. You remember my friend, Ed the vet? He called me this morning and....."

After hearing the whole story, Jim laughed and said, "I would have done the same thing."
Amos was peeking around the corner and listened intently. After hearing his laughter, the grateful bulldog came running over to Jim and sat at his feet. A long pat on Amos's head sealed the deal. Amos was a Capulet.

Then Barbara remembered Marie's gift. Sam asked if he could open it, and Barbara handed it to him.

After tearing away the wrapping, Sam said with some disappointment, "What's this? It's just an old book!"

Barbara took the book and read the title aloud, "It's *The Complete Works of William Shakespeare*!" Finding a note inside, she read that aloud also:

Dear Mrs. Capulet,

Joe and I like to read these plays to all our dogs. They seem to like them. Romeo and Juliet is Amos's favorite. Maybe Andy and your children will enjoy them as well.

Marie

"I think reading this book is an excellent idea for the whole family," added Jim.

Taylor rolled her eyes and Sam frowned, but as the years went by, they both grew to know and love that worn book of Shakespeare's plays.

* * *

The following summer, a one year anniversary celebration picnic was held at the Capulet's house. The two bulldogs had become inseparable. During the past year, Amos had the minor surgery to remove his tracheotomy tube, and Barbara had kept a diligent watch on his breathing hole. The picnic was a festive affair. I brought my family.

Our two older children, Eddie and Terri, headed for the pool with Taylor and Sam. Joe and Marie brought enough Italian food to feed the entire county. I relaxed in a comfortable chair next to my bulldog buddy. Amos was in his baby pool with about two inches of water, just enough to cover his paws. He was content with that and happy to watch Andy dive off the board.

Looking at me, he said, *Doc, watch Andy's new dive. It's called the swan dive!*

"Okay, I'm watching."

Still wearing her fluorescent pink life preserver, Andy turned and smiled at Amos. Then she ran and did her swan dive with head up and front legs out to the side. To my untrained eye, the dive looked remarkably similar to a *belly flop*. Amos loved it and that was all that mattered. I smiled and was quite pleased at how everything had turned out so well.

* * *

The years ticked by and the two bulldogs matured and shared their life together quite happily and deeply in love. After hearing Shakespeare's plays many times, they decided to change their names to Romeo and Juliet from their favorite play. It was their little secret. The rest of the family had no way of knowing about this name change so they still called them Amos and Andy.

Each night when getting into their comfortable dog bed, Juliet would whisper to Romeo, *Good night, good night! Parting is such sweet sorrow, that I shall say good night 'til it be 'morrow.*

Romeo would respond with various verses such as, *That which we call a rose by any other name would smell as sweet.*

Hey, that's Juliet's line! whispered Andy.

Sorry, I know, but I think of you as a rose, replied the now sleepy Romeo.

* * *

Romeo was the first to pass on. He developed cardiomyopathy, a serious heart disease. One morning, he just didn't wake up. Juliet didn't understand at first and tried several scratches with her paw on his still body, all to no avail. She went into the master bedroom and sat beside Barbara and whined repeatedly.

Barbara awoke and sensing trouble said, “Oh no!”

Jim and Barbara both threw back the covers and followed Andy into the den where their dog beds were kept.

Reaching down and feeling Amos’s lifeless and cool body, Barbara and Jim began to cry. It was then that Juliet realized that her Romeo was gone and gave him one last kiss.

Jim buried Amos in a peaceful place in the far back of the lawn near a shade tree and flower garden. He also made and erected a small grave marker that read: *Amos-- an English bulldog-- 1970-1982--*
Her Romeo.

Andy adjusted to being alone, just barely. Taylor was in a private boarding school and living away from home. Sam was in high school and interested in only girls and cars. Barbara and Jim were busy on most days and had little time for Andy. There was no more swimming and diving, she was too old for that. The Shakespeare readings at night ended as well.

Weather permitting, each afternoon for almost a full year, she hobbled on her arthritic legs to the back of the yard to lay by Amos’s grave.

It was the first week of November with a threat of an early snowfall, and Juliet made her afternoon trek. Looking at the grave marker, she sighed, *I’m getting pretty old. Everything aches; my back, hips and feet, and I’ve lost three teeth. I also have early cataracts and don’t hear so well either. Romeo, Romeo, where art thou my dear Romeo?...*

Hey, is this a new Romeo? A familiar voice echoed in her brain.

Is that you Amos, but...

Of course, it is! I'm a spirit, but I can still hear you, and if I try hard enough like now, I can speak with you like before, telepathically.

I wish I could join you, said a crying Juliet.

Are you sure that you are ready?

Yes, yes, I am.

Okay then, take a deep breath, then exhale it all out, close your eyes and stop your heart. Don't breathe anymore.

Andy did as she was instructed, and peacefully left her body while lying next to Amos's grave. Romeo and Juliet were finally reunited.

* * *

The light snow began to fall as the sun was covered with dark clouds, and evening was fast approaching. Barbara looked out of her kitchen window for Andy. "She must be down at Amos's grave, her usual spot," she said. Putting on her coat, she knew it was useless to call her anymore. She was practically deaf. Barbara briskly walked out to the rear of the house and past the dormant flower garden.

There she was lying by the grave site as she knew Andy would be. Barbara called loudly to her, but there was no response. Andy had a light dusting of snow accumulating on her fur. Bending over to touch her, Barbara knew what had happened.

Tears came to Barbara's eyes and dripped down onto Andy's fur. As she knelt down resting her head on Andy's back, they had a few moments together and one last embrace. Finally, picking herself up, she left Andy's body there for Jim to bury when he got home from work.

Jim made another marker for Andy to match that of Amos. The new marker read:
Andy -- an English bulldog-- 1971-1983 -- His Juliet.

Hanging on the back of the marker was an old worn out, faded, pink life jacket filled with memories.

So the circle of life was now complete, and some say that this is the end of the story. But, I think it may be just the beginning again.

Arrivederci, Romeo and Juliet.

12

Ziggy the Polecat

Until one has loved an animal, a part of one's soul remains unawakened.

Anatole France

In life, things are not all black or white. More often it's a little of each or shades of gray. Much to the delight of my fellow Libras, this story will be the exception. As you will soon see, it is, without a doubt, clearly both black and white.

* * *

Reviewing my appointment list for the afternoon and evening, my attention was drawn to the very last one of the schedule. It read: *6:45 p.m.-- NA (new account)-- Barrow-- two polecats-- checkup and shots*. I laughed out loud. The office staff was getting even for all the little jokes that I played on them for the past four years.

"Polecat!" I said to my assistant, Anne.

Then pointing to my list and 6:45 p.m. appointment, I asked her, "Do you know what a polecat is?"

"No, I don't Dr. Dionne," as she joined in on the laughter.

"Well, I've heard the term, but never stopped to consider that it was a real animal," I said still smiling.

"Same here," replied Anne.

"I bet Mike is behind this," as I picked up the phone and dialed the inter-office number.

Rosalee answered with a simple, "Yes."

"Rosalee, who made the appointment for Barrow, my last one of the evening?"

"That was Doris," she replied.

"Okay, please put her on."

Doris picked up and said sincerely, "Dr. Dionne, I made the appointment for Mr. Barrow. And I have no clue as to what a polecat is. Some breed of cat, I guess."

Sensing now that this wasn't an office practical joke, I replied, "Okay Doris, since you go home at 5 p.m., I will tell you tomorrow what a polecat is."

Before hanging up, Doris added one more thing, "Oh yes, Mr. Barrow is very hard to understand. He has a thick southern accent."

"Okay, thanks," I said before hanging up the phone.

* * *

Later, walking into that much discussed appointment, I introduced myself, "Hello Mr. and Mrs. Barrow, I'm Dr. Dionne."

Mr. Barrow extended his large beefy hand and answered, "Ya'll can call me Clyde."

Then he engulfed my small hand in a death grip and shook vigorously.

"This here's my wife, Bonnie. Ya'll got a nice office here, Doc. We just moved here from North Cackalacky," Clyde grinned.

"Stop it Clyde. I'm sorry, my husband likes to make up silly names. We're from Boone, North Carolina," Bonnie corrected.

The Barrows were quite a pair. Clyde was a huge man, maybe six foot three inches and in his late thirties. I guessed he was around 275 lbs., with short but thinning brown hair, hazel eyes, and a ruddy complexion. A friendly smile revealed a shiny gold tooth as his largest upper incisor. He wore a pair of bib blue jeans over a yellow tee-shirt and brown well-scuffed work boots.

A large bulge was in his left cheek. I assumed this was a plug of tobacco. I could see the top of a package sticking out of his jeans' pocket with the *Red Man* label. I hoped that he didn't have the urge to spit anytime soon.

Bonnie was about the same age, five foot seven inches and only 50-60 lbs. lighter. She had light brown hair, cut short without a curl in sight. Her eyes were blue, and she wore no makeup or lipstick. She wore a simple faded pink house-dress that bulged at the seams and a pair of flip-flops. They were both huge and occupied most of the space around the exam table.

Bonnie was more serious and quiet. She let the willing Clyde do most of the talking. Bonnie held, with both hands, a pink and white baby blanket close to her ample chest and neck. I was not able to see what was hidden inside the blanket. A polecat most likely.

In the middle of the exam table was a blue cat carrier; it was closed. A small wire window on each end allowed air circulation to the occupant. I could see flashes of white through the window and heard a great deal of scratching-- polecat number two.

"Who shall we look at first?" I asked.

"Let's do Iggy," was the unanimous opinion.

Clyde opened both carrier locks and lifted the lid slowly. Immediately, a small white head poked out. I still wasn't sure what kind of an animal it was. I knew it wasn't a cat.

"Hold your horses, Iggy. Daddy's gotcha," Clyde said as he lifted a white skunk out and placed him on the exam table.

The mystery of the polecat was revealed.

Iggy was actually more cream in color than white. His whitish color and absence of a stripe made him appear less threatening than his black and white cousins. His fur was long and coarse. Like all skunks, he had black powerful claws for digging. Iggy was the size of a house cat and appeared to weigh about ten pounds.

Being speechless for a moment, I then asked, "He is descented. Right?"

Clyde laughed and turned Iggy around so that his backside faced me. Lifting his tail, he said, "Here Doc, take a close up look."

Bonnie interrupted again, "Clyde Barrow! Stop this clowning right now! Yes, Doctor, he is descented and neutered."

Breathing a sigh of relief, I proceeded to make a patient record. Iggy was a one-year-old male that the Barrows had purchased from a licensed breeder in the Asheville area of North Carolina.

Iggy was ten weeks old when he joined the Barrow gang.

Examining a skunk, aka polecat, requires a great deal of patience. I proceeded with respectful caution. He was a slippery, wiggly patient, but fortunately didn't bite. I found him to be quite healthy and gave him a booster vaccination for distemper.

Iggy had a rabies vaccine at six months of age. He only went outside for short walks on a leash. Therefore, I didn't feel it was necessary for him to receive a booster on rabies. There is also no FDA approved rabies vaccine for skunks anyway.

They fed him primarily dry cat food plus a hard-boiled egg twice a week, some vegetable table scraps and fruit. A liquid vitamin supplement for cats was given daily. Iggy was trained to use a litter box.

I found the Barrows to be well-informed on skunk care and very attached to their cream-colored polecat.

Iggy was put back into the carrier, and it was time to meet the newest addition, Ziggy. Bonnie carefully placed the baby blanket on the exam table. Opening it up, Bonnie revealed a sleepy, twelve-week- old, black and white Ziggy.

"Doc, this *young'un* needs one more baby shot," Clyde said. "Oh yah, uh....we plum forgot to get him deodorized. What with the move up to Yankee territory and all."

I was half-way through the exam when this bomb shell was dropped. I was poking and prodding a lethal weapon.

"Don't worry, Doc, he ain't never sprayed yet," Clyde informed me with a proud smile.

I wasn't relieved.

Female skunks give birth in May to an average of 4-7 kits which are weaned at eight weeks of age. The best time to descent them is at 2-3 weeks of age. Dr. North's rule was *no descents* after August 1st.

Today was August 8th.

Ziggy was also quite healthy, and enjoying nibbling on my fingers with his sharp baby teeth. I informed the Barrows about the descenting cut off of August 1st.

Bonnie started to cry.

Clyde pleaded his case, "Doc.....Doc, what are we supposed to do? We're only a week late! Ya'll can see he don't spray yet. We can't just put him in the woods. He won't make it!"

Everything Clyde said was true. Most hunting animals like the wolf, fox and badger steer clear of a skunk. They know the consequences. One exception is the great horned owl. They will actively hunt the skunk because this owl has a poorly developed sense of smell. They don't mind being sprayed because their friends and family members can't smell anything either!

Dogs and the automobile are also a major threat. The skunk is often killed on the roads because they have extremely poor vision. They can only see clearly for about ten feet. They don't see the car until it is too late; although the skunk usually does manage to give one final squirt before departing.

Dr. Marshmallow relented. "Okay, I'll do the surgery."

Bonnie wiped her eyes and said, "Bless you, Doc."

Clyde was about to give me either a bear hug or another bone-crushing handshake.

"Hold it, Mr. Barrow! I have to do surgery tomorrow; need to protect the old pinkies. You can bring him in tomorrow, right?" I asked.

"Yup, you bet," they both said as they packed up and left happily for home.

Walking out of the room with a headache, I called Mike to schedule the surgery. I received the expected reaction.

"Are you nuts? Have you lost your mind, Doc?" he asked.

"I probably have. Just schedule the surgery. I'll do it outside behind the kennel runs."

CLICK.....Mike just hung up.

To make matters worse, this was my first de-scenting of a skunk. The skunk has two anal sacs located on each side of the anal area. They are located at approximately four and eight o'clock.

Skunks have the ability to spray their target from up to fifteen feet away. Plus, they have enough noxious liquid to spray 5-6 times. It takes about ten days to refill the sacs back up again to a full load.

I wasn't too worried about the surgery because I had experience removing anal glands from dogs. I had watched Dr. North descent a skunk, which was helpful even though it was three years ago.

* * *

The next day, I arranged my surgeries so that Ziggy the polecat would be the last one of the day. Behind the hospital and kennel was a fenced-in area. Miscellaneous items, such as lawn mowers, tools, garbage cans, and fencing were stored here.

Sandy had set up a make-shift surgery site. She placed the anesthesia supplies and surgical instruments that would be needed on a grooming table.

I carried Ziggy in a portable cage to our surgery spot. Naturally, he was scared and upset. The plan was to first sedate him with a tranquilizer, then administer a barbiturate for the anesthesia. I slipped on a pair of gloves and opened the cage.

Like a bolt of lightening, Ziggy alluded my grasp and sprang from the cage! The patient made a run for it, but the gate was closed-- no way out. We just had to catch him. I finally cornered him behind the garbage cans. He hissed and stamped his feet--the traditional skunk warning.

I didn't heed the warning.

Ziggy turned, raised his tail high and blasted away. I had the dubious honor of being his first victim.

The spray hit me like an *avalanche of stink.* My eyes were irritated and watered. The stench made me hold my breath for as long as possible. Backing away from my near-sighted patient, I lifted the plastic cover off one of our garbage cans.

"Okay, Ziggy, that was your *last spray* fella," I said and plopped the cover over his small body.

However, I was premature about the last spray. He managed two more weak squirts--one as the cover descended, and the second with the sedation injection.

Once Ziggy was snoozing peacefully, we performed the surgery without a hitch and removed the tiny but potent anal sacs. He was descented, and I smelled to high heaven!

The dutiful Sandy was a trooper through this whole pungent affair and didn't leave when the smell arrived.

Afterward, she said, "Dr. Dionne, you better go home and shower a few times."

I agreed wholeheartedly.

Before leaving, Sandy telephoned Tina and had her rush out for some tomato juice. Today, we would have used the much more effective *Skunk Off* to neutralize the skunk odor. Back then, however, soaking in tomato juice, letting it dry to a crusty state, then rinsing, was our only way to deal with the smell.

In my case, the whole process had to be repeated a few times. Standing naked in the bath tub covered with dried tomato juice, I can assure you was not a pretty sight.

The next day was worse with appointments all day long. I endured the *I told you so looks* from Mike and my co-workers. I reeked of deodorant and men's cologne.

Many of my clients said innocently,
"Dr. Dionne, I think I smell a skunk!"

Answering, "You know you're right, I've been smelling it all day today," I sheepishly replied. After a few days and numerous showers, I smelled normal again. I was getting tired of sleeping on the couch.

Bonnie and Clyde sent me a thank you note. Ziggy was fine.

To be continued...

13

Ziggy's Dilemma

Pets speak with meows and woofs.
They also communicate with their actions. Observe them closely. They may be trying to tell you something.
Author

Should we try to domesticate and make pets out of wild animals or leave them alone in the woods, fields, mountains, or natural habitats of their choosing? It is a difficult question that has brought forth various strong opinions, both for and against. I've wrestled with the problem myself, resulting in no satisfactory answer one way or the other.

But, what if the animals could choose for themselves? How would he or she tell their owner? Do we look closely enough at what they are trying to communicate to us?

* * *

The descented, squirtless Ziggy returned home and settled into a regular routine of eating, sleeping and annoying the older Iggy. Initially, Clyde and Bonnie took them both out for walks on a leash near their home. Later, they expanded their forays to include the park. Children and adults were fascinated with the contrast of a cream-colored Iggy and the traditional black and white Ziggy. Most kids were hesitant at first to pet them until one brave child would inevitably step forward to do so. The polecats became quite well known in the Bridgewater, N.J., area.

* * *

By late fall, Ziggy had grown to be slightly larger and much different than his adopted brother. Iggy preferred to be inside the house, whereas Ziggy longed to be outside, especially in the woods. Each evening, as Bonnie and Clyde slept, Ziggy roamed the house.

Every object was carefully inspected, and each nook and corner sniffed thoroughly.

Iggy, wake up! Are you sleeping? Come see what I found! he cried.

Go away, Zig! I'm not a night owl like you are, said his drowsy brother. Ziggy became more and more restless and frustrated as he now approached puberty. He was missing something, but had no idea what it was.

One cool, October evening, Ziggy climbed up onto Clyde's favorite recliner by the living room window. From there it was an easy step up onto the sill of the open window. A few swipes with his long black claws tore a large hole in the screen.

Ziggy thought to himself, *Should I? Why not, I'll be back before morning.*

Trying to leap gracefully out the torn screen, Ziggy fell four feet into Bonnie's favorite rose bush with a plop and thud.

Ouch! he cried. Ziggy slowly untangled himself from the prickly bush.

Outside at last, he thought.

A full moon and a starry, cloudless night illuminated the landscape for the near-sighted explorer. Having a keen sense of smell and excellent hearing, Ziggy delighted in all the chirps, croaks and other night sounds. With head close to the ground, he sniffed his way down the driveway and prepared to cross the road. He lifted his head and squinted to see two bright white balls off in the distance. They seemed to be coming closer.

Wow, look at that, he said and stepped out onto the road for a better look. A loud zoom and a rush of wind knocked Ziggy head over heels. A very close call.

The truck missed this polecat by only a handful of inches. Visibly shaken, he vowed to stay clear of roads and stick to the safer woods and fields.

Picking himself up, Ziggy looked around-- no white balls. Scooting across the road, he entered the *safe* forest.

In no particular pattern, Ziggy wandered and sniffed his way through the woodland for the rest of the evening. It was wonderful! He saw new plants like the fern, soft moss, mushrooms, fallen trees, and rocks of all sizes. The smells were the best-- decomposing leaves and a pot-pourri of animal scents. A well-traveled animal trail led him to a narrow stream.

Look at this! Water in the middle of the woods, he marveled.

While stopping to drink, Ziggy heard a rustling of the bushes. He looked up and saw a red fox, only a few feet away on the opposite side of the stream. They stared at each other momentarily.

Finally, the excited polecat said, *Hi, I'm Ziggy!*

The fox quickly turned and disappeared back into the bushes. He wanted no part of a skunk and his eye-irritating and sense-numbing spray.

Ziggy thought, *Gee, that wasn't very friendly.*

Undaunted, he continued his travels until the sun's red glow appeared on the horizon. Ziggy had no clue as to where he was or how to get back home.

I'm hungry. I wonder what's for breakfast? he foolishly thought.

Slowly it dawned on him that there would be no breakfast, or lunch and maybe dinner, if he didn't get home. Panic set in, and the woods didn't appear so friendly and enticing as last evening. His mind was confused, and his body very tired from the many miles that he had traveled. Finding a hollow log, he curled up and fell into a deep sleep. Upon waking, it was now late in the afternoon, and the sun was beginning its descent toward another evening.

What am I going to do now? he cried.

* * *

This was pretty much what the Barrows had said that morning when they discovered one polecat was missing. The tears streamed down Bonnie's face as she and Clyde scoured the yard and nearby woods. After three hours of frantic searching and yelling, they returned to the house in a state of depression.

Clyde made a promise to his wife, "Ya'll wait and see honey, we're going to find him. Don't worry!"

Bonnie picked up Iggy and rocked him in her arms.

Later that afternoon, I received a call from Clyde. He told me the sad news.

"Doc, I'm making a hundred reward posters for Ziggy. Can I put one in your office?"

"Of course, but what are you going to say?" I asked.

All I could envision was a poster saying, lost skunk-- all black with white stripe, answers to the name of Ziggy. How many people are going to walk up to a skunk and ask if his name is Ziggy?

I explained my concerns about the poster to Clyde.

"Ya'll got a point there, Doc," he said.

"What if we put his picture on the poster and explain that he is descented and not afraid of people. If they should see such a skunk, then they should contact you or animal control. We can distribute the posters to all the area veterinarians, humane society, pet shops and even the police. You can offer a nice reward and see what happens. It won't be easy, but not impossible either," I said hopefully.

"Thanks Doc, that's exactly what we're goin' to do!"

* * *

Ziggy had now started his second evening of freedom without the enthusiasm of yesterday. The noises and scents were now becoming scary. Hunger and being lost will do that to you. Sitting on a tree stump, tears were starting to well up in his eyes.

Then, a soft feminine voice from behind said, *Hi, I've never seen you before. Are you lost?*

Turning quickly around, Ziggy thought he saw an angel that looked just like him.

Yes, I'm quite lost and really hungry! There's nothing to eat in the woods, Ziggy complained.

His new dream girl politely said, *My name is Prudence, but my friends call me Prue for short. And there is plenty to eat in the woods. Where are you from?*

Ziggy introduced himself and explained his short life history to her. He also described, in detail, the events of last evening and his grand adventure. Prue listened intently to the story; she could never imagine a skunk living in a house and not in the woods.

Well, let me get you something to eat, said Prudence.

Jumping off the tree stump, Ziggy was re-invigorated. *Okay, let's go!* he said.

Prudence sniffed and found a couple of crickets and a few other insects. *Here you go Ziggy, have one.*

But these are bugs! Where's the cat chow? he asked.

Prudence answered, *What's cat chow? In the woods, we catch our food.*

Almost afraid to ask, Ziggy inquired, *What do you mean?*

Prudence patiently answered the city slicker. *Well, we eat worms, grubs, mice, frogs and occasionally snakes. In the summer, we have berries, nuts, roots, grasses and even leaves. Bird eggs are also very tasty.*

Ziggy wasn't sure if he was still hungry after hearing the menu. But, wanting to impress the lovely

Prudence, he went hunting with her and ate everything that she found.

* * *

Toward morning, with their stomachs finally full, Prudence invited Ziggy to her den to meet the *girls*. Female skunks often huddle up together to keep warm in cold weather and wait out the winter--no males allowed.

Ziggy and Prudence caused quite a stir when they entered the underground den.

Gladys asked, *What's he doing here? Prue, you know the rules. This den is just for us!*

The two other den-mates, Phyllis and Daisy, agreed.

Prudence stamped her feet and calmed everyone down. She explained that Ziggy was a lost, descented, domesticated skunk, who needed some serious training to survive in the woods. These female skunks were all *softies* and allowed Ziggy to stay with them in the cozy den until he was *educated.*

* * *

A week later on Tuesday morning, Clyde received an encouraging telephone call from Officer Wiggins, of the Animal Control Unit. They had cage-trapped a skunk only two miles from the Barrows' home. The skunk had been sleeping on the back porch of the Smith family for a few days. "Why don't you come on over and take a look at him. See if he's yours. We'll wait for you," said the officer.

"We'll be right over," Clyde answered while slipping on his shoes.

Bonnie was already out the door and headed

for the pickup truck. Minutes later, Clyde sped up the Smiths' driveway. Being so excited and in a hurry, they both practically fell out of the vehicle.

Not that their Ziggy was going anywhere, but what if he escaped or someone else claimed him? (a very unlikely scenario) They met Officer Wiggins and Mrs. Smith in the backyard. The possible Ziggy stood calmly in his cage unafraid and non-aggressive.

After a few minutes of close inspection through the cage, and "Hi Ziggy, baby--it's mommy!" the Barrows conferred and admitted that they weren't completely sure if it was Ziggy or not.

Bonnie suggested to Officer Wiggins that they take the caged skunk home, and see if Iggy recognizes his adopted brother. Surely, he could tell. The officer reluctantly agreed. The Barrows hopped in their pickup truck with their caged passenger, and returned home.

The curious Iggy inspected the new arrival through the wire screening. They showed no sign of aggression toward one another.

Clyde told Bonnie, "Wa'll that must be Ziggy, otherwise a wild polecat would have sprayed by now."

He then reached down and opened the cage door. "Okay, now let's see what happens."

Clyde made one major mistake. He didn't know that skunks do not spray each other! They will fight, especially the males during mating season-- but no spraying.

The unknown stranger walked out of the cage and all hell broke loose. The Barrows were both sprayed with the same squirt. The freed skunk ran through the living room, kitchen, bedroom and finally settled in the bathroom behind the toilet. Clyde closed the bathroom door until he could figure out what to do.

While he was *figurin'*, Bonnie called me.

I was in the middle of a dog spay so she had to wait for a return call. In the meantime, she went to look for Iggy, who had taken off when the *trouble* started. She found him in the guest bedroom underneath the bed. He was huddled in the far corner and trembling with fear. Despite the coaxing from Bonnie, Iggy wasn't planning on leaving his refuge anytime soon.

Clyde walked into the bedroom and announced, "Honey, ya'll stay right where you're at. I'm going to rid us of the polecat."

Bonnie looked up from her kneeling position by the bed to see what her husband meant. He was dressed in his green wader-boots that he used for fishing, a bright yellow rain jacket, a pair of goggles that he used for cutting wood, and Bonnie's rubber swim cap decorated with pink flowers. A white plastic clothespin was clamped over his nose. In his right hand, he held a broom. Clyde was so proud of himself; he had thought of everything.

Bonnie was speechless.

Before she could say anything, Clyde turned and clomped out of the guest bedroom, closed the door and headed for the bathroom. He had already opened both the front and rear doors as well as the screen doors.

Turning the bathroom door handle very quietly, he opened the door just enough to peek in. Clyde spotted his adversary's tail sticking out from behind the toilet. Closing the door again for a moment, he took one last deep breath and swung open the door.

Charging in, holding the broom low like a hockey stick, Clyde went for the black and white *puck.*

The not so nimble, 250 lb. plus, big man stepped into the bathtub to allow enough room for the wild polecat to escape. He then followed the skunk out, and it became a battle royal between the broom swinging hockey player and the squirting puck. Bonnie heard the commotion in the living room, and wished she could crawl under the bed with Iggy. Finally, three blasts of skunk spray later, the polecat found the open door and scooted out.

Clyde went to the spare bedroom and proudly said, "Ya'll can come out now, it's safe."

Bonnie walked out to the stench and began to cry. My phone call, ten minutes later, didn't help to improve the situation. They told me what had transpired. I couldn't offer that much help other than sympathy, having been sprayed myself-- by Ziggy no less. We discussed tomato juice, opening the windows, carpet cleaning and multiple washings of sprayed clothing.

* * *

The Barrows and their home recovered and winter arrived. The reward posters were taken down and thrown away. I was able to convince Mike, our office manager, to leave ours up for a few more months.

He reluctantly said, "Okay, besides, the clients get a chuckle at reading the poster."

* * *

Meanwhile, Ziggy was doing fine with his *schooling* from Prudence. He was becoming a wary and skilled hunter. Ziggy knew that being descented made him defenseless, so he only ventured out with Prudence. They became inseparable.

Now that winter was here, everyone stayed in the den on cold days. Skunks do not hibernate like bears and some other animals. They will continue to hunt on milder days.

Life changed for Ziggy in March. The *girls* all seemed different in some strange way--more attractive, especially Prudence. It was the skunk mating season.

Ziggy and Prudence were so happy that Clyde was a procrastinator about his *To Do* list.

Ziggy had not been neutered. Not needing any *teaching*, Ziggy fathered four beautiful kits that were born 66 days later in May. Ziggy and Prue moved to a new den of their own to raise the kits.

They named them Farley, Finn, Francine (the only girl) and Filbert.

Filbert looked a little different from his brothers and sister. Instead of a single broad, white stripe, he had two thinner, white stripes that ran parallel to each other down his back.

The kits were all born blind and deaf, which is normal. They opened their eyes at three weeks of age and were weaned at eight weeks. They would stay with their mother, and in this case, father, for almost a year before striking out on their own.

* * *

Friday was my last day of work before the Fourth of July holiday weekend. I was off for three days, and my family and I planned to spend the weekend relaxing at grandma's house in Pennsylvania.

Mrs. Ida Culpepper had brought in five of her ten cats for their annual checkups and shots. Ida was one of our frequent clients that loved animals, especially cats. Besides her own, she fed several feral cats each day on her back porch.

Mid-way through the appointment she asked, "Dr. Dionne, did they ever find the lost skunk on the reward poster?"

Taking the stethoscope out of my ears, I said, "No, they didn't."

"Well, I can't be sure, but for the last month, there has been a skunk eating our cat food outside my kitchen door. The strange thing is he also eats with my wild cats! They are not afraid of him. I started to let him see me at the door. I was nervous that he might spray me, so I kept one hand on the door and was ready to close it real fast if he turned around and lifted his tail. But, he just looked up at me and continued to eat. Now he's a regular and comes every evening at 6 p.m."

This was the first lead that we had in months. My appointments were until 5 p.m., so I got the directions to Ida's house, which was about seven miles from the Barrows. After the appointment, I excitedly called the Barrows. Bonnie answered, and I told her the news. Clyde would be home from work soon, and we agreed to meet at the Culpepper's home at 6 p.m.

Then calling Tina, I said, "Honey, we will be leaving for Pennsylvania a little later than we expected."

"Ed, what now?" she asked.

I explained the situation, and how I had to be there, especially if it turned out to be Ziggy.

"We will be leaving maybe one hour later, that's all," I promised.

"Okay, and I'll hold you to your promise," she patiently replied.

The Barrows and I arrived at the same time. We went in through the front door and met Ida. She told us to hurry because the skunk had arrived earlier this evening and was about to leave. He was about half-way down the lawn headed to the woods, when we saw him.

Bonnie stepped out and yelled, "Ziggy!"

We all followed out as well.

Upon hearing his name called, Ziggy stopped and turned around.

Clyde waved, and Bonnie decided to do her *test* first. No one wanted to make a mistake and get sprayed again. They had brought Iggy with them this time. She placed Iggy down on the lawn to see what would happen. Iggy walked straight down to meet his brother.

They met and Iggy asked, *Is that you, Zig?*

Happily, he answered, *It sure is!*

They rubbed up against each other like cats would do and Ziggy put his paw on his brother's head for a moment.

Iggy, I have to go now, my family is waiting for me.

Just then, Prudence and the four kits stepped out of the woods onto the very edge of the lawn.

Iggy said, *Wow, you're a dad!*

Yes, and I gotta go now. Good-bye, Iggy.

Ziggy turned slowly toward the woods and walked away from his brother.

Clyde called out to him one more time. Ziggy turned for one more look at his previous family, as if he was choosing what to do. In the end, he knew the answer and so did we. Ziggy rejoined Prudence and the kits and silently disappeared into the woods.

We thanked Mrs. Culpepper, picked up the confused Iggy, and walked back to our vehicles with mixed emotions. We were certainly happy that Ziggy had survived and had a family, but we knew that this was the last time we would see him.

The ever optimistic Clyde asked, "I wonder if Ziggy would let us have one of those baby polecats to raise?"

Bonnie yelled, "Clyde Barrow, you gotta get your head on straight!"

We all laughed and said, "Good-bye." I then went home to collect my wife and three *kits* to go to grandma's house.

Left to Right: Misty, Terri, Michelle, Eddie and Jason

14

Tilly - The Lonesome Boxer

Life is life ~ whether in a cat, or dog or man.
There is no difference there between a cat or a man.
The idea of difference is a human conception for man's own advantage.

Sri Aurobindo

There is an old saying that the dog is man's best friend. I'm sure that many people feel this way having seen evidence of it for many years. The question I've pondered, is *man* the dog's best friend?

* * *

Miss Harriet Beckman was better known as Hattie, the *boxer lady*. Today, she had a problem. Should she call the vet or not? Tilly was overdue to have her puppies. The normal gestation period for dogs and cats is 63 days, a mere nine weeks (normal range 61-65 days). This was her 67th day. She bent down and stroked Tilly's head, who was panting uncomfortably in her whelping box.

"Are you going to have those puppies or not?" she asked in a tone that seemed more like a demand than a question.

This was Tilly's third pregnancy, and she did not have any difficulties with the previous two litters. The fawn and white, five-year-old Tilly looked up at her owner with a sigh and thought to herself, *Miss Hattie, I want this over as much as you do*.

The thin, sixty-plus-year-old, Miss Beckman was getting more irritated and started to pace. She ran her fingers through her gray hair which was cut short in a pixie-style. Hattie had piercing blue eyes that made most people nervous to maintain eye contact with her for very long. She had a sharp pointed nose, and every other part of her body was very bony-hands, knees, elbows and legs.

Harriet was impatient with people, the government, traffic, red lights and just about anything that popped up in her life. A nervous tic developed in her left eye and lip just before she became visibly upset. Behind her back, some of the locals referred to her as *Crazy Hattie*. She spoke her mind with a loud raspy voice. Years of chain-smoking cigarettes had thickened her vocal cords.

Harriet had never married; however, she did have two or three promising boyfriends early on.

After a few tic episodes and tongue lashings, the prospects were soon scared off. Her inheritance from her father allowed her to purchase Fox Hollow Kennels in 1945 after World War II ended. The former boarding kennel was renovated and converted to a breeding kennel for boxers. Hattie had big plans to become a nationally recognized boxer breeder.

* * *

She purchased the best fawn-colored, female puppy that was available. She named her Violet, who later became Tilly's great-grandmother. Slowly, Hattie added more boxers to fill out her breeding stock. It was a tedious process that required careful planning. In the ensuing years, Hattie became well known in central New Jersey for selling outstanding boxer puppies.

Most of her puppies were *pet quality* which means that they made good pets, but were not quite up to the rigorous standards set by the American Kennel Club for show dogs. Tilly was one of the exceptions which all breeders look for in each litter.

The boxer breed was developed in Germany from cross-breeding the English bulldog with the now extinct Bullenbeisser breed. The boxer has a smooth, short coat and can be fawn, brindle or white in color. The males are 65-70 lbs., and the smaller females, 55-60 lbs.

In Fox Hollow Kennels, life for a boxer puppy was a little stressful. In Tilly's litter, she had three brothers and four sisters. One male and one female were mostly white with brown patches. Hattie's tic started twitching when she saw them being born. White puppies were not allowed to live for very long in Fox Hollow Kennels. This was also true in 1974 for most boxer breeders. White boxers could not be entered in dog shows, nor did breeders want them to be bred. They said it would *spoil* the breed.

Fortunately today, many white boxers are allowed to live and are sold as pets with a signed agreement that they will be spayed or neutered. Hattie would keep the two white ones around for a few days to see if Emerald, Tilly's mother, developed mastitis in one of her mammary glands.

White puppies were usually larger and very hardy compared to their colored litter-mates. Hattie had found that she could use the white puppies to nurse on the infected gland and *suck* out the infection. The fawn and brindle puppies would often get sick if they nursed on an infected breast, but not the white ones.

At 3-5 days of age, Hattie would make a trip to our hospital to have the puppies' tails docked and dewclaws removed. Undocked, the boxer would have a long whip like tail. The dewclaws are the *thumbs* on the front paws and sometimes can be found on the rear feet as well.

Hattie had been using Dr. Arthur North as her veterinarian as soon as she started breeding boxers in 1946. She *trusted* (sort of) the other vets on our staff when Arthur was not available. Hattie would have preferred to dock the tails herself and save the vet fees. But sharp objects like scalpel blades made her nervous which resulted in the inevitable eye and lip tremors. Today, I drew the short straw and got to deal with the touchy boxer breeder.

I walked into the exam room and said, "Hello, Miss Beckman. Another fine litter, I see."

Pointing to Tilly, Hattie said, "I think this one might turn out okay, the rest are just pets." Then looking with disgust at the two white puppies, she continued, "Of course, we have these two ugly white ones. You know what to do with 'em."

* * *

Having to bite my tongue and keep silent, I recalled the day, four years ago, of the monumental tirade. It was my first meeting with Harriet and her litter of newborn puppies.

I asked, "Why not keep the white ones and give them away? Or spay them?"

That was the first time I encountered the tic and its consequences. It was not a pretty sight. The next morning, Mike, the office manager, sat me down for a long talk about *do's and don't's* with Crazy Hattie.

* * *

I took the first pup out of Harriet's cardboard box. I liked to check each one for cleft palates, open fontanels, hernias and anything unusual.

"Doc, you don't have to do that. I've checked them already!"

I just ignored her and kept my mouth shut. I could imagine the scene if there was something wrong with a puppy that was discovered later on by another vet.

The six puppies were fine and I prepared to do the surgery. First, I shaved each tail with an electric clipper, washed the area with alcohol, applied a gauze tourniquet and injected a local anesthetic into the tails.

"You know Doc, that Novacaine is not really necessary."

"Uh huh," is all I mumbled, and thought, *I would like to see you have your tail removed without a local anesthetic!*

Miss Beckman assisted and gave advice as she held each wiggly puppy in both hands so that their tail faced me. Then, making a v-shaped incision between the tiny soft tail vertebrae, I removed approximately two-thirds of the first puppy's tail. The incision was closed with four absorbable cat gut sutures. The dewclaws were quickly removed and cauterized with silver nitrate sticks to stop any possible bleeding. The same procedure was repeated on the rest of the litter except for the white puppies.

This tail-docking method resulted in minimal-to-no scarring on the tails as well as the dewclaws. At the end, each gauze tourniquet was loosened, and I counted each severed tail-- six puppies, six tails.

* * *

Two years ago, I forgot to count and a six-year-old boy, absconded with a puppy tail. His teacher called me the next day. She didn't appreciate the tail trophy that she thought I gave him.

At show and tell the young *tail enthusiast* told his first grade class about his trip to the vet with his puppies. He ended with the *show* part of the story by holding up the severed tail by its tip for his class to see. It was met with a chorus of yuks and groans.

One little girl got sick to her stomach and vomited lunch all over her desk and had to visit the school nurse. It took some fast talking and many apologies to calm the teacher's ruffled feathers.

* * *

Finishing up with Harriet's appointment, most clients would have had some questions and words of thanks before leaving.

Not Hattie.

With only a slight twitch, she said, "You know Doc, this wouldn't be so dog-gone expensive if you didn't use that Novacaine! And make sure you take care of those two ugly white ones right away! Don't get any funny ideas about finding homes for them either."

She abruptly left and walked out leaving me holding two cute white boxers in each hand.

Later, slightly depressed, I thought, *Maybe I could do some other line of work. A bicycle messenger in New York City might be interesting.* I soon snapped out of my little fantasy and resumed what I do best—take care of animals.

* * *

Six weeks later, Miss Beckman, Tilly and the rest of the litter returned for their ear cropping. This surgery could only be done by Dr. North.

There were two reasons for this. First, Arthur did *show-crops* which were more difficult than ordinary pet-ear cropping. In show-crops, the ear is left longer with a sweeping curve up to a tapered tip. These crops require more artistic skill and more aftercare. Splinting was needed to get the ears to stand erect and not flop over. In pet-ear crops, the ear is cut much shorter and stands up much easier. The second reason is no one else on the staff including myself wanted anything to do with ear crops. We all felt it shouldn't be done at all.

Walking into surgery, I wanted to see how much Hattie's litter had grown. The surgery completed, Arthur was now finishing the first of the ear splinting. Dr. North devised his own splints which consisted of a trimmed down tongue depressor, wrapped in cotton and tape. He inserted this into the bottom of the puppy's ear canal. Each ear was then carefully wrapped with adhesive tape. Running across the top of the head, a thin strand of tape connected the tip of each splinted ear. The litter looked like little puppies from outer space.

I couldn't help but notice the pick of the litter-- Tilly. She stood out even to my untrained eye. Dr. North noticed my interest in Tilly and said, "This may be Miss Beckman's best one yet."

* * *

Arthur's prediction came true. Tilly grew up in the kennel while the rest of the litter were sold to happy, loving families. Tilly had plenty of attention from Hattie, excellent food, grooming and meticulous care. What she lacked was the chance to be a carefree puppy and most of all-- love.

Tilly often thought to herself, *It's not a bad life. The traveling to dog shows is exciting. The first place ribbons and trophies make everyone happy. Miss Hattie hugs me a lot when I win, but then we come back home to the kennel and my cage. That's when I get sad and lonely.*

Tilly did look forward to seeing Michael, the thirteen-year-old, part-time kennel boy. He came in on weekends to clean and take care of all the boxers. Tilly was Michael's favorite! After his chores were done, Michael took her out for a walk on the leash and some playtime. The bespectacled, socially awkward Michael liked to talk with Tilly.

He often said, "Tilly, if I had a dog, which I don't, it would be you. I'm saving my money that Miss Beckman pays me, and when I have enough, my mom said I could buy you. Then you can live with me, and we can play whenever we want!"

Tilly understood and jumped up on Michael and began to lick his face. The slightly built, brown-haired teenager was knocked off his feet. Tilly stood over him and continued with the face cleaning. Michael was laughing hysterically which stopped abruptly when Crazy Hattie marched out of the house to put an end to such foolishness.

Michael was ordered to take his favorite boxer back to her cage and finish up for the day. Before leaving, the shy teen said, "See ya, Tilly. Love you."

Tilly responded with a loud woofing as he left. The translation was, *Michael, take me with you - I love you too!*

* * *

Tilly's show career continued in New Jersey, Pennsylvania and Maryland. It finally ended in a large show in Columbus, Ohio. Tilly won a *major* after winning the Working Dog Group as best *bitch* (term for a female, *dog* being the term for a male). This gave her enough points to earn the title of Champion. A total of fifteen points must be earned to be recognized by the AKC as a Champion. Two of the wins must be considered a major win of three points or more.

Harriet was very happy for a change. She was congratulated by her best and probably only friend,

Charlotte, a fellow boxer breeder from Trenton. That evening the two friends celebrated over drinks and dinner at the most expensive restaurant that they could find in Columbus. The tipsy twosome left at closing time-- 11:30 p.m.

Tilly wasn't so lucky. It was the usual routine for her after a dog show. Back to the motel, a quick walk for a pee and the cardboard end of a match inserted into her butt. This crude, but effective, suppository made her poop. Hattie didn't want to clean up any *accidents* in the motel room. Tilly was put into her small traveling crate for the evening.

Some celebration, she thought and laid down to sleep.

What Tilly didn't realize was that this would be her last dog show and last trip out of the kennel. At two years old, she would now be used as a brood bitch. A puppy machine for Miss Hattie. Most female dogs of all breeds went into *heat*, or estrus every six months. The typical cycle lasts three weeks. During the first week, the female is attractive to males but will not allow mating with the exception of some most eager lovelies. Somewhere between the 9th and the 15th day of the cycle is usually the best time to breed. This can vary quite a bit according to the whims of the prospective mother and her two ovaries.

Tilly didn't fit into Hattie's plans of two litters per year. Her heat cycles were only once a year. The thought of only a single litter by her champion caused heart palpitations and almost non-stop twitching by her owner.

Fortunately, there were no problems with conceiving. Tilly had two outstanding litters: eight puppies at three years old-- four males, four females and zero white ones--happy Hattie! Next, she had seven puppies at four years old--three males, four females and two white ones-- twitchy Hattie.

* * *

However, this third litter was trying Hattie's limited patience. She didn't want to admit that she needed some advice from someone on our staff. Hattie took shortcuts.

She knew that the first question we would ask her would be, "What are your breeding dates?"

If she conceived on the second breeding this would change her due date, and maybe she wasn't overdue at all. Hattie had misplaced the paper with the breeding dates. All she knew was Tilly should have whelped by now.

The next question we would ask was, "What has her temperature been reading over the last few days?"

The normal body temperature of the dog is 101-102 degrees F. The pregnant female's temperature will usually drop as she nears parturition (birthing). When it reaches 98 degrees F. or below, expect puppies very soon as in the next twelve hours.

A clear vaginal discharge might also be noted (cervical plug or seal). This could happen a few days before whelping or the same day.

Hattie would not be able to answer a single one of these questions, and she knew it.

Turning to Tilly, she said, "Girl, it's high time that those puppies get born!"

Tilly rolled her eyes, *Oh no, what is she going to do?*

Hattie left for a few minutes and returned with

a syringe filled with a clear liquid. Hattie planned to give a *pit* shot to induce labor. *Pit* was short for Pitocin (oxytocin). Many breeders kept some around to help with the deliveries if their bitch was tiring after delivering several puppies, but was not finished yet. It would start the labor up again which would speed up the birthing process. Pitocin is a powerful drug and produces strong uterine contractions. It should only be given by a vet or under their supervision. I never knew how some breeders acquired the drug, but they did. This was the first time that I ever had anyone try to initiate labor!

Hattie bent over and injected the liquid into Tilly's thigh. Two minutes later, labor began. Tilly's abdomen contracted harder than in her previous two deliveries. The contractions came in waves one after the other. A few minutes later, Tilly vomited and felt light-headed. She tried to stand but wasn't able to get her footing. She slipped awkwardly back to the bottom of the whelping box.

"Tilly, what have you done!"

* * *

Hattie picked up the phone and called Somerset Veterinary Group. The answering service immediately called me, since it was my turn for emergency duty. On hearing the problem, I groaned. It was Sunday afternoon, and the division races in football were in full swing. I turned the television off and called Miss Beckman. She answered on the first ring, and we both spoke at the same time.

She said, "Hello," and I simply said, "What happened?"

"Something is wrong with Tilly, my prize

bitch. She's overdue to have her puppies. So I gave her a little pit shot to get things started. Now she's just laying here and not moving much."

Recovering from the momentary shock, I asked, "You did say a *pit* shot. Right?"

"Yes, but only half a syringe full."

Holy crap, I thought. That's more than two times the recommended dose. "Miss Beckman, don't argue with me, but you need to get her here right now!"

Before leaving, I alerted Sandy, our surgery assistant, to come in and get ready. There was trouble brewing, and I would need her help. I said good-bye to the family and hopped into our green station wagon. Arriving at the same time as Hattie, I helped her carry Tilly into the hospital and into Exam Room 3.

After examining my non-moving patient, my worst fear was confirmed. Tilly was going into shock. She most likely had a ruptured uterus from the pit shot.

"Miss Beckman, we need to do surgery immediately, and it will be risky. The puppies may not be alive, and I'm not sure if Tilly will be able to breed again even if she pulls through the surgery. She may have to be spayed."

For once, Hattie kept quiet and didn't twitch or complain. She lowered her head and said, "Do whatever you think best, Dr. Dionne."

I rushed out of the room and up the stairs carrying my patient. Sandy was there and had everything ready for the operation.

Sandy asked, "What's the plan here, Doctor D?"

"Get a unit of blood ready, we might need it.

Hook up an intravenous drip. I'm going to give her some atropine and face mask her down with *Halothane* and oxygen. Then clip her up and wash the abdomen. I'm going to put some local anesthetic in and start the surgery. Once she's under, you insert an endotracheal tube and connect her to the anesthesia machine."

"Got it!"

Moving as fast as I could, I scrubbed up and put on my gloves and surgery gown. A few minutes later, I opened the abdomen and found the uterus was indeed ruptured. Two dead puppies were in the abdomen. The other four were still in the uterus but also dead. I removed them and checked the uterus. Each puppy's placental attachment was bleeding slowly. Tilly was doing as well as could be expected.

"Sandy, start the blood. I'm going to spay her. The uterus is shot and may continue to bleed."

It was risky surgery removing such a distended uterus. Tilly could go into shock and die.

But fortunately, she didn't.

Finishing up, Sandy smiled, "Nice job! Doctor Dionne that was a close one."

"Couldn't have done it without you, Sandy, believe me!"

Tilly spent the next four days in the hospital and each day she got a little stronger. Hattie and Michael visited her every day. Finally, Tilly was released. It was back to Fox Hollow Kennels. Hattie and Michael led Tilly to her cage which was fixed up nicely with soft blankets for her to lie on.

Hattie looked at her champion boxer as she calmly said without any twitching, "Tilly, what am I going to do with you now?"

This was Michael's opportunity. He reached into his jeans pocket and pulled out seventy-six crumpled dollars and a few cents.

He handed it to his boss and said, "Miss Hattie, I would like to buy Tilly from you. My mom said it would be okay. This is all the money that I have saved from working at the kennel. Is it enough?"

Hattie said softly, "Yes it is....yes it is. She's yours. Take good care of her."

"Don't worry, I will."

Michael and Tilly left and walked slowly to her new home. That was the last day Tilly was ever in a cage, and the last day she was lonesome.

15

Showdown at High Noon

Yea, though I walk through the valley of the shadow of death...

Psalms 23:4

Each year the faithful make pilgrimages to cities like Jerusalem to celebrate Easter or pray at the Wailing Wall. The Kaaba is the small stone building in the court of the Great Mosque at Mecca which contains the famous Black Stone. Since the time of Mohammed, the Kaaba has been the chief object of pilgrimages of the Islamic world.

* * *

In 1968, I was to participate in my first rite of spring which occurs each year in central New Jersey. The annual pilgrimage of our *faithful* four-legged pets and their owners to the various rabies clinics is quite a sight to behold.

June's staff meeting of Somerset Veterinary Group was to be a lunch meeting in our small library on the second floor above the vet hospital. Having been gainfully employed for the past two weeks, this was my first staff meeting as a veterinarian. It felt very good not to be a student any longer. My excitement peaked at 1 p.m., as we all marched up the stairs and took our seats at the rectangular table. Dr. North sat at one end, and Mike with his agenda notes occupied the opposite end. The three other veterinarians, Ray, Richard and myself filled in along the sides. The subs and iced tea that we had ordered were in the center of the table waiting patiently to be distributed. Still in student mode, I was prepared to take notes along with Mike, our business manager. This was when everyone, except Dr. North and myself, lit up a cigarette for a pre-meal smoke fest. The small room quickly filled with a pungent smog.

We had no smoke detectors in 1968, but if we did, they would be working overtime at this luncheon. Then one of us, probably me, would have had to remove the smoke detector's battery because there would be no extinguishing the cigarettes.

The term, second-hand smoke, had not been coined as yet. Therefore, no one was overly concerned about the health ramifications of the smoke being shared by all. However, my watery eyes and nasal passages were getting a little peeved at the cumulus-sized cloud of smoke hovering over the lunch table.

Dr. North opened the meeting with a welcome speech and then asked, "How's everything going so far, Ed?"

"Well, everyone has been super helpful," I wheezed. "I'm still learning the routine, and where everything is. And it's great to be here!" I said with a very slight cough.

Mike then said, "Let's eat, then we can take care of business."

I reached eagerly for my now *smoked* tuna fish sub and carcinogenic iced tea. It was eaten with gusto. After lunch, it was time for another round of cigarettes to complete the meal. Mike ran down the business of the day fairly quickly and came to his last item on the agenda-- this Saturday's rabies clinic in the nearby town of Raritan.

The rabies clinics had started in May while I was still in veterinary school; I was finishing my senior year and preparing to graduate.

Mike explained for my benefit, "Rabies clinics are held each Saturday morning in a different town in our assigned area. A few clinics are also held in the evening during the week. The vaccination is required for dogs each year according to state law. Pet owners are able to receive a free vaccination for their dog or cat at a clinic. Their option would be to go to their veterinarian, but there they would have to pay."

Later, I learned that thrill-seekers, the uninitiated first-timers and those short on cash opted for the free clinics. The more sensible pet owners went to their veterinarian.

Wanting to make a good impression as a team player, I quickly volunteered for the Raritan clinic even though it was my weekend off. There was silence at the table, as my colleagues stared at me probably wondering, *What kind of nut did we just hire?*

"Are you sure about this Doc?" Mike asked.

"Absolutely," I said with confidence, plus with a six-week-old baby and a small school loan to pay off, the extra money would come in handy.

Dr. North informed his overly anxious neophyte, "Ed, this is one of our larger clinics. I will be there at the start for an hour or so to help with the early crowd."

"How many pets are we talking about?"

Looking at his notes, Mike said, "Last year we had a hair over 500 vaccinations. By the way, the clinic starts at 8:30 a.m., so plan on being there at 8:00 a.m. to set up. Sandy will be your assistant and draw up the shots."

"What time is the clinic over?"

"Officially, it's over at noon, but you can stay longer to get any stragglers if you want to."

Doing some quick math in my head, *500 dogs and cats in 3 1/2 hours, that's about 2 1/2 vaccinations per minute. But, Dr. North will be there for an hour-- so, okay-- I need to do an animal every 30 seconds. Hmm..... I gotta be quick.*

Mike continued on, "Next week on Wednesday evening our last clinic will be from 7 to 9 p.m. It's a small one at the Martinsville Fire House. Last year we did 118 animals."

"I'll do it," I said for the second time.

"Way to go Doc, meeting adjourned. Back to work," Mike ordered.

As we filed out and down the stairs, I heard someone ask Mike, "Did you tell Ed about Thor on Saturday?"

Mike laughed, "No, he likes surprises."

Then everyone chuckled. I wasn't sure what was so funny, I meant to ask Mike about Thor later on, but forgot.

The next day in surgery between cat spays, Sandy and I had a mini-meeting about the upcoming rabies clinic.

"So Sandy, you know what to do. Right?"

"Dr. Dionne, this is my first one. I'm clueless," she admitted.

"Okay, how hard can it be. We'll load two grooming tables into my station wagon on Friday evening. One table is for Dr. North and the other table is for me. You can have the card table for the vaccines, syringes, cotton and alcohol. We'll keep the vaccine in a cooler. We will need a box to throw the empty syringes in. Oh yes, Mike has a ramp for each table for the dogs to walk up, get their shot and jump off."

"I'll talk to Mike this afternoon and get everything ready for Saturday," Sandy said.

"Great, I'll meet you at the hospital at quarter to eight so we can be at Raritan by 8 a.m. and set up."

Saturday morning came and everything was going smoothly. We pulled into the fire station's parking lot right on time. We met with the three volunteer ladies, Agnes, Mary and Sharon, who would be handling the paperwork, vaccination certificates, rabies tags, dog licenses and questions.

Mary had brought a large box of assorted doughnuts and coffee. The firemen provided a table and chairs for the ladies. It was very well organized.

I then heard the noise and saw the line forming which stretched half a block. Sandy and I quickly unloaded the station wagon and set up our tables.

In order to meet the 8:30 a.m. start time, we pre-loaded several syringes with vaccine.

With a few minutes to spare, we were ready. Just enough time to have one of Mary's chocolate covered doughnuts and burn my tongue sipping their very hot coffee.

It was now 8:30 a.m., time to start, and Dr. North was nowhere in sight. The neighbors on each side of the fire station were coming out of their homes to have coffee on the porch. The porch-less ones used lawn chairs.

There was no parade with marching band expected this day. But we had plenty of our own music-- high-pitched woofs, low growls, ear-deafening barks, meows and lots of yelling--good girl, bad boy, sit, stay, down boy, stop it, heel, I said heel!...

The line started to move. The small and medium-sized dogs were picked up and placed on the table by their owners. I would walk up behind both of them, quickly hold the dog's hind leg, give the shot and walk away. Most animals and owners didn't realize the vaccination was over.

The larger animals took more time. Some walked willingly up the ramp; most were pushed and pulled to the top and onto the table. A few nimble ones ran up and immediately jumped off the other end of the table without receiving the rabies shot. On the second or third attempt, I grabbed the pooch and gave the shot in mid-air as he was diving off the table. The really large ones were done on the ground.

Dr. North finally arrived at 8:30 a.m. his time, a.k.a. 9 a.m. our time. Half the line moved over to his table. His old clients wanted to see him and chat a bit.

After two weeks of employment, there were no old clients in my line. I did have a variety of dogs-- the outside-living hunting dogs, obedience school *dropouts,* and a handful of rough customers. This is the group that the neighbors wanted to see.

The beagles howled, the pointers didn't point and the retrievers held something like a ball in their mouth. It hadn't rained in a week so none were bathed for the occasion. All had a distinct aroma.

The obedience school dropouts included a wide variety of breeds and mixtures of all sizes and shapes. The one thing they all had in common is that not one listened to their owner for more than a few milli-seconds.

A few dogs were able to slip out of their collars during the tug-of-war contest with their masters. Once free, they provided much amusement to the crowd of onlookers. Owner chasing their dog, dog chasing other dogs, some finally captured, others headed for home or parts unknown.

The rough ones had names like Satan, Rex, King, Killer, Queenie (beware of dogs with this name), Lobo, and Flash. Some wore muzzles that didn't fit all that well. Most bared their choppers and were ready to fight or bite anyone that came too close like the vet. More excitement for the crowd.

At 10:15 a.m., Dr. North left for home. We continued to use his table for the few brave cats and gentler dogs. Sandy was able to draw up vaccine and direct traffic to the proper table. As we approached noon, the line was dwindling, but the spectators were increasing in number. Mary replenished my now cold coffee and left a doughnut on a plate. Not that I wanted to touch the doughnut after handling a multitude of unkempt hind legs.

I overheard Mary tell Sharon that Thor should be coming soon. Then I remembered the name, and how I forgot to ask Mike about Thor.

At 11:45 a.m., I heard a spectator say, "There he is!" and another announce with awe and fear, "Thor's coming!"

All porch people turned to look up the street, the lawn chair people moved back closer to their house, the meager line of canines and their owners parted like the Red Sea, and Mary, Agnes, and Sharon quickly left their table and moved toward the fire station.

Agnes said, "I hope they can vaccinate him this year!"

Now I was curious. *What kind of beast is coming down the street?* Leaving my empty table, I stepped out into the middle of the street to get a better look. I witnessed two strong young men lowering the tailgate of their pickup truck. The side of the truck said, Jessie and Frank James, *Used Cars, Parts and Towing.*

I quickly surmised Thor was their guard dog. However, he was no ordinary junk yard dog. Thor was the largest and most heavily muscled Rottweiler that I have ever seen. He was black and tan with a massive head and neck attached to his 150 lb. frame. Around his neck was a spiked collar with two long, thick towing chains attached. Wearing sturdy work gloves, each James boy held one of the chains tightly with both hands.

Thor was pulling Frank and Jessie down the middle of the street. He was looking straight at me standing in his way. Thor's eyes seemed to be glowing red, his huge mouth was open, teeth bared, and saliva frothing from both sides of his jowls. He looked like a dog with rabies!

It was now *high noon*, and Thor was looking for a fight. Today, would be the modern version of *The Gunfight at the OK Corral*. Jessie and Frank managed to stop the beast about twenty feet from me.

Thor and I tried to stare each other down; neither of us turned and ran. The townsfolk stood in hushed silence. Mothers held their children tightly. A few of the men were making bets among themselves. All were prepared to run if Thor broke loose.

I was remarkably cool and calm, unless you count the fact that my knees were knocking, hands trembling, and there was a flood under each armpit.

Thinking to myself, I said, *Okay, Wyatt Earp, what now?*

Frank James broke the silence, "Where do ya'll want him, Doc?" Jessie stood patiently with a slight grin remembering last year's failed vaccination attempt.

Scanning the area for some type of help, my eyes fell on a nearby sturdy telephone pole. Now it was my turn to grin.

"Take him over to that telephone pole and wrap one of the chains around it one time, but still hold the end tightly."

Then pointing to Jessie, "You hold your chain off to one side away from the pole. Thor will be caught in the middle."

As Frank and Jessie were re-positioning their guard dog, I turned and walked back to my assistant.

"Sandy, put a full load in my *gun*, I mean syringe."

She handed me the syringe and said, "Be careful out there, marshal."

"Sandy, I'm going to need your help. Get two doughnuts from Mary, walk around the James gang, but stay about ten feet in front of Thor. On my signal, start tossing pieces of doughnut to you know who."

I concealed my weapon/syringe in the palm of my right hand and walked back toward the non-vaccinated growling outlaw. When everyone was in place, I nodded my head to Sandy *Doc Holiday*. She started with the doughnut-tossing and Thor gobbled each piece as it arrived.

Timing the toss, I put my thumb on the end of the plunger, and walked up behind the distracted Thor. It was not the normal technique for giving an injection. I used the old stab and push the plunger into the hamstring method. I then turned and quickly walked away ignoring the loud snap of teeth behind my leg.

Thor was *shot* and his ego wounded. It took a moment for the spectators to respond with clapping and cheering. The James gang returned to their pick-up, the vaccinated Thor hopped into the back, and they drove peacefully out of town.

Sandy and I gently vaccinated ten more animals, said good-bye to Mary, Agnes and Sharon, took a doughnut for the trip home and rode off knowing that the good townsfolk of Raritan would be safe for another year.

16

Cleopatra

Thousands of years ago, cats were worshipped as Gods. Cats have never forgotten this.
Anonymous

Rabies is a dreaded disease that has struck fear into the hearts of men and women for many centuries. There is a great deal of confusion and misunderstanding about the disease. A brief synopsis is in order. Rabies is a viral disease of warmblooded mammals including humans. The virus causes an encephalitis resulting in an almost 100% mortality. Vaccination of our two most common pets, dogs and cats, has controlled rabies for the most part in the United States. The raccoon, skunk and the bat are the main rabies carriers in our wildlife population, although it has been reported in many other animal species as well.

Each week, we would receive calls from

worried parents, "My Johnny's gerbil bit him in the finger. Will he get rabies?"

The answer is No!

There has been no known cases of rabies transmission to people from rodents such as the squirrel, hamster, guinea pig, rats or mice. Upon being bitten by a rabid animal, the virus attaches itself to peripheral nerves. The brain is the target site for this nasty virus. The process of getting there takes awhile-- weeks to months. Fortunately, the infected person has time to get necessary treatment.

* * *

In the center of the small town of Martinsville, the volunteer fire department was located on the busy main street. A few acres of woodland were located behind the building. Volunteer firemen kept the two fire engines spotlessly clean and ready to respond to any emergency at a moment's notice.

Sandy and I arrived twenty minutes early to set up our tables. This time we were both veterans of one rabies clinic.

Driving into the parking lot, I quipped,
"After Raritan on Saturday, this clinic will be a piece of cake."

Sandy responded, "There's no one even here yet! Last week, it seemed like some people had camped out the night before."

I laughed and said, "Mike told me at the staff luncheon that Martinsville had just a little over 100 animals last year. We can take our time and not rush."

We met our helpers, Ann, Fred and his wife, Tracey. The animals and their owners started arriving shortly after 7 p.m. The crowd came in dribs and drabs. The line was always short and manageable. There were a few *toughies* but nothing like Thor. One six-foot, 200 lb. gentleman decided to walk up the ramp onto our table to show his reluctant Brittany spaniel that it was safe. My back was turned at the time of his ascent to the table top. Swinging back around with a needle and syringe in my hand, I grabbed the towering giant's calf and almost gave him the shot.

As nice as possible I said, "Sir, I'm not sure this table is going to hold your weight. How about you get off and we will help lift your fine looking Brittany up and take your place? Unless you plan on biting someone, I don't think you need a rabies shot."

* * *

A light blue, 1964 Volkswagen Beetle was parked in the lot near the front of the fire hall. It had been there for the past hour. James Riley and Thelma Forbes were seated in the vehicle and watching the rabies clinic with great interest. Thelma was waiting for that moment when there would be no animals present and an empty line. She planned to spring from the Volkswagen and run to our vaccination table with her cat, Cleopatra. Once the shot was given, they would hurry back to the car and with great relief head for home.

The twenty-four-year-old Thelma was a secretary for Dr. John Wade, a busy orthopedic surgeon in Somerville. The slender Thelma had bright red hair which was slightly curly and hung down to her shoulders. Her emerald green eyes and abundance of freckles made her quite attractive.

James, her fiancee, had recently graduated from law school and was studying for his Bar exams. He was hired by the law firm of Werner, Scullin, Meckley and Hall on a trial basis until he passed his exams. The twenty-five-year-old James was also slender in build, with blond hair and light blue eyes. After graduation from Seton Hall, James had moved into Thelma's apartment two months ago.

That's when the problems began. The three-year-old Cleopatra did not like James moving in at all. He took her spot on the bed and couch. James did not like Cleopatra either, but it was part of the agreement that he made with his bride-to-be.

"Take me, take my cat for better or worse!" Thelma joked.

James and Cleopatra grudgingly accepted each other for the most part. James could not pet or pick up the fussy feline. The few times that he tried were met with a hiss or a growl. He grew to dislike *Cleo* and teased her or stepped on her tail when Thelma was out of the room.

Tonight at the clinic, Cleo was sitting somewhat impatiently on Thelma's lap. She didn't like to be in the car or outside for that matter. She was quite happy in her cozy two bedroom apartment.

* * *

Three years ago, Thelma adopted her from the nearby humane society. This was Cleopatra's lucky day because her two week adoption time was running out. Everyone at the kennel wanted to be *chosen* and taken home by a new family. Those that weren't *chosen* went through the black door at the end of the kennel never to return.

Cleo was young enough at ten weeks of age, and cute enough with her orange stripes. She had a white mustache, white paws and a white bib that started under her chin and ran down her neck and chest to her abdomen. Many potential owners stopped to admire her in the cage, but soon moved on after Cleo hissed and spit repeatedly. The kennel volunteers had little hope that anyone would adopt this little *spitfire*.

On day thirteen, Thelma walked into the Humane Society and said, "I would like to adopt a kitten. Maybe one that might be hard to place. I'm not fussy."

John, the attendant, thought for a moment and said, "Well Miss, we do have one for you to consider. Let me show you."

He took her back to Cleopatra's cage for an inspection.

"Oh, she's so beautiful, and her fur matches my hair!" Thelma laughed.

"I must warn you, she doesn't like most people. I think she may have been abused, or maybe she thinks she's a queen or something," John guessed.

"Well, I'll just name her Cleopatra, Queen of the Nile."

Thelma opened the cage and just picked up the future queen without any trouble--no hissing, spitting, or scratching.

John said, "I don't believe it! She really likes you."

Thelma bought a cardboard pet carrier, signed the adoption papers, took her home and had her spayed when she was six months old.

* * *

It was after 8 p.m. and the sun was beginning to sink below the treeline behind the fire hall.

James was finding it increasingly difficult to study in the tiny vehicle any longer.

"Thelma, we've been here over an hour. Let's go home."

"I know, I know... let's give it five more minutes. There's only three dogs in the line."

"Honey, there's been three dogs in line for the past hour. They just keep on coming."

"James, hold on. Look! There's only one dog left, and I don't see any other car in the parking lot but us. Let's go!"

Holding Cleopatra wrapped in a small blanket over her shoulder like a baby, Thelma and James walked quickly to Sandy and me.

"Doctor, could you give my cat the rabies shot while I hold her like this?"

Before I could answer Thelma's question, Bobby Rodgers came running around the side of the fire hall with his dog, Bruno. He didn't want to be late for the clinic. Bruno pulled Bobby right up behind Thelma. His dog saw Cleo and gave a loud bark.

The queen hissed and dug her sharp claws into Thelma's shoulder and chest.

"Ow!" Thelma cried in pain releasing her grip just enough that Cleopatra was able to jump over her shoulder. Once on the ground, Cleo ran toward the fire hall, with Bruno in hot pursuit.

The two escaped pets were chased by Bobby, Thelma and James. All three were calling to their pets, "Come back!" to no avail.

Bobby managed to catch Bruno by the collar. Thelma and James saw Cleopatra run into the woods.

The future attorney stopped at the edge of the woods while his fiancee plunged headlong into the trees, bushes and brambles.

Sandy and I looked on in amazement, but we had to get back to work because five more animals with owners in tow had just arrived.

We did hear Thelma holler, “James, don’t just stand there. Come help me!”

James entered the woods reluctantly; he still had on his good clothes and new shoes that he had worn to the office earlier today. Sandy and I continued the vaccinations while every two minutes we heard Thelma call out for her cat.

It was slowly getting darker.

We then heard James and Thelma having a loud disagreement.

“Thelma, I’m leaving. Let the cat go. She’s wild anyway. We can get a new kitten--a nice one. So what’s it going to be, me or Cleopatra?”

Thelma didn’t hesitate. She turned and yelled, “*Cleo!*”

“Stay there then and look for your darn cat! I’m going to my brother’s house.”

“Go ahead, I’m finding Cleo. By the way James, do you know that you’re standing in poison ivy?”

James jumped out of the patch of ivy as though he was about to be run over by a train and stomped out of the woods. Sandy and I watched James cross in front of the fire hall. He kept his head down and cursed to himself.

Upon reaching his VW Beetle, he hopped in, slammed the door, revved the engine and pulled out of the parking lot leaving a trail of flying gravel and dust.

Two volunteer firemen were worried about Thelma. They walked to the woods, entered and found Miss Forbes still searching for her lost feline. The firemen tried in vain to bring her out; she was on a mission. The unsuccessful firemen returned shaking their heads.

* * *

At 9 p.m. the clinic was over and fairly dark. A full moon and a clear night provided a welcome illumination.

Sandy asked, "What are we going to do about the woman in the woods?"

I started to answer when David, a third volunteer fireman, limped out of the fire hall with two flashlights.

"Hey Doc, let's go help that crazy lady. Maybe we can find the lost cat or at least guide the woman out. It's starting to become a dangerous situation. Oh, I'm David Bell by the way."

We introduced ourselves, and I looked down at his cast and walking boot on his right foot.

"Are you going to be able to walk okay in the woods?"

"Yup, no problem, just a hairline fracture in one of my ankle bones. Let's go find her."

I guessed that David was around thirty years old. He had brown eyes, wavy brown hair, broad shoulders and large impressive biceps.

David must spend quite a bit of time in the weight room, I thought to myself.

We found Thelma on her hands and knees looking under a bush.

David said kindly, "We came to help you, Miss."

"David, let's start checking the trees. I don't think her cat would stay on the ground."

We split up and shined our flashlights up into the tree branches. After a few minutes of searching, David found a pair of shining eyes looking down at him.

"I found him," he yelled. Thelma corrected him, as though it made a difference.

"She's a girl, her name is Cleopatra."

Thelma tried to coax her cat down, "Cleo, it's me, mommy. Please come down."

Fat chance of that, I thought. She was a good fourteen feet up in a sturdy elm tree. She was sitting on the crook of a large branch close to the main tree trunk.

"Doc, I would climb that tree if my foot was okay."

I looked at Sandy. "Don't look at me, Dr. Dionne. I'm not about to climb up there!"

"I know, I'm just teasing. I'm going."

David, the muscular fireman, moved close to the base of the tree and interlaced his fingers forming a step to boost me up. I latched onto the first branch and pulled myself up. Sandy and Thelma held the flashlights as I climbed up two more branches.

I made one mistake. Reaching for Cleo with my right hand, I thought she would welcome being rescued.

Not so!

Faster than you can blink an eye, a paw with four razor-sharp claws raked my forearm. Pain radiated up to my shoulder and warm blood dripped down underneath my forearm.

Using another more careful technique, I planted each foot securely on two tree limbs and leaned my body against the trunk. I reached my left hand around the tree and grabbed Cleo's tail.

As I pulled her tail back, she tried to hold on to the branch with her dangerous claws. This gave me the opportunity to reach up and grasp the scruff of her neck with my right hand.

Cleopatra let out a blood-curdling meow followed by hissing and spitting.

I held the fractious feline tightly and as far out from my body as possible. Slowly and carefully I started to descend using only my left hand to hold onto any convenient branch.

Thelma yelled, "Please don't hurt her doctor!"

I thought, *Don't hurt her, what do you mean, I'm the one who's bleeding!*

In the meantime, Sandy had left, ran to my car and brought back a pet carrier to put the captured little *tiger* in. Using David's strong hands again as a step, I stepped back down onto mother earth. Thelma rushed to her cat before I could stop her. She became the second victim of the evening. Cleo threw a right hook and slashed Thelma's left cheek.

"Cleopatra, that was not nice; you're a naughty cat!" she scolded.

Sandy opened the pet carrier, and I dropped Cleo in quickly and closed the top as fast as I could. The four of us trudged and stumbled out of the dark woods and back to the fire hall.

David cleaned my scratches and put on a light bandage. He spent much more time tending Thelma's cheek, actually more time than was necessary.

David and Thelma's heads were close together. They were making eye contact. Sandy nudged me with her elbow and smiled. David also volunteered to drive Thelma and Cleopatra home.

"Don't take your cat out of the carrier until you are safely inside your house," I ordered.

Sandy and I packed up our supplies from the *easy* clinic and went home ourselves. I was glad that the rabies clinics were over for another year.

* * *

This story ended happily. James moved out for good, the engagement ring was returned and Cleopatra was declawed.

A few months later, Thelma moved in with David. Cleopatra actually liked her new house, especially David's two fish aquariums. She spent hours watching the fish swim by the front of the tank. A goldfish seemed to be her favorite. Thelma named the fish Marc Antony, after the lover of the famous Cleopatra.

The easy-going David and feline queen became friends. Cleo allowed him to pet her, and she often sat on his lap.

Later, I noticed the wedding engagement in the paper-- Thelma Forbes to marry David Bell. The wedding took place in the fire hall next to the woods where they first met. All their friends and relatives were present, except for Cleopatra who stayed home with Marc Antony.

17

Squeaky

Brutality to an animal is cruelty to mankind ~ it is only the difference in the victim.

Alphonse de Lamartine

According to *Wikipedia*, the online encyclopedia, the term to *bully* is described as-- *the use of force or coercion to abuse or intimidate others. This behavior can be habitual and involve an imbalance of social or physical power. It can also involve verbal harassment or threats.*

* * *

In 1969, Billy Harper was twelve years old and had several nicknames. He grudgingly accepted the names but didn't care for any of them except for *Pee Wee.*

The famous Pee Wee Reese was an all-star shortstop for the Brooklyn Dodgers and later the Los Angeles Dodgers from 1940-1958. He was the favorite baseball player of Frank Harper, Billy's dad. Frank grew up in Brooklyn near Ebbets Field, and he went to see the Dodgers play whenever he could.

Frank told Billy that *Pee Wee* got his nickname not from being short. He really wasn't at five feet ten inches. As a child, Harold Reese, his real name, received his nickname because he was an outstanding marble player. And a small marble is referred to as a *pee wee.*

So Billy thought that nickname was okay. But, runt, shrimp, midget, tiny, squirt, pip-squeak, peanut and shorty were all names that Billy despised. On any given day at school he would be called each name at least once, usually followed by a mocking laugh.

Yes, Billy Harper was short. The shortest student, boy or girl, in the seventh grade. The doctors thought that Billy must have a pituitary problem-- not enough growth hormone. They also told Darlene, Billy's mother, the pituitary might start working once he reached puberty in his teenage years. He might then catch up to the other children.

Billy was a nice kid but very shy and quiet. He had light brown hair, hazel eyes and wore eyeglasses encased in a thin wire frame. Billy didn't smile very much; he was too self-conscious because of the thick metal braces attached to his teeth. He was also fairly thin, and the boys in gym class called him *chicken legs*.

* * *

Tuesday was his favorite day of the week. This is the evening when his Boy Scout Troop met at a nearby church hall in Somerville. Billy had more merit badges than any other twelve year old in the troop. This included his biggest tormentor, Anthony *Big Tony* Romano, who often made his life miserable.

The one merit badge that eluded Billy had to do with pets and animal care.

The Harper family had allergy problems. The entire family including his parents and younger sister, Tracy, was allergic to the usual seasonal pollen--trees, grasses and ragweed. But pet hair and dander were the worst. So any discussion of getting a dog or cat was quickly nixed by Billy's dad, Frank.

What Billy really needed was a friend his own age. His younger sister, Tracy, was okay, but she liked to play house, have tea parties and dress up her dolls. Billy could only take so much of that type of play--maybe thirty minutes at the most.

He would then retreat to his room and do his homework, read a book or listen to the radio. He liked *Rock 'n' Roll*, especially the *Rolling Stones*. Billy spent a good deal of time imitating the lead singer, Mick Jagger. Whenever a Stones' song came on, Billy strutted across the bedroom and practiced his cool dance moves. Standing in front of the mirror, he tried in vain to pull his lips out further in a futile attempt to resemble Mick. Inevitably, he would tire and plop down onto his bed.

"I wish I had a pet. Why do I have to be so

short *and* have allergies? Maybe if I have a little pet the allergies wouldn't be so bad."

He laid on his bed and stared at the ceiling trying to come up with a solution to his *lack of a pet* problem.

He remembered the goldfish disaster. *Goldie the fish didn't last two weeks before she died,* he thought to himself. "Fish aren't any fun anyway," Billy said aloud.

Standing in front of his dresser's mirror, Billy asked himself, "How about a snake? They don't have hair so probably no allergy problems either. I could get a python or a big boa and take him to school. If *Big Tony* calls me names and makes fun of me, I could wrap my boa around him and have my snake squeeze him a little until he stops teasing me."

The thought of a snake wrapped around Big Tony made Billy laugh.

"Nah, snakes aren't any fun. Actually they're kinda creepy. They just lay around in some big fish tank, and you have to feed them little mice. The poor mice."

"Hey, that's it! Why didn't I think of that before-- a pet mouse. Now that would be very cool. They're little like me, and how much allergy stuff could a mouse have?"

Getting more excited, Billy said aloud, "I could train him and everything! And I could get my pet merit badge!"

That evening as the family gathered around the kitchen table for dinner, Billy pleaded his case for a pet mouse. Darlene and Tracy seemed to be in agreement with Billy. Frank was skeptical but listening.

Frank had spent four years in the army as a Staff Sergeant. He was used to listening and giving orders. He still wore his hair short in an army-style crew-cut. Dark brown eyes, a deep cleft in a prominent chin and a close shave gave the ex-sergeant a military appearance.

Frank wasn't very tall himself at five feet seven inches, but his muscular arms and broad shoulders made him appear taller.

After several minutes of discussion, dad smiled and said, "We'll give it a try as long as no allergy problems arise."

"It's a deal!" Billy shouted with glee.

"Doesn't Mr. Sharbaugh, our neighbor, work in one of those drug research companies in Piscataway?" Darlene asked. "I bet he might know something about mice."

"I'll talk to him tomorrow after work," Frank offered.

* * *

The next day, Frank went over to Paul Sharbaugh's house to talk about mice. It turned out that Paul knew a lot about this tiny animal since his company did use mice for research studies.

"We have just received a new batch of New Zealand white mice. I think we can spare one for Billy."

"The mice are from New Zealand?" Frank asked.

"No...no, that's just their breed name. Well, tomorrow is Saturday, and no one is working except for the animal caretakers. So let's go then. How about around 10 a.m.?"

"That would be fine, but this is Billy's pet so I'm letting him go all by himself with you to pick out his mouse," Frank answered.

* * *

Even though it was Saturday, Billy was up at 7 a.m., and he had dressed, eaten breakfast and brushed his teeth by 8 a.m.

Darlene found him at the breakfast table. "Billy, why are you up so early? You're not leaving for another two hours."

"Mom, I'm so excited that I couldn't sleep any longer. So I'm making a list of things that I have to do and questions for Mr. Sharbaugh."

"Like what?"

"Like--what's a good name for a mouse?"

"How about Mickey?"

"Mom! Get serious. This is a *real* mouse that I'm getting."

After much discussion, Squeaky was the name chosen. The other question, like how to care for a mouse, would have to wait until 10 a.m. and Mr. Sharbaugh.

The clock ticked slowly and finally reached the appointed time. Billy was out the door and ran to the Sharbaugh's residence.

On the drive over to the research facility, Mr. Sharbaugh was peppered with mouse questions. And the answers were recorded by Billy in his school notebook.

Mr. Sharbaugh said, "I think the best place to keep your mouse is in an aquarium rather than a cage. The aquarium will be easier to clean, and your mouse will stay warmer than in a drafty cage. Mice really like to be warm. I brought an old aquarium that you can have. It's in my car trunk."

"Wow, thanks Mr. Sharbaugh!"

"We'll pick up some cedar shavings at the lab. It makes a good bedding for your mouse."

"What should I feed my mouse?"

"If you go to the pet shop in Somerville, they can help you. But hamster and gerbil pellets are good. So is rabbit and guinea pig food. Mice also like seeds, and it's okay to give them parakeet seed. And they also really love raw sunflower seeds."

"How about table food?" Billy asked while writing quickly in his notebook.

"That's a good question. You can feed uncooked cereal grain like oats. They also like lettuce and other raw vegetables and small pieces of fruit like apples."

They soon reached the lab and Paul took the aquarium out of the trunk to bring the selected mouse home.

Entering the animal area, Billy saw several cages of white mice, rats, guinea pigs and rabbits.

"I've never seen so many animals before!" said the amazed twelve year old.

"Do you want a male or a female mouse?"

"*Boy!*"

Paul pulled out a cage containing eight white mice-- all boys.

"These guys just arrived. They're about four or five weeks old."

The mice all looked cute to Billy with their tiny ears and long hairless tails. All the mice, except for one, were missing some hair in spots and had little sores on their bodies. The one with no hair loss or sores was a little bigger than the rest and had a beautiful shiny white coat.

"Mr. Sharbaugh, I like the big mouse with the nice hair."

"Do you know why that mouse looks so good and the rest look so bad?" asked Paul.

"No."

"That big mouse picks on the smaller mice and bites them. So we're going to have to move him anyway, unless you take him."

"What! He's a *bully!*" said an angry Billy. "I don't want him. I'll take the smallest one then."

"Okay, let me show you how to pick him up."

Mr. Sharbaugh reached in and grabbed the small mouse by the base of the tail and put him in the aquarium. The little mouse squeaked when he was picked up.

Billy laughed, "Well I guess Squeaky is a good name for you after all."

The two of them and the adopted white mouse left the research lab. Billy and Paul discussed mice on the way home while Squeaky was content to hide in the cedar shavings.

"Did you know that mice are color-blind just like dogs?" Mr. Sharbaugh asked.

"No."

"Yup, they just see black, white and shades of gray."

"How long does a mouse live?" Billy asked.

"As a pet, they could live to four years old and maybe longer."

With all the conversation and mice knowledge being shared, they arrived home quickly. Billy thanked his new teacher and friend and rushed into the house with Squeaky.

* * *

Over the next few months, Billy learned as much as he could about mice. He kept Squeaky in his bedroom and fixed up the aquarium with assorted items to keep his pet active. He used various sized stones, small branches and even fashioned a tiny pond to make it seem like Squeaky was not in a cage.

Squeaky became *trained* and didn't have to be picked up by his tail any longer. He readily jumped onto Billy's palm. Then came the big test; Billy put on a shirt with a deep pocket. He put three pumpkin seeds into the pocket and dropped Squeaky inside hoping that he would not try to jump out.

The little mouse grew to love being in the shirt pocket. It was warm, dark, and there was always a treat inside. He occasionally would pop his head out of his *pocket-apartment* for a look around. But quickly withdrew and hid if he saw anyone. It was *safe* in his little home.

Billy and Squeaky would walk around the house together. His parents and sister laughed when Squeaky would take a quick peek from his pocket home and squeak.

A few weeks later, Billy bravely took his mouse outside. He didn't know what to expect, but his mouse calmly stayed put in Billy's shirt pocket.

One Tuesday evening, Billy, the mouse trainer, decided to take him to Boy Scouts. He wanted to show the Scoutmaster his pet, and that he was working on his pet merit badge. The other Scouts were impressed and excited to see the white mouse, and how well-trained he was. They never imagined a mouse would stay in your pocket.

All the attention being given to Billy made Big Tony Romano jealous.

Tony turned to one of his buddies and said, "Give me your pencil."

Tony and his two friends then walked over to Billy when he was alone and the Scoutmaster was in another room.

"Hey *Shorty*, whata ya got in your pocket?"

Before he could answer, Big Tony took the pencil and jabbed the bulge in Billy's pocket.

There was a loud squeak, then silence.

Tony then pushed Billy knocking him to the floor. The three laughing bullies walked away before the Scoutmaster returned.

Billy was distraught. Looking into his pocket, he saw Squeaky was not moving. There was some blood around his left eye. Before he started to cry, Billy left the Scout meeting and ran the several blocks to his home.

Once home the tears flowed down his cheeks.

Frank said, "What happened? Why are you crying?"

Darlene asked, "Are you hurt?"

Between sobs, Billy explained to his parents what Big Tony had done.

Darlene placed a hand towel on the kitchen table and said, "Billy, take him out of your pocket so we can see if he's okay."

Billy then carefully lifted Squeaky out of his pocket and placed him gently on the hand towel.

Squeaky was now moving but very slowly. His left eye was all swollen and red. The family stared at the injured mouse for several minutes not sure as to what to do.

Darlene asked, "Should we call a vet?"

"Are you crazy, no vet's going to see a mouse at night," Frank asserted.

"Mom, please call," Tracy asked for her brother.

Darlene picked up the telephone book and checked the yellow pages under veterinarian. She picked our office because we were close and offered emergency service.

* * *

I was still in the office finishing up with a case when the answering service called me.

It was Angel, the operator, who asked, "Dr. Dionne, do you take care of mice?"

"Why? Don't tell me someone is calling about a mouse."

"Yes, Mrs. Harper has a pet mouse with an injured eye."

"Angel, I was just about to go home, but I'll call them right now before I leave."

I then called the Harper residence; Mrs. Harper explained the problem and our conversation was quite brief.

"Mrs. Harper, bring your little mouse right in, I need to see what's wrong with his eye."

In less than ten minutes, the entire family was huddled around the table in Exam Room 2.

Darlene said, "Thank you for seeing us, Dr...."

"Dionne," I replied.

I took out my penlight and flashed the light at

the injured eye. It was quite clear as to the problem. Squeaky had a *proptosis* of the eyeball. The eye had been knocked out of its socket and became swollen and severely damaged.

Squeaky was blind in that eye.

I explained all of this to the Harpers.

"Aren't there any eye-drops that you can use to make it shrink and go back into place?" Darlene asked.

"No, not really. The only thing that could be done is to enucleate or remove the eyeball."

"Billy, we can talk to Mr. Sharbaugh tomorrow and get you a new mouse," Frank offered.

Then the tears started again this time from both children.

"I want Squeaky. I don't care if he only has one eye," Billy said as he held his little friend in the palm of his hand.

"Dr. Dionne, is it possible to operate on a mouse? How much will it cost?" Darlene asked.

Not expecting this response from the family, I stared down at the *two dollar* mouse and thought for a moment.

Mike really is going to hit the roof this time, I thought.

Looking at the family, I said, "It's possible to operate, but it will be risky with the anesthesia. The eye needs to be removed, and the eyelids will have to be sutured closed, otherwise an infection will get in. I've done the surgery on both dogs and cats, but never on a mouse. So I don't really know how it will work out."

"As far as the cost, I will do it for *free*. We'll chalk it off to a learning experience."

Big smiles appeared on everyone's face. Even Squeaky looked happy.

It was a go.

"You folks wait in the exam room, and I'll take this little guy to surgery."

* * *

First, I set out our ophthalmic surgery instruments on a tray and put on the necessary suture material. I then turned on the bright surgery lights and placed a binocular loupe on my head.

The loupe looks like a pair of funny eyeglasses; the lenses of which are like magnifying glasses so the surgeon can do close-up work and see during the operation.

The biggest problem was going to be the anesthesia. The anesthesia machine was turned on and connected to a face mask. The mask was made to fit a dog or cat, not a mouse. I dropped Squeaky into the mask's chamber and plugged the opening with cotton. Within a few minutes, my tiny patient was anesthetized.

Reaching into the mask, I removed Squeaky and placed him on a surgery drape to begin the operation. Working quickly, the eye was removed and its blood vessels tied off.

Every few minutes, Squeaky was put back into the anesthesia chamber for more gas to keep him *asleep*.

The final step was to suture his eyelids closed. Using a small but very sharp pair of ophthalmic scissors, I removed a few millimeters of the top and bottom eyelid. This created a fresh wound for closure.

Very fine ophthalmic sutures were used to join the upper and lower eyelids.

The operation was over fairly quickly and the one-eyed white mouse woke up a few minutes later.

Returning triumphantly to the exam room with my patient, the Harpers let out a collective "Squeaky!"

Squeaky went home and healed well.

I was in trouble with Mike again, but not too badly.

* * *

Billy visited the veterinary hospital a few times in the ensuing weeks to work on his pet merit badge. Squeaky came along each time but was perfectly happy to stay hidden in Billy's shirt pocket.

His last visit was about a year later. I noticed that Billy had grown several inches, and his voice was starting to change.

After the hospital visit, we went out for a hamburger and a milk shake. Billy said, "Dr. Dionne, I have to tell you a story."

"Okay," I said as ketchup dribbled down my chin.

"My dad has been taking me to his gym and teaching me how to lift weights." And he flexed his biceps to show me his *new* muscles.

"Wow, I think they're bigger than mine."

"My dad doesn't want anyone picking on me any more so I'm also in a martial arts class."

"Does Squeaky take the class also?"

"No," as we both laughed.

"But listen to this," Billy said, "that bully, Big

Tony Romano, the other day at school, tried to push me in the pocket where Squeaky stays."

"Yes."

"Well, I was ready. I turned my body sideways as he was trying to push us. Then I grabbed his wrist and forearm and pulled him forward. He was off-balance and tripped. He landed flat on his face on the floor. And everyone laughed at him for a change."

"I wish that I was there to see that," I said.

"Squeaky popped his head out of my pocket and kept squeaking at him." I think he said, "Take that you big bully!"

As we left the restaurant, I put my arm around Billy and said, "You know, I think that's exactly what Squeaky said."

18

Clarence Monteith

When we show our respect for other living things, they respond with respect for us.
Arapaho Proverb

Today was the first Monday of May, in 1974. My ten-month-old daughter, Michelle, had slept through the night. It was a reason for a tired mom and dad to celebrate. The seven-mile drive into work was pleasant this morning. The rain had finally ended, trees were blooming, my nose was running and my eyes were starting to itch. A sure sign that spring had officially arrived.

It was going to be a good day I thought to myself. Pulling into the parking lot along side the hospital at precisely 8 a.m., I was full of energy and eager to start the day. Monday was my day to be a *floater*-- to do a little bit of everything. For the first hour, animals having surgery that day were checked by me during a quick office exam, then admitted. This was important; you had to make sure the owner didn't give their pooch or kitty any food that morning. They could regurgitate their breakfast under anesthesia or upon waking up. This could result in a potentially serious aspiration pneumonia.

Sometimes the surgery had to be postponed if Lassie was in the middle of a *heat* cycle. We didn't spay dogs at this time because the uterus is swollen and filled with blood. Too risky.

Or the type of surgery might be changed because Thomasina, the female cat, was actually Tom, a potential lover-boy.

Imagine the embarrassment to be in the middle of the abdominal spay operation and discover no ovaries or uterus. An assistant would be called upon to peek under the surgery drape to identify the correct sex. *Oops!* was usually heard from the surgeon as he sutured the unnecessary incision. I can proudly say there was never an *Oops!* in my career.

After everyone was admitted for surgery, I then became the assistant surgeon. My job was to anesthetize the animals for the doctor doing surgery that morning. Sandy and I would have the next animal prepped and ready so the surgeon could go right to the next operation. It was pretty much like an assembly line.

At 11 a.m., I would leave to do ward rounds. Mike, the business manager, would stroll out of the office, refill his coffee cup and round up the kennel help. He carried a stack of records of every medical patient in the hospital. The kennel crew would bring in one patient at a time for me to check. After my exam, Mike would write up the report for the owners who would be calling this afternoon after 3 p.m. He would also write down any treatment that may be needed for each animal that day. The lucky ones that were going home often needed medication to take with them and a possible return office appointment. After ward rounds, I would return to surgery to continue to assist. Later, after lunch, I would be busy seeing office appointments from 2 to 7 p.m.

On this fine spring morning, my normal schedule was disrupted by a very *unusual* emergency. The nervous Rosalee, our receptionist, met me as I walked through the office door.

"Dr. Dionne, I'm so glad that you're here. You have an emergency coming in right away. It's a new account, Ellen Fitzpatrick's duck was bitten by her dog!"

Rosalee didn't handle emergencies that well. She would work herself up into a tizzy and become upset.

"Okay Rosalee, leave Exam Room 1 open for the duck, and put the pre-surgeries into rooms 2 and 3. I'll check them in until Fitzpatrick arrives."

"Okay Dr Dionne, will do. Oh, I hope that poor duck will be all right!"

Thinking to myself, *God, I hope this won't be like the last duck that I saw four years ago.*

* * *

July 1970

The Monteith family brought in a mallard duck that was living in their pond. This mallard, named Clarence, returned to their pond for the past three years along with one or two female ducks. They arrived in the spring and migrated south as winter approached. The Monteith children made sure that the aquatic threesome were well-fed with duck pellets and treats that they purchased at the feed and grain store.

The previous year, one of the females laid nine eggs and hatched nine fuzzy little ducklings or fledglings. The baby ducks took to the water right after hatching. They stayed with mom for quite awhile and if one started to stray, a loud quack brought the baby back to the flock. After two months, the baby duck is considered a juvenile and is now capable of flight.

But on this memorable day in 1970, Clarence was sick. He was found by the kids at the edge of the pond and unable to walk. When I walked into the exam room, Edith, the mother, was holding this beautiful mallard in a bath towel on the exam table. The duck was a male or also called a drake.

Clarence's head was a glossy green with gray wings and belly and a distinct white collar circled his neck. On the rear of each wing was a section of iridescent blue feathers.

Female mallards are brown-speckled in color with a smaller patch of blue feathers on their wings. Edith's own brood of five children all under twelve years old consisted of two *drakes* and three *hens*. The kids were gathered around Clarence giving him words of encouragement.

"Don't worry, you'll be okay. The doctor will fix you up!"

Clarence was my first duck, so my experience with treating this type of bird was very limited, or to be more exact-- nil. I checked him over and could not find any obvious problem.

"Let's see if he can walk now," I suggested.

Picking Clarence up carefully, I then knelt down putting my left knee on the floor. My right knee and shoe were directly behind the sick bird. I placed Clarence on the floor so his head faced away from me. The kids stood a few feet in front of the patient and encouraged him to walk.

"Come on, Clarence. You can do it!

As I was about to let him go, he had an explosive blast of diarrhea all over my fairly new right shoe, right sock and a good portion of my right pant leg.

The smell was sickening!

The kids all gagged and held their noses. Two Monteith drakes and one hen ran from the room and into the waiting room. I could hear them announcing to the waiting patients that their duck had pooped all over the vet. Momma and the two remaining hens were able to bravely stick it out. I wanted to run out with the kids, but felt it might be unprofessional. At least I now knew the diagnosis. Clarence had enteritis or some type of bacterial infection like food poisoning. This resulted in the diarrhea and difficulty walking. I opened the exam room windows and called the office for a *clean-up* in Exam Room 3.

"Mrs. Monteith, I'll be back in a few minutes. I need to change my clothes."

* * *

Stepping out the employee entrance, I thought about running up to the nearby car wash and walking through. Instead, I grabbed one of the kennel hoses and turned the spray on my right foot and pants.

Most of the diarrhea was washed off, but now I was soaking wet from my right knee on down to my shoe.

In 1970, our family still lived in the apartment above the hospital. Walking and squishing up the back steps to our small porch, I knew that there would be no entering Tina's clean living room in this condition. I quickly removed my right shoe and sock. Then I carefully looked around like a potential burglar might do for any witnesses. There were none, so I unbuckled my belt, looked around one more time, stepped out of my pants and ran into the apartment.

Tina had a look of shock on her face when she saw her husband standing there with a stethoscope around his neck, white top, white undies *(Fruit of the Loom)*, and only one shoe and sock. No pants.

"Ed, you didn't go to work like that did you? What happened?"

"Well, it's a long story, but the short version is a duck crapped all over my shoe and pants. I left them out on the porch."

"I hate to tell you, but you still smell quite a bit," she said and laughed.

My two-year-old son, Eddie, held his nose like the Monteith kids, and said, "Daddy, you *'tink like poopie*."

"Great!" I hurried into the bathroom and put my right foot in the tub. Turning the water on, I lathered up my foot and leg up to my knee. After drying myself, I applied a liberal spray of deodorant on my offended foot. I rushed into the bedroom to put on one sock, clean pants and a new shoe.

Hurrying to the door, my observant wife noted, "Ed, your shoes don't match and neither do your socks."

"No one will notice," I hoped and ran down the steps and into Exam Room 3.

Edith said, "Doctor, I think Clarence is feeling a little better."

All the Monteith *ducklings* had also returned to their mother and were busy petting Clarence. First, I explained the mallard's malady to Edith. Then I excused myself once again to get some liquid antibiotics for Clarence.

Ann, my assistant, got the medicine and said, "Nice footwear, Dr. Dionne."

"Thanks," I said and returned to the exam room.

I gave Clarence his first dose of the medicine to show Mrs. Monteith the best way to administer it. I also explained the importance of confining Clarence to the house or garage until he was better. An old playpen turned upside-down could be used as a cage for Clarence.

At this point, I felt repeated tugs on my right pant leg. I looked down at the six-year-old Monteith drake, who was missing his two front teeth. He spoke with a slight lisp, "Hey, Mister Doctor, your shoes look funny!"

I thought to myself, *What's wrong with one brown loafer and one black dress shoe?*

Clarence and his flock left for home, and I ran back upstairs to get a matching shoe and sock.

Four days later, a note in my mailbox read that Clarence had recovered nicely.

* * *

In late fall, while standing on my small porch, I heard a loud quacking sound. I looked up and saw several ducks flying south. I knew it had to be Clarence and his expanded family when a big duck turd landed near my new shoes. I swear that I could hear him laughing.

19

Noodles and Bingo

A righteous man cares for the needs of his animal.
Proverbs 12:10

What makes some creatures, including we humans, have a strong survival instinct and others very willing to give up? I asked myself this question while watching a National Geographic television special on African lions. The program followed a pride of lions over the course of several months as they hunted various species of animals including zebras, gazelles, gnus, antelopes and even young and old elephants.

The hunted had one thing in common. They all ran for their lives, but if pounced upon, most accepted their fate and death with grace. Occasionally, one wouldn't give in so easily and fought back with a flurry of kicks and bucks. Their attempt to ward off the lion was usually futile. The strength of the skilled feline hunter with its sharp teeth and claws soon overpowered the weaker animal. The *law of the jungle* prevailed.

But sometimes by fate, pure luck or stubbornness, the hunted managed to escape and survive even though wounded. The program ended with the narrator extolling the many virtues of this pride of lions. This was certainly true, but I couldn't help but smile and cheer for the fortunate critters that got away.

* * *

Monday, May 1974

I snapped out of my reminiscing about my first duck case back in 1970 concerning Clarence the mallard and my ruined shoe. Rosalee's shrill voice had seen to that when she loudly announced, "Dr. Dionne, the Fitzpatrick duck is going into Exam Room 1."

I hurried into the exam room and met Ellen Fitzpatrick. She was holding her black and white duck, wrapped in a blood stained towel, securely on the exam table. I glanced at the patient record that the office prepared, *Noodles-- Muscovy duck-- female-- 7 years old.*

"What happened?" I asked.

Ellen was quite composed for being in the midst of her duck emergency. I guessed that she was in her early twenties. Her hair was light blond, uncombed and pulled back in a pony tail. I suspected that she had jumped out of bed, threw on an old gray

NYU tee-shirt and a pair of black gym shorts. She was also barefoot. Emergencies produced all types of interesting attire. She had very well defined biceps and calf muscles and appeared to be very physically fit.

Ellen proceeded to answer my question and gave me a little background history. She lived at home with her parents in Middlesex. They raised and trained German wire-haired pointers for field work--primarily bird hunting. They also kept a few Muscovy ducks on the premises as pets.

"My dad bought a new puppy, Bingo, who is ten months old and untrained. Our three other pointers and the ducks all get along very well. They are used to each other."

"How long have you had Bingo?" I asked.

"We've had Bingo for about a month, and today he was able to sneak out of the house. He saw Noodles and went right for her. I was in bed, but my mother heard the ruckus and looked out the window."

"What happened then?"

"Noodles fought back by flapping her wings and even kicking. Her wings have been clipped so she wasn't able to fly away. She tried to run for the pond, but Bingo was too fast and grabbed her and bit her badly. If it wasn't for my mom, he would have killed her."

Tears started to well up in Ellen's pretty green eyes. I sensed that she was a real animal lover.

"Okay, let's see how bad the bite wound is," I said and reached for the towel. "You can keep a hand on Noodles as I unwrap her."

I was amazed at the severity of the wound. Thinking to myself, *How is this poor duck still alive!*

Starting below her left wing, a large chunk of her feathers, skin and muscle were gone-- ripped away. The bite produced a circular tear, four to five inches in diameter, and so deep that I could see her breastbone or keel. There was no way it could even be sutured. Noodles stared at me stoically and didn't move. I swallowed hard and tried to hide my sense of dread.

She looked like a Thanksgiving turkey that someone had started to carve, and all the white meat on one side of the breast was now missing right down to the bone.

I had little hope for her.

"Miss Fitzpatrick..."

"Call me Ellen, Doctor."

"Okay Ellen, we can't do surgery, there's nothing to suture. The chance of an infection is quite likely. I'm not sure if such a large wound will even heal. So your options are..."

"Don't even go there. She will not be put to sleep without our trying to save her." Ellen had a look of steely resolve to do everything possible.

Noodles had the same look and said telepathically, *Listen to the lady, Doc. I'm not ready for the big pond in the sky just yet!*

"I understand completely, but we always have to discuss the options and the cost and time involved in taking care of her."

"Money is not a problem, and I have the time," she said.

"Well then, let's get started," I said with a smile.

I opened a sterile suture pack and removed some gauze sponges to clean the wound. Hydrogen peroxide worked best for removing the dirt and debris still present on the little muscle and tissue still remaining. While cleaning, three small blood vessels started to bleed. I took a small mosquito hemostat out of the pack and clamped each one for a minute which stopped any further bleeding. Once the wound was cleaned, I knew it had to be bandaged and protected. I chose a topical antibiotic that had the consistency of butter and melted at body temperature.

My feeling was that it would be best to keep the wound moist so that it wouldn't dry out. I packed the wound, put on some sterile gauze pads to cover the opening, then wrapped Noodles with gauze and elastic tape. After I had finished, she was quite a sight-- a wounded *combat duck.*

"Let me get you some liquid amoxicillin to give her at home. Tastes like bubble gum, so she should like it. I'll need to change the dressing every-day for the next few days until it starts to heal," I said optimistically.

Ellen said, "I'll keep her in a dog cage and put her in my bedroom. And thanks for trying. Noodles is only a duck, but she means a lot to me."

* * *

Over the next few days that turned into weeks, Ellen, Noodles and I became friends. Each visit was a learning experience for me with regards to Muscovy ducks. People tend to think that they originated in Russia; instead they are native to Mexico, Central and South America.

The males are larger and weigh 7-15 lbs. The females are one-half the size and weigh 4-7 lbs. The drake may be white, black and white, or brownish with a wide variety of patterns. The hen has the same colors and patterns but not as glossy as the males.

The most distinctive markings of the Muscovy are the prominent red knobs on the head above the bill that often extend up to and around their eyes. The knobs look like bizarre tumors growing out of their face, or a severe case of acne. Pink or red wattles around the bill add to the colorful bumpy head. The feet are webbed like other ducks, but they also have three long claws extending out from each foot.

The Muscovy was once known as the Barbary duck. They can be quite aggressive and will fight over food with other Muscovy ducks. They rarely quack like other ducks unless they are put under stress like Noodles was.

* * *

Each week, the injury was slowly healing, and new tissue started to fill in the once gaping wound. Skin started to creep in from the edges working toward the middle. After six weeks the bite wound was healed except for the feathers which came in several months later.

During this time, Ellen and her father Bob, had started an intensive training program in obedience and manners for the misbehaving Bingo. They didn't want any repeat performances with any of their other pet birds.

A good hunting dog will gently carry a bird back in its mouth to the hunter. A chewed up quail or duck is not very appetizing for dinner.

At night, Bingo was confined to a cage in the

family room. As Noodles began to heal, she was moved to the family room and put in a cage next to her former attacker. At first they eyed each other warily; then a truce was made. Over the ensuing weeks, a friendship began to blossom from one cage to the other.

* * *

When Bingo was finally trained, Bob and Ellen brought in their older dog, Gretchen, and the much discussed, Bingo, for shots and checkups. They were both outstanding examples of liver and white German wire-haired pointers. Gretchen was a champion in the show ring and excelled in the field as a hunting dog. It was Gretchen's job to teach Bingo the proper hunting etiquette. The young one-year-old Bingo was full of energy and eager to learn.

Ellen introduced her handsome father to me. Bob was a retired Air Force officer who now worked for a large bank in New York City. He was well over six feet tall with green eyes like Ellen and had a well-defined cleft in his chin. Bob also kept himself in very good shape and had the demeanor that you would expect from a military officer.

Bob extended his hand and said, "Doctor Dionne, I've heard a lot about you for the last two months, and we can't thank you enough for working on our little feathered friend."

"Should I call you by your military rank or would you prefer Mister Fitzpatrick?"

"Son, you better call me Bob!"

"Aye, aye, sir," I saluted and laughed. "Well, let's start with Gretchen."

Bob lifted her up onto the exam table, and she stood obediently for the exam and booster shots.

"I wish they were all as easy as her to examine," I said when finished.

"Okay, next," I said and looked at Bingo.

Bob snapped his fingers and pointed to the table. His now-trained pointer jumped easily right up onto the table top.

"Wow, that was impressive!" I said.

"Doctor Dionne, how would you like to go pheasant hunting with me this Saturday? I want to show you how this guy is doing as a hunting dog."

"I don't really hunt, Bob."

"That's all right, I'll do the shooting and you can watch Bingo in action."

"That will be great. I'll look forward to it," I said.

* * *

Saturday was a picture-perfect day. The air was cool and crisp and the sun shone brightly in the blue sky. Bob was dressed in proper hunting attire with a red hat and water-proof boots and pants. He also wore a vest containing several pockets for his shotgun cartridges, whistle and other miscellaneous items related to hunting and training.

I, on the other hand, did not resemble a hunter at all-- more like someone going to a football game, with a Penn State sweatshirt, blue jeans and non-waterproofed sneakers.

Bob took Bingo out of the back of his truck and said, "Doc, this dog has the best nose that I have ever come across in a hunting dog. Watch this."

He walked over to the nearby stream, and bent

over and picked up one of the several small, smooth white rocks that lay in the stream bed. Bob held the small, one-inch stone tightly in his hands for a few seconds, then reached into his vest pocket and pulled out a marking pen. He placed a small dot on one side of the stone and tossed it into the stream.

Releasing Bingo from his leash, he said, "Fetch." His pointer jumped into the stream and began to sniff and hunt for the stone among the hundreds of similar stones. Fully submerging his head for several seconds at a time, Bingo finally emerged after 4-5 minutes of searching. He returned to Bob and sat down in front of his master.

Bob put out his hand and Bingo dropped a small white stone into his palm. I couldn't see the dot until the stone was turned over and there it was.

All I could say was, "I don't believe it!"

Dogs have an extremely well-developed sense of smell. Search and Rescue dogs are able to find drowning victims by standing in the prow of a boat and barking when they pick up the scent. But I had never heard of or observed anything like Bingo's demonstration.

For the next few hours, Bob hunted and I watched and stayed out of the way. Bingo worked like a seasoned veteran being able to both point and retrieve. It was beautiful to watch a working dog in action. We came home with three plump pheasants that day.

* * *

We returned to his house in Middlesex. While Bob was dressing out one pheasant for me, Ellen said, "Let's go look at Noodles."

She then snapped a leash on Bingo and handed it to me. We entered the house and went to the family room. Opening the cage, our healed Muscovy duck waddled out.

"Okay Dr. Dionne, let Bingo off the leash. This will be the first time that they have been together out of their cages."

"Ellen, are you sure about this?" I asked.

"Yes!"

Oh boy, here we go again, I thought.

Ellen nodded her head, and I unsnapped the leash.

Bingo walked over to his new friend and sniffed. Ellen then said, "Bingo, sit."

After sitting obediently in front of Noodles, Ellen commanded, "Give paw."

The right paw came up in the handshake position. We now waited for the duck's reaction. After a few tense seconds, Noodles walked over to her roommate and bit him in his extended foot. It wasn't hard or serious because ducks don't have teeth like a dog.

Bingo jumped, *Ouch, what did you do that for?*

Noodles answered, *Now we are even, and we can be friends-- no hard feelings.*

She then turned and waddled back to her cage.

Ellen and I had a good laugh. "It was sure worth the effort, partner," I said.

"Definitely," she said and gave me a warm hug.

I left soon afterwards saying good-bye to my new friends.

The next day, Tina cooked up the pheasant and we had an early Thanksgiving-like dinner. The pheasant was delicious except for the several shotgun pellets that we had to keep spitting out!

20

The Bad Luck Week

Murphy's Law: If something can go wrong, it will.
Anonymous

Monday, May 4, 1970... Elizabeth and Timothy Jackson have been married for three years. The twenty-seven-year-old Timothy is currently employed as a used car salesman for the Ford dealer in Somerville, New Jersey. Timothy is in a constant state of unhappiness which all started when he reached the age of fourteen.

This was the year that his eyesight took a turn for the worse. He needed a pair of eyeglasses with thick lenses in order to see. His classmates thought that he was a bit weird anyway, but now with the heavy-duty glasses, they teased him with name-calling.

"Hey four eyes" or "Nice *Coke* bottles you're wearing there, Timmy."

As he grew into adulthood, his disposition became surly and pessimistic.

Now, even his talkative, scatter-brained wife hasn't helped matters. She wants to have children and soon. This has led to numerous quarrels, and as Tim would say, *nagging*.

This past April was a slow month for car sales, due in part to the rainy weather. Standing in the doorway of his small office, located in the middle of the lot, he was lighting up his fourth cigarette of the morning. He had already downed two cups of coffee. He cursed silently at the rain that was expected to last all day.

"No customers will be coming out in this crappy weather," he said and walked back to his disorganized desk and uncomfortable chair. After one last drag, Tim snuffed out the remains of his cigarette into a littered ashtray of dead *Camel* butts. He flipped open this morning's newspaper to the Classified Section. He scanned the Want Ads for a job that he might like-- one that paid well with good hours, no nights or weekends, vacation time, and other benefits. Timothy looked every day, but never found anything that met his requirements. The truth was that he really wasn't qualified for the so called *good jobs*.

Today promised to be very slow. The phone hadn't rung once all morning. Tim continued to peruse the rest of the Classified Section. One ad caught his eye.

It read: *Free to a good home-- one-year-old, male squirrel monkey. Cage included.*

An idea suddenly blossomed in Tim's brain. *If Liz wants a baby so badly, and I need her to keep working at the beauty salon to supplement my lousy salary, then the monkey might be the next best thing to a real kid. At least it would stop the nagging, and what do I have to lose-- it's free!*

Tim answered the ad and spoke with Mrs. Wanda Conroy, the monkey's owner, and made arrangements to pick up Chester, the monkey, after work this evening.

* * *

The anxious Mr. Jackson drove to Plainfield and found the Conroy's home, the last one on a dead-end street. The white house was small and not well maintained. Plastic sheets were used as storm windows. Various toys and rusting bicycles lay scattered about the pot-holed driveway. The lawn hadn't been mowed for quite awhile as evidenced by a lawn mower stuck in the middle of the long grass waiting silently for gasoline.

What a dump, Tim thought as he knocked on the door.

The hefty Mrs. Conroy, dressed in her usual attire-- pink housecoat and slippers, answered the door. Her three young, sniffling children, hid behind her ample backside and pleaded for Chester not to be given away.

The house had a peculiar smell to it, like a zoo-- more precisely the monkey house.

Timothy said, "I'm here for the monkey."

On hearing this the kids cried louder.

"Would youse kids just shut up a minute!" Wanda yelled.

Then looking at Tim, she said, "I have a book on monkey care that you can have for ten bucks."

"I thought everything was free," Tim complained as he pulled out his wallet to pay the lady.

"The book is extra," as she grabbed the ten dollar bill and stuffed it down the front of her pink housecoat.

Wanda then shuffled into the living room to get Chester while Tim waited impatiently by the front door. This prompted another chorus of crying from the kids.

"Why am I so *unlucky* to have three kids that cry all the time?" Wanda asked herself.

Out of frustration, she raised her right hand and threatened to whack all of their rear ends if the racket didn't stop right now. It did.

Wanda returned to the front door with Chester who was squealing in his cage. This was the first time that Tim had ever seen a squirrel monkey.

Chester was about one foot tall and skinny--maybe two pounds or so in weight. He had very dark eyes and a black circle of fur surrounded his mouth and nose. The rest of his coat was olive in color over the shoulder area and yellow-orange on his back, arms and legs. His hair was somewhat curly especially on his head. His ears and around his eyes were devoid of hair, making these areas look a pinkish white.

Chester was wearing an old white cloth diaper held in place with two safety pins.

"Does he have to wear a diaper all the time?" the surprised Tim asked.

"No, but then he's going to do his business all over the place which is hard to clean up."

"Oh."

Timothy thought for a moment about not taking the diaper-wearing monkey, but then changed his mind. It would give Liz something to do just like with a real baby.

Wanda didn't tell Mr. Jackson that if Chester's diaper became too full, he would reach down into the diaper and throw the poop out of the cage. Sometimes those brown missiles were directed at Wanda or one of the kids.

"Is there anything else I should know?" Tim asked before leaving.

"Everything is in the book. Oh yes, he must have caught a little cold from one of the kids. His nose is running, and he's coughing a little. He'll be better in a couple of days."

Timothy carried the large cage and the excited Chester back to his pickup truck, placed him inside the cab and drove home.

* * *

Elizabeth was in a state of shock when she came home to find a monkey in her living room. Tim used his best car salesman's speech to *sell* his wife on the benefits of having a slightly *used monkey* as a pet.

"It will be good practice for when we have our own kids some day," he said.

Elizabeth was skeptical at first; then she studied Chester in his cage who reached through the wire and gently grabbed Liz's finger.

"Oh, how cute," she smiled.

The bonding began, and Elizabeth read the entire book that evening and fussed over Chester like a real baby.

Timothy's nagging problem was solved, but now he had extra expenses-- buying diapers, a leash and harness so Liz could let Chester out of the cage, a pole for him to climb and perch on, special monkey food and vitamins.

Chester's cold didn't go away, in fact it was getting a little worse each day. Liz wanted to take him to the vet.

"Let's give it another day or two," Tim said each time the subject was brought up. *This free monkey is starting to get expensive*, he thought to himself.

Chester finally stopped eating over the weekend.

On Monday, Liz said, "When I get home tonight if he's not better I'm taking him to a vet."

This was her day to work late at the salon--8 p.m.

* * *

Arriving home that evening Liz found Chester curled up in the bottom of his cage. He was not moving and unresponsive.

"Oh my God!" she cried and opened the cage.

After wrapping her *baby* up in a blanket, she marched into the living room and found her husband eating peanuts and watching a basketball game.

"Timothy, did you check Chester when you got home from work?"

Tim put down his beer and said, "Of course, he was sleeping so I didn't disturb him."

"You got home at 5 p.m., so he's been sleeping for over three hours! I'm calling a vet. You care more about basketball than baby Chester!"

* * *

After receiving the message from the answering service, I groaned, "What luck, a sick monkey."

The upset Elizabeth answered the phone on

the first ring, "Dr. Donnie, my Chester is real sick--he's barely breathing!"

"What kind of a monkey do you have?" hoping it wasn't something big like a chimp or a future King Kong.

"He's a one-year-old squirrel monkey; we got him a week ago. Chester has had a cold the entire time, but my husband wouldn't let me bring him to the vet." Then glaring at Tim, she rambled on, "He's too cheap!"

Suspecting a possible pneumonia, I said, "Mrs. Jackson, bring him in right now and I'll take a look at him for you."

Tim and Liz rushed to the car and headed for the hospital. Mike and Doris were working late in the office doing the monthly bookkeeping and receipts. They let the Jacksons in just moments before I arrived.

Elizabeth was holding Chester wrapped in the blanket. She talked softly to her baby saying, "Everything is going to be okay, Chester."

Tim paced the exam room wondering what this visit was going to cost him.

After introducing myself correctly as Dr. Dionne, not Donnie, I made out a patient record and went over the history once more.

"Let's look at Chester," I said realizing something didn't look right about our sick monkey.

Liz asked, "Can you examine him while I hold him? I don't want you to scare him!"

As she gently unfolded the blanket, I could clearly see the problem.

Chester was dead!

His pupils were dilated and glassy. Rigor

mortis was setting into his muscles. Knowing that there would be no heart beat, I still put my stethoscope into my ears to listen, more for the Jacksons' sake than the deceased.

After a minute or so of listening to various *non-functioning* parts of Chester's anatomy, I removed the stethoscope and pronounced gravely, "I'm sorry Mr. and Mrs. Jackson, but Chester has died."

I expected a bit of the usual crying and remorse on hearing these sad words. Instead Liz asked, "Doctor, isn't there anything you can do?"

This was the first time anyone asked me this question, so I was at a loss for words.

Before I could re-explain the gravity of death another way, Liz said, "Look Doctor, he just took a breath!"

I put my stethoscope back in my ears and listened.

Nope, still dead.

"How about heart massage or something?"

"Mrs. Jackson, your pet has been dead at least a few hours. See, his fingers are curled up and everything is getting stiff. This is rigor mortis."

Liz started to cry as she re-wrapped her baby. On the way out, she stopped once more and said, "You're sure he's dead because I think he just took another breath?"

"I'm sure."

The Jacksons left, and Liz started in on Tim. It was all his fault for bringing a monkey home in the first place, and for not watching him and on and on.

* * *

The next morning, Elizabeth busied herself in the house gathering up Chester's cage and supplies for the trash man. Tim had the job of burying Chester in the backyard. Unfortunately for the unlucky Tim, it was still raining during the grave digging and burial. He was now completely drenched.

He looked down at his wet clothes and thought to himself, *I'm soaking wet, my shoes and pants are muddy, and I'm burying a dead monkey during a rainstorm.*

A light went on somewhere in Tim's brain.

He started to laugh, a real hearty laugh and said, "If I didn't have such *bad* luck, I would have no luck at all."

When he finished the last shovelful, Tim marked the grave with stones, placed a small bouquet of Liz's plastic flowers in the center, and said a little prayer for Chester. Then the sun peeked through the clouds for the first time in days.

Putting back his shovel, the suddenly happier Tim walked into the house with a smile. After giving Liz a big hug, Tim invited her to sit down at the kitchen table.

"Okay honey, let's talk about starting a family."

THE NEWS
FREE TO A GOOD HOME:
SQUIRREL MONKEY
• Male
• 1 Year Old
• Cage Included

21

Bad Luck Week...
Tuesday and Wednesday

The greatness of a nation and its moral progress can be judged by the way its animals are treated.

Mahatma Gandhi

Tuesday, May 5, 1970... My wife and I each had trouble sleeping last night. Our ten-month-old Terri was cutting two teeth which made her wake up every two hours and cry. Tina and I took turns trying to soothe her until I gave up. Baby Terri just wanted mommy.

Relieved of duty, my mind still wouldn't allow sleep to settle in. It felt a need to replay the bizarre emergency call of last evening-- *The exam of the dead monkey*. I half-expected another call saying Chester took another breath, or worse yet that he was awake and doing fine this morning.

Last evening, Mike and Doris were still working in the office after finishing with the monkey, and

I knew they would be interested in knowing what was wrong with the monkey. They were both surprised to find out that he was actually dead, but the fact that I didn't charge the *unlucky* Jacksons for the emergency call resulted in me being chewed out once again by Mike.

"Doc, you're too softhearted. You need to stop giving away free services!"

The words stung and echoed repeatedly in my restless mind. Some time after 5 a.m., I drifted off into a deep dreamless sleep. The kind of sleep where drool dribbles out of your mouth and onto the pillow-case. Tuesday was my day off so my plan was to stay in bed as long as possible.

My almost two-year-old son, Eddie, had his own ideas about how long his father should sleep. He woke up every morning at 7 a.m. when the dogs were put out into the kennel runs. Their barking bothered his sensitive ears.

Eddie managed to climb out of his crib this morning and proudly walked into our bedroom. Standing alongside our bed, he wondered why mom-my and daddy were still sleeping. After waiting patiently by my side of the bed for a lengthy minute or so, he extended his tiny index finger and touched his dad's closed left eyelid. Maybe poked would be a better word. This was not my preferred method of waking up, but I must admit it was very effective.

"Ouch!" I yelled and catapulted to an upright position.

This started a chain of events on this *Bad Luck Tuesday*. My loud screech of pain made Eddie cry which woke his baby sister, who then joined in the wailing, which woke my tired wife who scolded me.

"Ed, what did you do to Eddie?"

Holding my hand over my rapidly swelling left eye, I tried to explain to my upset wife.

"Tina, I didn't do anything; Eddie poked me in the eye while I was sleeping!"

"Uh, huh," she mumbled while trying to console our two children.

The children recovered quickly and stopped crying when Tina asked, "Who wants some pancakes?"

* * *

It had now stopped raining and the sun was finally peeking out while we were having our pancake breakfast. The now happy Eddie was sitting in a chair, face covered in maple syrup, feeding himself and making a mess. I was feeding our daughter who competed with her brother in the *mess-making contest*.

I carefully cut up small pieces of pancake for Terri and placed them neatly on top of her highchair's white tray. Using both hands, she eagerly stuffed them into her mouth. For every piece eaten, two were squeezed to death in her hands by chubby little fingers. Once properly squashed, she tossed the pancake balls overboard in various random directions.

Miss sticky-fingers was declared the winner of the mess-making by grabbing hairs on her head causing them to be instantly glued together and point out in odd spikes.

Our daughter began to resemble a baby porcupine having a *bad-hair day*. At this point, Tina the chef had enough and relieved her beleaguered husband. I was free to enjoy my cold pancakes covered with non-melting butter and drizzled with the few remaining drops of maple syrup.

After breakfast, Tina gave the kids a non-planned bath. I busied about sweeping, scraping and washing the sticky kitchen floor. The blue highchair and white tray were untouchable. I carefully carried both outside and washed them down with the kennel hose. The clean highchair and tray were left to dry in the sun on our small deck. Our maple syrup induced *sugar-high* kids were then dressed and packed into our green station wagon.

* * *

Today was going to be our initial *shopping adventure as potential first home buyers*. We scoured the Somerville and Bridgewater areas without any luck. The few *For Sale by Owner* properties that we did see were either too big, too small, and mostly too expensive for our meager savings.

"No luck today," I said.

"How about we eat out for lunch and treat ourselves?" Tina suggested.

I was about to say sure when a squirrel ran out in front of the car. The gray squirrel would have made it easily to the other side of the road, if she hadn't stopped for no apparent reason as only a squirrel would do.

She then turned and tried to run back across the road. The sickening thump under my right front tire took away our appetite for lunch. The streets of Somerville held the remains of many deceased squirrels.

The kids had also run out of patience and crackers. We drove silently back to the hospital and our apartment. As a vet I was supposed to save lives not take them. We each had a peanut butter and jelly sandwich, and settled for a one hour nap.

* * *

About three miles away, Mrs. Alice Heffelfinger was waiting for the yellow school bus to drop off her two children at their designated spot. Her children, Tommy and Lydia, were fraternal twins and ten years old. Alice walked them home and listened to the school news each day.

The talkative, blond-haired, blue-eyed Lydia played with one of her pigtails as she rattled off the latest school gossip and romances.

Whereas, her one-hour-younger brother was more introspective and preferred to let his older sister do the talking.

Once home while munching on their after-school snacks, Mom suggested, “Since the rain has stopped, why don’t we change our clothes and go for a bike ride.”

This woke Tommy out of his deep thoughts, “Good idea, mom. Let’s go.”

Lydia changed quickly; Tommy took his time. He had to comb his hair, pick out just the right biking outfit and matching sneakers.

The *girls* waited and Lydia tapped her foot and said, “Mom, why is Tommy so fussy about his clothes? He’s worse than a girl!”

“Who knows,” Alice said.

Finally Tommy appeared, ready to ride. He wore a new pair of white sneakers, white athletic socks with red and blue trim at the top, white shorts with gold trim, a blue and white New York Yankees tee-shirt, a pair of cool shades and a blue New York Giants ball cap over perfectly combed blond hair.

* * *

Meanwhile, three blocks away, a tiny six-week-old gray squirrel crawled out of his nest in a towering old oak tree that provided ample shade for the adjacent sidewalk and a portion of West Cliff St. His mother left early that morning in search of breakfast which usually consisted of seeds, nuts, certain edible leaves, caterpillars, fruit if possible, and even roots. His mother was weaning him slowly onto solid food.

But she had not returned which was highly unusual.

As luck would have it, the Heffelfinger bike caravan was rapidly approaching this magnificent oak tree. At the same time, our little squirrel spotted an unrecognizable gray lump in the middle of West Cliff St.

Mom! Is that my mom? he wondered and proceeded to climb farther out on a large branch to get a better look.

Being young and not sure-footed as yet, he unwisely leaned too far off the branch and lost his grip. His fifteen-foot fall was broken by the front wheel of Tommy's bike.

The shock of a squirrel landing on his bike caused Tommy to lose control, hit the curb and do a head-over-heels tumble into a handy low-lying bush.

Alice and Lydia arrived at the scene a few seconds later and simultaneously screamed, "Tommy!"

Throwing down their bikes, they rushed to the bush, "Are you all right?" his worried mother asked.

Tommy had a few scratches but no significant injuries. He was mainly crying because of the tear in his New York Yankees tee-shirt.

Once mom and Lydia determined that everything was indeed okay, they turned their attention to the roadway. The small squirrel was dragging himself toward the gray lump in the middle of the road.

"Look mom, it's a baby squirrel!" Lydia pointed.

"I see that. I wonder if that was what we saw fall out of the tree and cause the bike accident," said Alice.

"It is mom, the squirrel hit my tire, and now he's hurt," Tommy informed his family.

Now it was Lydia's turn to cry. She had a warm heart for a cold nose. The three Heffelfingers carefully surrounded the baby squirrel and peered down.

"His legs must be hurt or broken," mom diagnosed.

"Do you think that run-over squirrel was his mother?" Tommy asked.

"Oh my, how unlucky if it is-- no mom and injured legs."

"What will happen to him ?" Lydia asked as tears began to flow again and trickle down her cheek.

"Let's take him home and take care of him," Tommy pleaded.

"Okay, but I don't know if he's a he or she's a she. I hope he doesn't bite so let me pick him up," mom ordered.

The fashionable Tommy took off his favorite baseball cap and handed it to his mother. Alice picked up the squirrel's tail and gently scooped the injured squirrel into Tommy's cap. She then quickly lifted the cap with squirrel into the basket on the front of her bicycle for the short ride home.

The trio rode slowly and made it safely home without any further animal encounters. Lydia found a cardboard box in the garage and lined it with towels. Wearing a pair of work gloves, Alice picked up the no-name baby squirrel and transferred him from the cap to his new nest.

"We should give the squirrel a name," Alice said.

"I hope it's a girl. We can call her Princess," Lydia said hopefully.

"No, I know he's a boy and his name is Elvis," Tommy said with confidence.

They carried the box into the kitchen to keep an eye on Princess/Elvis. Sunshine, their nine- month-old calico cat came running in to check the contents of the box. She looked in and meowed softly, but didn't hiss. A good sign.

"Well, I was worried about how Sunshine was going to accept her," Alice sighed with relief.

* * *

Sunshine hadn't been a member of the Heffelfinger family for very long. She was adopted five weeks ago from the Somerset County Humane Society. Lydia wanted, actually needed, a pet and convinced her parents that adoption would be a good thing. George, her dad, finally agreed after some persuasion by the rest of the family. He knew that if it came to a family vote, there would be no chance of his winning anyway.

The agreement with the Humane Society stated that their adopted pet would have to be spayed. Alice made the arrangements with our veterinary hospital, but on the pre-surgery check, Dr. Coburn found that Sunshine was pregnant. Alice and Richard Coburn were friends-- they sang in the church choir together.

The tall, slender red-haired Dr. Coburn was number two man in seniority on Somerset Veterinary Group's staff. He was a very influential mentor for me especially in surgery. He was my assistant and patiently guided and *taught* the novice the best way to do various surgical operations.

Alice and the kids did not want to spay Sunshine when she was pregnant. Dr. Coburn said it could wait until after the kittens were born. But unfortunately, just last week Sunshine delivered three stillborn, premature kittens. She was too young, and not fed properly before the Humane Society had picked her up. Poor Sunshine didn't quite understand the loss of her kittens, and she had spent the past few days meowing and looking for them.

* * *

Dad, a.k.a. George, came home this evening and saw the little squirrel in his cardboard box.

"What the heck is this? A squirrel!" he said.

Alice explained what had happened and told her alarmed husband, "I've made an appointment with the vet first thing tomorrow morning to see what's wrong. So don't worry."

That evening the scared, hungry baby squirrel huddled in his cardboard nest and chattered softly. Hearing this, Sunshine came running and hopped up onto a kitchen table chair then jumped down into the box. At first the squirrel and the kitten-less cat sniffed each other carefully. Sunshine then licked the baby's head and laid down; she still had some unused milk left in some of her mammary glands. Slowly, the injured, hungry orphan pulled itself over and started to nurse.

Something very special happened that evening.

In the morning, Alice and kids found Sunshine and Princess/Elvis curled up together in the box.

"Wow!" was the general family consensus.

"Mom, we have to keep her," Lydia pleaded.

"He's a boy!" Tommy corrected his sister.

"Don't get your hopes up, we'll see what the vet says this morning," said Alice.

* * *

Checking my morning appointment list, I couldn't help but notice the injured squirrel at 9:15 a.m. *Here we go again*, I thought, but didn't complain to the office any longer-- it never did any good anyway.

I walked into Exam Room 3 and introduced myself to the Heffelfingers. I then slipped on a single leather glove to protect my left hand. Squirrels have two upper and two lower central incisors that are quite sharp. The constant gnawing by this member of the rodent family wears the incisors down, but it's not a problem because these teeth continue to grow throughout their life.

Squirrels can live up to six years in the woods, but in a city setting most don't live more than a year-- victims of the automobile.

The first question to be answered was the sex.

"Male," I announced.

"Hurray," the neatly dressed, school-skipping Tommy shouted.

I held the now officially named Elvis in my hand and checked his injuries. There were no fractures in either leg, but the bad news was the lack of sensation and paralysis of both legs. Somewhere in his lower back was a possible fracture or dislocation with injury to the spinal cord.

What bad luck, I thought.

The good news was Elvis could urinate and defecate, but the little guy was not going to walk again let alone climb a tree.

The Heffelfingers took the news bravely-- no tears.

To the surprise of her children, Alice said, "Well then, I think we'll try and keep Elvis as a pet. Dr. Dionne, do you know anyone else that has a pet squirrel?"

"No I don't. But since he's so young, Elvis will probably imprint on you as his extended family," I said.

"Elvis and our cat, Sunshine, slept together last night, and she allowed him to nurse a little. She's the cat that miscarried last week and Sunshine still has some milk to give."

"That's wonderful because he still needs two to three more weeks of nursing before being completely weaned."

I recommended that they go to the library and read up on gray squirrels to learn as much about them as possible. Which they did.

* * *

In the next few months I saw Elvis twice more for minor problems. The Heffelfingers were excellent pet owners.

Lydia informed me, "I want to be a veterinarian when I grow up."

Her brother said, "I want to be a famous fashion designer."

"Well, I wish you both luck in your future careers," I said with a smile.

Sunshine, the calico cat was spayed a few weeks later. She and her new best friend, Elvis, continued to sleep together. They both shared the dry cat food. Elvis liked his nuts, Sunshine did not.

The cat meowed and Elvis chattered in a language that only they could understand. Each night they curled up together in their cushioned dog bed.

Sunshine meowed, *Love you, Elvis*, and he chattered in response, *Love you too, mom*.

And so bad luck did not last very long in the Heffelfinger household.

22

The Orphans

I am in favor of animal rights as well as human rights. That is the way of a whole human being.
Abraham Lincoln

The white-tailed deer is native to North America originally, but is now found on all continents with the lone exception being Australia. The deer historically has been a very important animal for indigenous people and provides a valuable food source. The skin or hide, skeletal bones, ligaments, antlers and even hoofs are utilized in some manner as well.

The deer is also a central figure in Buddhism. The Buddha was thought to be able to turn himself into a deer and is often depicted in such a manner. Wisdom, gentleness and insight are traits of this beautiful animal.

* * *

July 17, 1970

Candace *Candy* Wells woke at 6 a.m. this Thursday as was her usual custom. She meditated for fifteen minutes then proceeded to stretch and awaken her sleepy muscles with a half-hour of yoga, ending with the invigorating *Sun Salutation.*

She then had a light breakfast of juice, fruit, a small bowl of raspberry low-fat yogurt, one slice of wheat toast and a cup of green tea. The slender, twenty-eight year old quickly dressed for work-- khaki pants neatly pressed, black belt, short-sleeved khaki blouse embroidered with New Jersey Division of Fish and Wildlife, gold badge and a name tag-- Candy Wells, Park Ranger.

A quick brush of her short black hair, no make up, no perfume and no jewelry was needed. In fact, with her job they were all frowned upon. The dark-eyed, olive-skinned ranger was quite beautiful without all the feminine accessories. After lacing up her sturdy work boots, Candy ran out the door to her white Dodge Dart and headed to work.

Sitting at her government issued metal desk, she first checked her phone messages. "Nothing urgent," she whispered.

She then reviewed the current list of animals at the center. Some wildlife were being rehabilitated to be eventually returned to their natural surroundings. Others might not be so lucky-- too sick or injuries too severe. Candy's main interest was the deer pen. Her master's thesis at Rutgers University was *The Biology and Habitat of the White-Tailed Deer in New Jersey.*

It was a beautiful day, and Candy felt the need to be outside in the sunshine. Leaving the small ranger station, she strolled down to the deer pen. This enclosure was a three acre, mostly wooded area. It was surrounded by an extra high chain-linked fence to keep the deer in and predators out.

Feeding stations were set up just inside the fence near the ranger station and also in the middle of the wooded area for the people-shy new animals. Today, the residents included seven doe and one fawn-- no bucks.

The oldest resident was Desiree or *Desi* as Candy called her. She was four years old with a beautiful, reddish-brown coat and large soft brown eyes.

* * *

June 6, 1966-- Four years earlier

Desiree had a sad story. Her mother had been shot out of season by Butch Chambers. Butch had a small five acre farm in rural Clinton, New Jersey. Not that he grew any crops or raised any livestock-- too much work.

One thing that Butch did do was to fish and hunt without a license. In season or out of season, any animal that ventured onto his property was fair game.

Deer usually give birth to one to three fawn in May or June each year. Desi was orphaned in early June. Her mother was a victim of a well-aimed bullet from the rifle of Mr. Chambers.

Desiree was hidden in the tall grass earlier by her now deceased mother. When she didn't return, she began to bleat softly. Butch stumbled upon Desiree as he walked back to his farmhouse to get help carrying his trophy (Desi's mom) back home.

"Well, what do we have here," he laughed without an ounce of sympathy.

Before the tiny fawn could stand and attempt to run, Butch grabbed her. He carried her back to his small rundown barn and placed her in an old horse stall. His fifteen-year-old son, Junior, went back with his father to help drag the doe back to the farm.

After the non-professional butchering task was completed, Butch cracked opened a beer and lit up a cigarette. He offered a cigarette to his son who readily accepted.

"Hey pop, how about a beer for me?" the hopeful teenager asked.

"Junior, you know the rules. How many times do I have to tell you? No drinking until you're sixteen!"

"How about a sip of yours?"

"No! And don't ask anymore or I'll cuff ya one," Butch said as he raised his right hand and threatened to make good on his vow.

"Ain't you goin' to school today?" Butch then asked.

"Takin' a sick day."

"Okay, but you're not goin' to lay about the house. Get the wheelbarrow and take the remains of that doe into the woods and bury them deep. Don't want no one snoopin' around and finding them."

"But dad, I really ain't feelin' that good."

"Don't sass me boy, and do as I say. I'll fix some bacon and eggs for breakfast."

On hearing the word breakfast, Junior started to feel much better, and proceeded to fetch the wheelbarrow from the barn. Butch watched his gawky son walk off and thought to himself, *That no good wife of mine left me a lot of work raisin' that kid.*

Butch's wife, Brenda, left five years ago for better pastures and hasn't been heard from since--not even a Christmas card.

* * *

Junior reached the edge of the woods with the doe's remains in the middle of the wheelbarrow. He was tired of pushing it so far through the bumpy field. And now it would be worse, trying to maneuver in the woods over rocks, tall grass and fallen branches. Then there was the digging. He looked back at their farm house some 200 yards away. *No dad in sight.*

Must be in the kitchen, he thought.

Junior pushed his load just inside the woods, dumped it and shoveled leaves and branches over the remains.

No grave digging.

He sat down on the grass and leaned his back against an oak tree. Junior lit up another cigarette that he had snitched from his father's pack. He relaxed and blew out several smoke rings.

Junior had to kill some time because if he returned home too soon his father would become suspicious about the burial.

Butch was deep in thought as he scrambled the eggs. He wondered what to do about the captured fawn. *She's gotta be worth some money to someone, but who? I bet the hide would make some real soft deerskin gloves.*

After breakfast, he made the *sick* Junior get some grass, hay and leaves for the herbivorous prisoner. But, what the fawn really needed was her mother's milk. She hadn't been weaned as yet. The speckled fawn laid curled up and partially hidden under some straw in the far corner of the stall. She bleated softly to no avail.

* * *

The next day, the now healthy Junior was back in school. In homeroom this morning, he bragged to his friend, John, about the doe his dad *bagged* yesterday, and there was a baby fawn locked up in the barn.

As usual, Junior was a little too loud. Two seats over, Margaret Dinsmore was listening intently while pretending to read her history book.

That evening she told her father, Jack the state trooper, what she had overheard in homeroom. He in turn notified the local authorities and the Fish and Wildlife Department. Candy Wells was eventually contacted by her superiors to assist with rescuing the fawn.

A search warrant was easily obtained thanks to the animal-loving Judge Prescott. The Clinton Police Department had been waiting a long time to finally catch the slippery Butch Chambers in something illegal. Sheriff Mack Powers led the team of two squad cars-- three officers and one K-9 officer, a German shepherd named Duke.

Candy drove the fish and wildlife pickup truck with a padded cage anchored securely in the bed of the truck. She brought along her medical supply kit which included a sedative for the fawn if it was needed. Nina Suslyk was another park ranger and Candy's friend, who came along to assist with the deer.

* * *

The blond, blue-eyed Nina was a big woman. She stood some six feet tall and was slightly heavy with very large shoulders, muscular arms and *tree trunks* for legs. Nina's family was of Russian heritage with strong ties to the former homeland.

Her younger brother, Bogdan, was an outstanding wrestler in high school and earned a wrestling scholarship to Lehigh University. This year he is a co-captain of the team.

Nina's older brother, Sergei, is a weight lifter and a construction worker for the state of New York. Nina learned the art of wrestling and weight lifting from each brother. *No one messes with Nina Suslyk.*

If the police had any trouble with Butch Chambers, Candy knew that Nina would step in and take him down with a *half-nelson* and wrap those tree trunks around him in a *cradle*-- her favorite wrestling move. She would then squeeze slowly until Butch gave up or passed out. Fortunately for Butch, Nina's services were not needed.

* * *

At 8 a.m., the convoy of law enforcement vehicles roared down the half-mile dirt drive to the Chambers's farm and caught Butch with his pants down-- literally, he was sitting on the toilet.

The raid was all over in less than one hour. The search warrant was presented to the outraged Butch, the house and premises searched by the officers. Candy and Nina went straight to the barn for the fawn. And Duke, the police dog, found the deer remains after twenty minutes of sniffing.

Park rangers, Suslyk and Wells, carried the

frightened fawn back to their truck, and Butch was handcuffed and placed in the rear seat of Officer Powers's squad car. Nina walked over to the squad car, glared at Butch and said, "So long, sucker!"

Once back at the center, Candy worked day and night to nourish and calm her new arrival. She named the fawn, Desiree. A rather unusual name for a deer, but this was an unusual circumstance.

Desi the deer grew, but she could never be placed back into the woods. She didn't have the instincts or survival training from her mother.

Desi became a people person. Children and adults could feed her, and she allowed the gentle, quiet ones to pet her for a few seconds before gracefully bounding back to the wooded area of the pen.

* * *

My association with Candy Wells started four years later in 1970. Her black cat, Licorice, was having problems urinating. Licorice was a spayed, two-year-old Persian cat. She wasn't feeling sick, but she wouldn't use her litter box and frequently *peed* small amounts on the carpet.

Candy finished work early in order to make her 4:30 p.m. vet appointment. She was dressed in her park ranger uniform and standing in Exam Room 3. She was holding her *leaky* cat waiting patiently for me.

I said, "Hello," then took the kitty's history and started the examination. Licorice appeared to be quite healthy, and I felt quite confident that all she had was a simple cystitis or bladder infection.

Speaking to Candy, I said, "I have some antibiotics for Licorice to take. She may be better in forty-eight hours, but don't stop the medication until it's finished or the infection may flare up again. If she isn't better by then let me know, and I'll take an x-ray to check for possible bladder stones and probably do a culture on her urine."

"Don't worry about me not calling, Dr. Dionne. Licorice is my baby." Candy followed up the promise with a kiss and hug for her ebony cat with the yellow eyes.

Sensing that there would be no hugs for the vet, I asked, "I see that you're a park ranger by your uniform. What do you do?"

"Well, do you make house calls?" she asked with a smile.

"It could be arranged, I'm sure. Are you having a problem?"

"We have a new deer, Abby, and something is wrong with her skin. And I don't want it spreading to the others if it's contagious."

"How do you plan on catching her?"

"I'm going to *dart* her with my rifle to knock her down and sedate her for a few minutes. That's where you come in and do your thing. Maybe you can tell what's wrong with her skin."

"Yes, maybe," I said hopefully. *Then maybe not*, I thought to myself. *I didn't exactly specialize in skin diseases of the white-tailed deer.*

* * *

The next afternoon before leaving, Mike gave his blessing and warning, "Doc, try and stay out of trouble and keep track of your time so we can bill the State."

Arriving at the park ranger station, I met Candy who was standing outside the deer pen with a serious looking rifle in hand.

"Hi Dr. Dionne, Licorice is not *peeing* on the carpet any more," she said happily.

"That's good. I'm glad she's better since you're carrying the rifle. I wouldn't want to be darted if she wasn't."

Candy laughed and promised that I would be safe-- no darts.

We walked to a spot near the feeding station and waited patiently for the new deer with the skin problem to appear. When she finally did, Candy took out a dart that contained the sedative that would cause a temporary muscle paralysis.

Candy took a careful aim and fired. The dart found the target and stuck in the doe's rump. One or two minutes later, the deer became unsteady and wobbly, followed by her hind legs buckling under her. She then completely collapsed onto her right side.

It was now my turn. We walked into the pen and knelt down beside the immobile doe for a better look. Her coat looked moth-eaten. There were irregular patches about the size of a quarter and larger scattered about the trunk of her body.

I opened my black doctor's bag and pulled out a scalpel blade and four glass slides. Using the blade, I gently scraped the surface of the skin and transferred the skin layers to the glass slides. I covered each of the four scrapings with a cover slip. The rest of the deer looked fine.

Upon completion we hurried back to the office where my microscope was waiting. After putting a drop of immersion oil on the cover slips, I placed a slide under the microscope. The diagnosis was easy. The deer was infested with a mange mite, *Psoroptes Cuniculi*.

Planning ahead, I had brought along an insecticidal dip. We mixed the concentrated solution up in a plastic bucket and hurried back to the deer pen. The doe was in the process of waking up but still unable to stand. Wearing gloves and using sponges, we sloshed the dip over every available part of her body.

When she finally stood, Candy and I did her abdomen and other side. Abby was going to be fine and not spread the mite to her pen-mates. This doe and most of the others would be returned to the forest except for Desiree.

She was not going anywhere.

* * *

June 2, 1971

Almost a year later, I received an urgent call from Candy.

"Dr. Dionne, I need help with a fawn that probably has a broken leg. It was hit by a car in Middlesex and is now lying just off the side of the road. I can get Nina, another ranger, to come and help me get her. We can bring her to the ranger station or the hospital if you can take a look at her."

"Candy, I have office appointments for another hour. Take her to your office, and I'll come as soon as I finish here."

Before leaving the hospital, I gathered a few supplies and drove to the ranger station. Candy introduced the scrawny vet to the *Herculean* Nina. I was very impressed with her biceps muscles that were about the same as mine. Not my biceps, mind you, more like my calf muscles or maybe thighs. Candy had the rescued fawn in a small pen in the corner of the office. She needed to be close by in order to feed her.

She made a special formula for orphaned deer. A mixture of goat's milk, one egg yolk, honey and two tablespoons of unpasteurized yogurt were all mixed together in a blender.

She then warmed the formula to body temperature and put it in an infant nursing bottle. She planned to feed the fawn every four to six hours for two days and then decrease the feeding gradually as she began the weaning process. A baby cereal mixture and a banana also mixed in a blender worked quite well to start the transition to solid food. Next, finely chopped carrots and apples were usually given and readily accepted. Deer like the sweet taste.

I looked at the small fawn and admired her beauty.

"Look at all those white spots on her sides. They're like large freckles!" I said.

"That's it!" Candy said excitedly. "I've been trying to find a name for her. We'll call her Freckles."

Of course, we knew that these white spots would slowly disappear as she grew into a doe. But somehow Freckles seemed an appropriate name.

It was now time to get down to business and check her leg. Her left front leg was obviously fractured. Freckles's cloven or split hoof was facing out 90 degrees to the rest of her leg.

"Candy, I think we should sedate her slightly so I can check Freckles over without scaring her. If she panics and thrashes about, she may cause more injury to the leg."

"Yes, whatever you think is best," Candy replied.

It took about ten minutes for my injection to work. First, I checked the rest of her body. Sometimes if you concentrate on the obvious problem, you may miss a broken rib, hernia, mouth laceration or some other important injury. In this instance, Freckles had no other injuries that I could find.

Now, I concentrated on the leg. She had a mid-shaft radius and ulna fracture. The overlying skin was not broken which was very fortunate. Compound fractures, where the skin is broken and one of the bone fragments may be sticking through the skin present the real possibility of a complicating and potentially serious bone infection-- osteomyelitis.

Freckles's fractures appeared to be at an oblique angle which was also good-- providing a greater surface area for a callus to form. I then set the leg into its proper alignment.

So far so good, I thought. *Okay, how are we going to keep it in position?* I asked myself.

Speaking to Candy and Nina, "If I make a plaster of Paris cast, it would be sturdy, but too heavy, and she might try to chew it off."

"Well, we are on a limited budget, so anything fancy like surgery with a pinning is not possible," Candy offered.

"I could fashion a splint out of a piece of 3/8 inch plywood. I brought what I needed with me and a jigsaw to cut the plywood. It might work."

"Let's try it," Candy smiled. Nina didn't smile but nodded her head in agreement.

Using a pencil, I sketched the outline of Freckles's leg onto the plywood. It included the bend at the shoulder joint and the elbow in a slightly flexed position. First, I cut out the splint for Freckles with the jigsaw. Next, I wrapped cotton padding and gauze around her leg, then laid the cut plywood splint over this followed by more gauze and finally adhesive tape.

I left Candy a large plastic Elizabethan collar to be put on Freckles's neck if she tried to gnaw at her splint. The collar would be cumbersome, but it would prevent Freckles from reaching the splint.

"You'll need to lift her to a standing position, but once up she can be walked on a leash and nurse from her bottle."

Candy and Nina seemed happy. I was hoping that Nina Suslyk would be. I feared her wrestling moves that Candy had told me about-- especially the cradle. Being squeezed to death by a Russian park ranger would not be pleasant.

Freckles adjusted to the splint and did not need the Elizabethan collar. She walked with a clunk each time the splint landed on the wooden floor. After a week, Candy decided to put her in the deer pen for short periods of walking as she held the leash.

Desi was the welcoming committee. After residing in the deer enclosure for the past four years, she considered the pen to be her home. It was the only place she could remember.

Freckles was momentarily frightened by the large, fully matured doe and hid behind Candy. Desiree's gentle manner and kind deer thoughts soon won the fawn over. Both orphans looked forward to their daily walks together with Candy.

Freckles was growing fast, but the splint was not. I knew she would need to have the splint removed. Three weeks of splinting might be enough, I hoped.

* * *

Nina, Candy, Desiree and I met in the deer enclosure to take a look. Using bandage scissors, I snipped here and there and removed her bandage and splint. Holding my breath, I ran my hands down her leg and felt the fracture site. There was a firm callus and no pain or movement. We all smiled at the good news. Desi gave a snort followed by a grunt.

"Most people think that deer are silent and can't make any noise, but as you just heard they do make sounds. Deer have acute hearing and eyesight. They lift and flick their white tail when danger is present," Candy commented.

"They also stomp their feet and communicate that way," Nina added.

"Keep walking her on a leash for another week until the muscles in her broken leg get stronger. Then you will be able to set her free in the pen with her new friend. Desi will look after her."

We walked back to the office, and since it was after hours and the three of us were now *off duty*, Nina said, "Let's celebrate!"

Opening her purse, she pulled out a small but potent bottle of vodka and three small glasses. She poured Candy, the non-drinking vet and herself a half of a glass of the clear spirits.

We toasted each other, then Desi and Freckles with a *na zdorovja*.

Nina was ready for a second glass, but Candy and I raised our hands in surrender and shook our heads no. Candy was still coughing from the first glass, and my lips, throat and stomach were still on fire.

A few minutes later, I recovered from the vodka and said good-bye.

Candy gave me a warm hug and said, "Thanks."

Nina gave me what I would call a Russian bear hug which opened up my blocked nasal sinuses. A week later, Desiree gave Freckles a tour of her new home. The once-lonely orphans became inseparable and very happy.

23

Truffles

When you love your pet,
it's like sharing both your hearts.
Author

The word *miracle* is often used rather loosely in our every day speech. We tend to exaggerate the significance of simple events in our life as miracles. According to *Mirriam-Webster's Intermediate Dictionary*, a miracle can mean:

1. an extraordinary event taken as a sign of the supernatural power of God.

2. an extremely outstanding or unusual event, thing, or accomplishment.

In sports, the success of the United States Hockey Team at the 1980 Olympics at Lake Placid, New York, is often mentioned as an example of a miracle. The United States team was made up of amateur and collegiate players and led by coach, Herb Brooks.

They defeated the mighty Soviet team, who had won nearly every World Championship and Olympic tournament since 1954. The U.S. Team then continued on to win the Olympic gold medal by defeating a powerful team from Finland. But, was it a *miracle?*

* * *

December 1974

Nigel Sutton had three dogs-- all poodles. He was bringing all of them into our Pluckemin outpatient clinic on a dreary day in early December. Nigel was a fifty-five-year-old stonemason of Scottish and English descent. He lived close by in Bedminister, New Jersey.

Prior to this, he was born and lived his entire life in the Yorkshire Dales area of England. Nigel's father and uncle were also stonemasons, and he became their apprentice at the early age of fourteen.

Upon graduation from the English equivalent of high school, Nigel married his sweetheart Margaret and settled in Hawes to be close to both their families.

The Sutton men were kept busy stone-framing the outside of homes and repairing the numerous stone walls that crisscrossed the entire area. For hundreds of years, farmers cleared their fields of rocks and painstakingly constructed stone walls to serve as both fence and property lines.

Nigel also loved to hunt with his brother Hugh and trek the surrounding hills with Margaret and their dogs. Four years ago, tragedy struck; Margaret died in an automobile accident on her way to work- victim of a careless driver. Life was not the same for Nigel, alone after thirty-two years of marriage. He endured several months of depression, then decided that a change of scenery was needed. He immigrated to the United States with his two-year-old black standard poodle Henry, and his one-year-old female miniature poodle named Twinkle. She was parti-colored-- all white with a solid brown patch on each side of her chest extending back to include her flanks.

* * *

There was plenty of work for a skilled stone-mason in Bedminister and the many estates in this area of New Jersey. These large estates had familiar stone walls. The United States Equestrian Center was nearby, and fox hunting was a popular sport, except for the fox, of the privileged residents. In many respects, this area seemed like merry old England.

Two years ago, his small family of poodles expanded to three, when he purchased an apricot-colored toy poodle puppy, whom he named Truffles. Nigel's three dogs all needed rabies vaccinations. In England, rabies vaccination is not necessary for dogs because there is no rabies in their wildlife. Anyone moving to England with a dog is required to put their pet into quarantine for six months to be sure he or she is not incubating the deadly virus.

* * *

This happened to be my day to work in our Pluckemin office which thankfully was only one mile from our home. I could sleep twenty minutes longer on Thursdays. This branch office had two exam rooms and a small waiting area-- no surgery or kennels. Mr. Sutton was my last appointment of the morning. I could take my time; there was less stress and emergencies at this location.

Walking into the exam room, I had to look twice at the sight before me. Nigel sat on one of the office chairs wearing typical English attire including tweed pants, waist coat, white shirt, bow tie, cap, and walking boots. An unlit pipe nestled in his right hand. Nigel was fairly small in stature, five feet seven inches or so, medium build with strong-looking calloused hands. I suspected that he had male-patterned baldness which was hidden by his cap. His side hairs were a salt and pepper gray. A thin pair of wire-rimmed glasses was perched on the bridge of his pointed nose. On the second chair to his left sat Truffles and Twinkle. Henry, the large black standard poodle sat obediently on the floor to Nigel's right.

All eyes were on me as I introduced myself. Wishing that I had a camera, this was a photographic opportunity worth mounting on my family room wall. Besides the obvious size and color variations, each dog was also groomed differently.

Truffles was trimmed in a typical poodle clip with a pom-pom on the top of her head and on her tail. The tail-wagging Twinkle was neither clipped nor shaved. Her white and brown coat was much longer and evenly trimmed. No pom-poms.

Henry was not trimmed at all; his coat was allowed to grow long to the point where most people would not know that he was even a poodle. His black fur was twined together in cords or braids that appeared to be in early stages of dreadlocks. Henry looked more like a Hungarian puli than a poodle.

"This is a fine looking family you have here Mr. Sutton," I said.

"Aye, indeed they are very good mates," Nigel replied while patting Twinkle on her head.

"Whom shall we do first?" I asked.

"How about this bloke," as he stood up, put his pipe into his jacket and in one fluid movement easily lifted Henry up onto the table. It was no problem for a man that had been lifting rocks most of his life.

"So Mr. Sutton, I assume that you're from England?"

"Yes, you are spot on there Doctor." Then Nigel seized the opportunity to give me an in-depth history of his life and journey to the United States. In the meantime, I kept myself busy by examining and vaccinating Henry.

"Mr. Sutton, why is Henry not clipped like a poodle?"

Nigel looked at me like I didn't know anything about poodles and asked, "Dr. Dionne, do you know where the poodle originated?"

"France," I guessed.

"Good try mate, but it was Germany. You're half-right though. The French standardized the breed. The larger standard poodles were bred down to the miniatures and then further still to get the toy size."

Nodding my head in agreement, I said, "Yes, I know."

Nigel continued on, "The standard poodle like Henry and even the wee minis were and still are used for hunting in Europe. They are an excellent working and retrieving dog. Henry is a good bird dog for grouse, pheasant, and quail. But he likes duck hunting the best. Twinkle and Henry are both excellent swimmers and will doggy-paddle out to retrieve the duck. That's why I keep their coats long. They don't get all scratched up and stay warmer in cold weather."

"Mr. Sutton, this is very interesting. I never knew this about poodles! Hold on one minute, I have to tell Sarah, our receptionist, something."

* * *

I walked out of the exam room and the hungry Sarah looked at me and then at her watch. "We've been talking so much that I've only done one dog and the appointment time is almost over. Please call Tina and tell her that I may not make it home for lunch today. Turn the phone over to the answering service, then take your lunch hour."

I re-entered the exam room for more poodle education and conversation. Nigel was a delight to talk to, and I didn't mind missing lunch if need be.

"Okay, I'm back. Let's do Twinkle next."

The future Rastafarian Henry was put back onto the floor and replaced with the two-colored Twinkle who was well named. She tried her best to sit still, but her wagging little tail and butt had minds of their own. Anyone coming within one foot of Twinkle received a thorough face washing with a tongue that seemed excessively long for her size.

"This little Twinkle is not what I would picture as a swimmer and retriever," I said.

"You would be quite surprised then. She swims faster and better than Henry. I only use her for ducks. That's her specialty."

Twinkle had a small umbilical hernia which was not a problem, and a mild otitis in her left ear. I cleaned and plucked some hair out of both ears and gave Mr. Sutton some drops to use at home. I then shared some of my knowledge with Nigel.

"The dog's ear is shaped like the letter L. It goes straight down then makes a right angle bend to go into the ear drum. So it's safe to put a q-tip in your dog's ear as far as you can see to clean out wax or dirt. Just hold the ear flap so they can't shake their head."

I finished her exam and vaccination. She was one that I would have liked to take home to my family to play with.

Placing her back on her chair, I switched and picked up Truffles. Nigel stood up and said, "I'll need to hold onto her for you, Doc. She's going to want to jump right off that table of yours."

This little apricot dog looked more like the type of poodle that I was used to seeing.

"So what does *she* hunt?" I joked not expecting an answer.

"Truffles," Nigel answered.

"Yes, Truffles," I repeated.

"Doc, you asked and I said truffles."

Now being totally confused, "Do you mean to say that your dog, Truffles, hunts truffles?"

"Yes, yes of course, now you got it," Nigel replied. He then asked, "Do you know what a truffle is?"

"It's some kind of a .....uh.....no, actually I don't know what a truffle is," I finally admitted.

Nigel just looked and smiled at the stammering vet. *These American colonists have a lot to learn*, he thought.

* * *

He patiently explained, "The truffle is the fruiting body of a mushroom that grows beneath the ground. It prefers to grow near the roots of the trees like the oak, birch, poplar and pine trees. In Europe the truffle is held in high esteem by discriminating chefs for French, Spanish and Italian cooking. Just a thin shaving off a truffle adds a most delicious taste to pasta, meats, salads and especially fried eggs."

"That's something that I didn't know," I said.

Nigel continued, "There are black truffles, and the most sought after white ones. They can sell for one to two thousand dollars a pound and even much higher. When I was a boy, my father would take me and two of our small poodles to Alba in northern Italy. We would leave England in October and spend six weeks in the mountains truffle hunting. We had a secret area that we systematically scoured each season."

"Amazing," I interjected.

"Our toy and miniature poodle would sniff each tree and dig up the spot where a truffle was buried. The tiny feet of small dogs didn't harm the truffle which is usually around the size of a golf ball. Some of the locals in other countries used trained pigs to root out truffles, but you just can't beat a good poodle for my money."

I was mesmerized by Nigel's storytelling and almost forgot to examine his last dog named in honor of the expensive mushroom.

"So how about this Truffles. How's her hunting going?"

"She's still young at two years old, but I took her up to Vermont into the Green Mountains last year as a youngster to start her training. This year we returned, and she did rather well and sniffed out about a dozen truffles. Next time will be her time to shine. I'm sure of it," he said proudly.

Trying harder to focus on the four-legged

apricot Truffles, I checked her over and asked, "Did you know that she's starting her heat cycle?"

"I thought so, Henry's getting a little interested in her." Then letting out a deep sigh, "Now I'm going to have to mate her. I really don't want to, but the agreement that I had with her breeder was that she had to have one pregnancy. The breeder then gets the pick of the litter. Then I'll have her spayed."

It was now 1:50 p.m. Sarah returned from lunch and peeked into the exam room, "Dr. Dionne, you're still here!"

The Sutton appointment lasted 1 1/2 hours, and it was time to get ready for my afternoon appointments starting in ten minutes.

I shook hands with Nigel and thanked him for the education on poodles. We planned to check Truffles after she was bred.

"The best time to check for pregnancy is at 28 days," I informed him.

Taking out a small notepad, he wrote the information down and left with his merry band of strange looking poodles.

* * *

Truffles was bred by the breeder's best male poodle and now it was time to see if she was pregnant. On our second meeting, Mr. Sutton insisted that I call him by his first name. This time Henry and Twinkle were left at home. Truffles was already on the exam table.

Examination for pregnancy was done by palpating the abdomen. No ultrasound or quick urine tests were available in 1974 for veterinarians. I spoke briefly to Nigel and patted and stroked Truffles to relax her. If the potential mom was tense or uncooperative, it wouldn't be possible to tell her pregnancy status.

Truffles was relaxed.

Using my right hand, I gently palpated her abdomen and uterus for any distinct golf ball size swellings. There was one!

I announced to Nigel, "Truffles is pregnant, but I can only feel one puppy. That doesn't mean that there can't be more. Part of the uterus is difficult to feel so there may be one or two that are hidden."

"Why don't you just wait until the fifth or sixth week of pregnancy? Wouldn't it be easier to feel them then?" Nigel asked.

"No, not actually. The uterus expands so much with fluid, and with increased blood supply it just feels big. After eight weeks we could then x-ray them because the unborn puppies' bones are fully formed and calcified so they show up easily. Dogs also get false pregnancies and look and feel pregnant when they are not. So four weeks is the best time to check them."

"Now that we know Truffles is pregnant, what do we do now?" Nigel asked.

I spent the rest of the appointment discussing diet and vitamins, exercise, preparing a whelping box, figuring her due date, and the importance of taking her temperature. In the dog, their body temperature will usually drop from 101 degrees F. to 98 degrees F. or below to give a clue when labor is about to start.

"Nigel, most deliveries seem to be at night, but that's generalizing. They can come at any time. It's better to call if anything seems strange and definitely alert us if she's in labor with contractions and no puppy is delivered within an hour. Then we will want to see her."

Nigel wrote everything down in his little note-pad.

* * *

February 1975 - Five weeks later

The answering service called me at 8 p.m. exactly on Truffles's due date-- her 63rd day-- nine weeks. All quite normal.

The only problem was that Truffles had been in hard labor for possibly three hours with no puppy being delivered. Nigel was not at home when labor began. He was stuck on a job that took longer than he had expected. The young woman who was taking care of Nigel's three dogs didn't realize that Truffles was in labor. She was too involved with watching a movie on television.

Nigel called the hospital as soon as he arrived home and discovered his exhausted and distressed poodle. I was at home when the answering service called. I phoned my worried English friend and told him to go straight to the hospital in Somerville, not Pluckemin, and we would meet there.

Suspecting a major problem, I asked Tina to come with me. Our surgery technician, Sandy, was on vacation. Fortunately Tina's sister, Barbara, was visiting with us and she volunteered to watch our three children. Like most veterinary spouses, Tina had lent a hand on quite a few emergencies.

Nigel and Truffles arrived at the same time as we did. I unlocked the hospital door, and turned on the lights to Exam Room 2. Nigel placed the exhausted Truffles on a towel. My exam was fairly quick. The puppy was too large and in a breech position. Truffles was too small to try to re-position the puppy. She needed surgery.

"Nigel, we have a problem. Your dog is in trouble. She needs a Cesarean section right away, and it may be risky."

"Yes I know, try your best Doctor Dionne. I should have brought her in much sooner," he lamented.

Tina had the surgery lights on and was waiting for me. I gave our patient some *Demerol*, and a local anesthetic. We kept her warm with a heating pad, set up an intravenous fluid drip and gave her oxygen through the anesthesia machine and into a face mask. The anesthetic part was turned off, but it was available if we needed it. Surgery had to be as quick as possible, and it was.

Truffles only had one puppy to remove, a fairly large male. The amniotic sac or water bag had already ruptured during the labor. I picked up the newborn puppy, wiped the tiny nostrils and mouth with a gauze sponge to clear away any amniotic fluid, double clamped the umbilical cord with hemostats and cut between them releasing the puppy from the uterus. Tina held a plastic wash basin with a soft towel inside. I turned and dropped the puppy and attached hemostat into the basin.

"Tina, dry the puppy off right away, and rub him until he cries. Then keep stimulating him until he is fully awake."

After removing the placenta and remaining umbilical cord attached to the second hemostat,

I concentrated on suturing the uterus. Then the abdomen and skin. The puppy was now fully awake and squeaking. I removed the first hemostat from the puppy's umbilical cord and placed him in our infant incubator to keep him warm.

But, Truffles did not look very well and was fading. Her heart was weak and breathing shallow. I opened her mouth and inserted an endotracheal tube, and gave her some medication for shock. She did not respond and stopped breathing, so I began to breath for her by squeezing the oxygen bag to inflate her lungs. We were in trouble, and it became more serious as her pupils were dilating. If I stopped breathing for her, she was gone. Realizing that she was basically dead and her spirit was leaving or had already left-- I needed to do something more.

I needed a *miracle*.

* * *

"Tina, go down to the exam room and bring Mr. Sutton up to surgery. I want him to see Truffles and the puppy."

A few minutes later, Nigel walked in and looked at his poodle lying on the surgery table. Tears started to drip down his face.

"Does it look bad, Doctor Dionne?"

Not wanting to answer his question, I said, "Nigel, this is what I would like you to do. Stand by Truffles's head, and tell her how much you love her. I'll stand on the other side and keep breathing for her."

Nigel leaned over and spoke softly and passionately to his little dog. "Truffles, I don't want you to go, but if you must, my Margaret will take care of you. She's a fine woman who loves poodles like I do."

Nigel continued on for the next five minutes. I kept checking her heart periodically. Then the small flap on the anesthesia/oxygen machine moved, indicating that Truffles took a breath on her own. Her heartbeat steadily grew stronger. Then there were more breaths.

"Nigel, keep talking-- she's coming back. Tina, bring the puppy over so her mom can hear her."

I washed one of Truffles's nipples off and let the puppy nurse. She needed the colostrum, the important first milk from the mother that contained all of the important maternal antibodies.

Two minutes later, I was able to remove the endotracheal tube. Truffles was awake.

The three of us spent the next two hours sitting on the floor watching the new mother nurse and fuss over her baby. We had put them into a makeshift cardboard whelping box. When the new mom was able to stand, walk, wag her tail and *pee*, I knew she and her baby could go home.

Nigel looked at me and let out a sigh of relief. It isn't often an owner gets to see the close calls in the surgery room.

"Doc, that was the most amazing thing that I have ever seen! She was dead, wasn't she?"

"I think so, but not quite. Your voice and kind words brought her back," I said with a smile.

Nigel then shook my hand, and hugged and thanked Tina. We all walked down the surgery steps and carried our two patients to Nigel's car.

My last words were, "Call me if there are any

problems, and we need to remove the stitches in ten days."

* * *

April 1975 - Two months later

I was in Pluckemin for my weekly outpatient appointments. Sarah smiled when she handed me one more patient record. It said: *Sutton-- new puppy-- male-- 8 weeks-- toy poodle-- check up and puppy shots.* I laughed and walked in to see Nigel and his new puppy. Truffles, Henry and Twinkle had come along for the ride.

"What a pleasant surprise!"

Mr. Sutton held a familiar looking apricot puppy.

"Nigel, is that Truffles's puppy?"

"Yes it is. And a fine looking laddie he's turning out to be."

"What happened? I thought the breeder wanted the pick of the litter?"

"Aye, that was the agreement, but she wanted a female. So I bought this puppy from her. We named him Archie."

I checked the non-clipped, fuzzy Archie over and found no problems. He gave a little yipe when he had his vaccination which made his mother a little worried.

Before leaving, Nigel said, "My family has a few presents of gratitude for you."

He handed Henry an oddly shaped package, and told me to call him.

"Henry, come!" I commanded.

The retrieving Henry walked to me and dropped the package at my feet. I picked up the package which was quite cold. It was a frozen, dressed out duck-- ready to be cooked. Nigel then gave Twinkle a smaller package and nodded to me.

"Twinkle, come here girl," I called and bent over.

She ran excitedly to me and jumped into my arms. "Thanks Twinkle," I said and opened her gift-- it was a small book.

The title read, *Poodles-- All You Ever Need to Know.*

"Thank you very much."

"We're not quite done yet," Nigel winked and put a small pair of saddlebags on Truffles and pointed at me, "Go to Dr. Dionne."

There was a small bulge in each bag.

"Go ahead and open them up, Doc."

I unzipped each bag, and there neatly wrapped was a white truffle from mom and in the other saddlebag a small black one from Archie. Now *I* was the one with tears in my eyes and speechless. Sarah was peeking in the door and quickly got a tissue.

The Sutton family said good-bye after one more face-lick from Twinkle and drove home.

* * *

February 1980 - Five years later...

Sitting in front of the television, I was watching the United States Olympic Hockey Team defeat the Russian squad and heard the announcer ask if the viewers believed in *miracles*.

Thinking back to Truffles, I smiled and said, "I sure do!"

24

Domino and Shirley

Kindness is the language which the deaf can hear and the blind can see.

Mark Twain

"What we've got here is a failure to communicate" is a line in the famous 1967 movie, *Cool Hand Luke*, starring Paul Newman. There are so many varied ways to communicate with each other, but what if you couldn't? Anyone who is alone and friendless might slowly go mad if she or he cannot give or receive information, or express feelings and thoughts with others in some manner. How many simple problems, disputes and major conflicts could be avoided by simply listening.

Some animals can face similar problems if placed in an isolated unnatural confinement like in a poorly run zoo, research facility or tied up in someone's backyard. This next case was very *unusual* and presented a major communication challenge for all the concerned parties.

* * *

Ivan Horvat sat at the kitchen table drinking a cup of tea while his wife, Maja, prepared breakfast. Today, Ivan was both happy and sad. His mood vacillated back and forth between these two emotions. His thoughts were in a state of flux and competed for his attention.

The Horvat family lived in Yugoslavia before the country was divided into Croatia, Bosnia and Herzegovina and Serbia. They lived in the beautiful area of Dalmatia, the mountainous western region of present day Croatia. Dalmatia borders the Adriatic Sea directly across from Italy. Ivan's ancestors had always lived here as far back as he could trace. The men in the Horvat family bred, raised and trained Dalmatians for over 100 years.

Ivan and Maja were both fifty-two years old, so there would be no further children added to the family. Their only child, Markus, was twenty-four years old and a recent graduate of the University of Zagreb. Markus was the first Horvat to attend college and excelled in his engineering studies.

Ivan became sad when he thought about Markus leaving his family and moving to the United States. But then he became happy knowing that he met a nice girl, Danielle, his senior year in college. She was an American studying history at the university. They fell in love and married last month.

"Maja, how can you get married two times to the same girl?" he asked. "Isn't once enough?"

"Ivan, you already know the answer. They married in our church for our family. Then they will marry in New York for hers. Now our little Markus can be an American citizen and get a good job."

"But what if we don't see him again?" Ivan asked moving back to the sad side.

Handing him a plate of eggs and sausage, Maja ordered, "Here, you eat now and go take care of the dogs and puppies and stop this foolish talk about Markus!"

After breakfast, Ivan went into the kennel. He had two males, four females and a litter of seven ten-week-old puppies. Originally there were eight puppies, but three weeks ago he gave the best male puppy to his son and new wife as a farewell present. Markus promised that he would start his own kennel and use his father's puppy to improve the Dalmatian bloodlines in America.

Ivan knew that this puppy would grow to be well-muscled and 60-65 pounds. He was white with black spots, but two of his litter-mates were white with brown or liver spots. At birth, Dalmatians are all white and the spots start to appear at four weeks of age and can continue to appear and develop in some cases throughout adulthood.

Ivan laughed and thought to himself, *I should have sent a long-haired Dalmatian with Markus that would have really surprised the Americans.*

Dalmatians can have a variety of eye colors ranging from brown, amber, blue or mixed-- one eye blue and the other eye a different color.

Danielle immediately fell in love with the puppy whom she named Domino.

Ivan, the new father-in-law wondered to himself, *I know what a domino is. It's part of a game and each white piece has black dots. But what kind of a name is this for a dog? What's wrong with Ilrio, Roko or Ante? These are good Croatian names for dogs!*

* * *

The next day the newly married couple flew to the United States with the tiny Domino snuggled in a small travel cage. The puppy and cage just fit under the passenger seat in front of them. The following month, Danielle and Markus were married again for the bride's family.

Domino attended the ceremony and barked approvingly when Markus said, "I do." The puppy also had two *accidents* at the reception, but no one seemed to mind.

* * *

I met Markus and Danielle in July when it was time for Domino's next vaccinations. Markus was a handsome man with black hair, brown eyes and a dark stubble of a beard. He was about my height, six feet and 170 lbs. He looked athletic having played soccer most of his life and in college.

Danielle, his red-haired, blue-eyed wife was loaded with freckles; many more than Domino would ever have in black spots.

There was something about Markus, whether it was his heavily accented English or his amicable demeanor that made me want to be his friend. Danielle, with her contrasting New York accent, didn't hesitate to tell me about her husband's background with Dalmatians. She explained how famous his family was in the Yugoslavian dog world.

Later, I had to agree with Danielle as I saw Domino mature into a magnificent well-trained male Dalmatian.

* * *

Markus kept his word to his father and three years later in 1973 started a small breeding kennel for Dalmatians in Basking Ridge, New Jersey. Domino, as predicted, easily earned an AKC Champion title and later became a Grand Champion.

Other Dalmatian owners were eager to breed their females to the famous Dalmatian from the Dalmatia area of Yugoslavia. Markus was very careful as to whom he would accept for mating. He studied their pedigree very carefully before accepting them.

Many females were sent to Horvat Kennels by airplane from far away places like California, Texas and even Canada. Markus would pick them up usually from the airport in Newark, New Jersey. He then boarded them at his kennel until it was time for the mating. Occasionally, he would need my services if there were any problems or questions such as determining the best day of the heat cycle for the breeding.

* * *

Over the years, Markus *taught* me the history of the Dalmatian. He explained in detail their early origins in Dalmatia and their versatility as a working dog and as a devoted family pet. "Dalmatians need exercise every day or they get into mischief. The more the better, you can't tire them out."

That's quite accurate with all dogs, I thought to myself.

"In Europe, especially in the larger cities, Dalmatians along with small terriers were once used to hunt and kill rodents like rats. They are also very loyal to the family, so Dalmatians are excellent watchdogs."

I had never pictured them necessarily as having these traits. Each meeting with Markus, I could usually pick up some tidbit of knowledge.

"Dr. Dionne, do you know why the Dalmatian is the mascot for firemen?" Markus asked during one office appointment.

"I cannot tell a lie, Markus, I don't. Maybe the firemen like their spots."

"No...no, I will tell you," he said proudly with his usual accent.

"Dalmatians like horses and the two get along very well together," he said.

"That's it? Firemen have the Dalmatian as a mascot because of horses?"

"Yes, but you forget your history my friend," he scolded gently. "In America, fire-wagons were pulled by horses in the early 1900's, especially in the big cities. The Dalmatian would run in front of the fire-wagon to lead the way. If the horses were not going fast enough, the dog would circle back and nip at their heels to make them run faster. Once at the fire, the dogs would stand guard and protect the wagon and the horses. These horses were very valuable, so the Dalmatian would sleep in the firehouse at night to protect the horses in their stalls from thieves who might want to steal them. Today, even though there are no horses used anymore, the Dalmatian, out of respect and honor is still their mascot."

"Very interesting, Markus." There wasn't a

day that went by that I didn't learn something from my two and four-legged friends.

* * *

November 1973

Rosalee caught me just before I entered the exam room for my next appointment-- a new account with a puppy for her first shots. She was in her usual tizzy over something as she whispered from the pharmacy area and motioned urgently for me to come with her.

Wondering what the top-secret might be as we entered the doctors' lounge, I asked, "What's up Rosalee?"

"Dr. Dionne," pausing as she looked around in case someone was eavesdropping, "your next clients, the O'Connors, are all deaf! I didn't know this until they checked in for their appointment and had to fill out a new patient sheet. They must have had someone else call for them to make the appointment. I thought I better let you know..."

Finishing her sentence, "So I don't embarrass myself like usual," I said. "Thanks Rosalee, it will be okay."

Rosalee fluttered back into the office, and I walked into the exam room. There were four O'Connors--mother, dad, brother and sister.

All were deaf.

I smiled and said, "Hello."

The twenty-something daughter, Roberta, and her brother Franklin, were able to read even my mumbling lips, but were not able to speak very well themselves. I handed her a paper and pencil, and we *communicated* in this fashion.

The kids then *signed* to their parents with a blur of moving hands and fingers back and forth. It was dazzling to my eye.

I wished that I could have joined in with the signing, but my sign language was rather limited. I was quite adept at waving hello, bye-bye, and flashing a mean peace sign, but that was about it.

The question-and-answer paper method worked quite well. I learned that their new Dalmatian puppy was a twelve-week-old female. Her name was Shirley.

They purchased her one week ago from a pet shop in Pennsylvania. The blue-eyed Shirley was quite cute but something didn't seem right about the puppy. I couldn't put my finger on it at first.

* * *

The physical exam revealed that everything was quite normal, but she seemed a bit more excitable and jumpy than the usual puppy. I became suspicious and hoped that I was mistaken.

I wrote a note to Roberta, "Please put Shirley on the floor and have everyone ignore her."

I wanted to see what she would do. Roberta lifted the puppy off the table, and I knelt down as she let her go. It took a minute or so for Shirley to tire of chewing my shoelaces and pant cuff. Becoming bored, she turned around and faced away from me.

This was what I was waiting for and let out a low whistle. I repeated the whistling twice more, each time a little louder. There was no response from Shirley.

She was *deaf!*

* * *

Deafness is an inherited problem in the Dalmatian breed. In any litter, there might be two or three puppies that are deaf. These pups are usually not permitted to live by Dalmatian breeders and certainly are not sold.

Thinking to myself, *How do I tell these nice people that they have a deaf puppy?*

I did not want to embarrass them or hurt their feelings because of their own hearing impairment. It was a bit of a predicament.

The normal recommendation would be to return the puppy to the pet shop for a refund or exchange it for another puppy. This might sound too cruel as if being deaf made one worthless. And I certainly didn't want to tell them what normally happens to deaf Dalmatians.

Taking it one step at a time, I informed the O'Connors with a paper message, "Shirley is deaf. It is not uncommon in this breed."

The note was simple, straight-forward, not eloquent, but it was the best that I could do at the moment.

Roberta turned and flashed her fingers. The rest of the family answered.

She wrote back a note, "Okay, is it a problem?"

I wrote a follow-up note, "Well yes, training Shirley will be more difficult, and she will need to be kept on a leash outside to protect her from danger like cars, other dogs or people running or riding bicycles."

"Dr. Dionne, this doesn't sound like too much of a problem. We face this everyday ourselves. Please don't tell us we have to take her back."

Roberta's eyes were starting to glisten with a possible tear starting to form. I could see that the rest of the family members were in agreement about not wanting to return their deaf Dalmatian.

After giving Shirley her vaccination, we continued our note writing and I answered the typical puppy care questions. Shirley was to return in one month for a recheck and her last shots.

* * *

One month later, the O'Connor family were all smiles when I entered the room. Franklin held up his hand and pointed to Shirley who had grown quite a bit since the last visit. He pointed to his eyes then to me.

I watched.

Franklin moved his hand and fingers-- Shirley sat, then another move with his fingers-- Shirley gave Franklin her paw. Another signing and she laid down, then another and she barked.

The note from Roberta said, "How's that for one month of training?"

"Great!" I said and smiled as they read my lips.

I felt relieved and cautiously optimistic. Many older dogs become hard of hearing or even deaf and seem to adjust okay. But this was just a puppy.

Shirley was spayed at six months of age. At nine months of age, the problems started.

* * *

Shirley was becoming bored and didn't get nearly enough exercise. She became destructive when left alone. There were numerous *accidents* starting to happen each day. Roberta had her neighbor make an appointment for her to come in and discuss the problem with me.

By this time, I could sign, *Hello, how are you* and *good-bye*.

I walked into the exam room. Roberta was alone, no Shirley. It was obvious that she was upset.

She handed me a typed letter that summarized the problems and closed with, *We need help, Dr. Dionne*.

Sitting down next to her, I wrote, *Do you still want to keep her?*

"Yes, I think so," she responded.

This time the dam burst and tears flooded her cheeks.

I grabbed a handful of tissues from the desk which were there for such events.

"Shirley needs some specialized training and more exercise is definitely needed. Nine months of age is equivalent to being a rebellious teenager. Let me call a friend of mine, Markus Horvat. His family has bred and trained Dalmatians for years."

The tears slowed to a trickle, and a slight smile decorated her pretty face. This time *I* read *her* lips that mouthed, "Thank you."

I arranged to call her neighbor when I had any news, and we signed *Good-bye*.

* * *

That evening, I called Markus and explained the complicated problem. I could picture his engineering mind go to work.

After a few moments, he said, "Dr. Dionne,

remember when I told you about Dalmatians and horses?"

"Yes...yes," I said as my mind also swirled with possibilities.

"You said her name is Shirley?" Markus asked.

"Yes, that's right."

"I will give her some training using hand signals that we use for obedience work and hunting. And she needs to meet my Domino. He will tire her out for sure."

"Thank you Markus, this will make the O'Connor family very, very happy," I said and almost shouted with excitement.

* * *

This story had a happy ending because of overcoming *communication* differences and caring. The Horvat family and the O'Connors became friends. Danielle became an effective signer so there was no need for note writing.

The luck of the Irish smiled on Shirley. A horseback riding stable was in walking distance from the O'Connor's house. The owner of the stable took the deaf Dalmatian under her wing.

Each afternoon, Shirley visited the stable and became friends with Apache and Belle, the two most gentle horses. The children that came for riding lessons also liked to play with and pet Shirley. The no longer bored Dalmatian loved to run with the horses inside the fenced-in training area and even went out for a few trail rides.

Each week, Markus worked with Shirley who eagerly copied everything that Domino would do.

Meanwhile, Markus, the engineer, worked to try and modify the recently developed shock collar for training and correcting bad habits in problem dogs.

He was able to change the collar so that instead of a shock it would deliver a simple vibration. When the O'Connors wanted Shirley's attention, a simple press on the radio controlled remote receiver was all that was needed. A simple Morse Code system was worked out. A single dot or buzz meant one thing, a longer dash meant something else.

The O'Connors learned a new way to communicate with their deaf pet.

Not wanting to be left out of the fun, I had an idea for both Shirley and her best friend, Domino. I contacted several fire stations in the area.

"Do you have a Dalmatian mascot?" I asked.

Most said no, they did not.

"How would you like to have two well-trained Dalmatians ride in any parades or events that you might have?"

* * *

The usual large crowd gathered for the Fourth of July parade in downtown Somerville. Markus and Danielle, Roberta and the O'Connor family and my family stood together on Main Street. We waited nervously for the fire engines to appear.

Finally, two red hook-and-ladders came down the middle of the street just behind the high school marching band. Domino rode atop the first truck and was held by a volunteer fireman. He wagged his tail and barked loudly when he recognized Markus and Danielle.

Shirley rode proudly upon the next hook and ladder. She also posed with a fireman.

The fact that Shirley could not hear the spectators cheer was not a problem. The children and adults communicated to her with their smiles and signed with a multitude of waving hands.

Domino and Shirley each wore a medal of appreciation attached to their collars for all the previous Dalmatians that served this country as fire dogs.

25

Home Is Where The Heart Is

To understand a man, you've got to walk a mile in his shoes.

Anonymous

The Mekong Delta occupies fifteen-thousand square miles in the southwestern portion of Vietnam. The Mekong River is the main river that courses through this area, and numerous tributaries branch off the Mekong to supply the entire delta. During the monsoon season, from May through September, these waterways swell and often cause flooding to the surrounding agricultural land and rice paddies. The Mekong River which originates in Tibet, travels through six countries and eventually empties into the South China Sea. This entire area was strategically important during the Vietnam War from the time the United States entered the conflict in 1965 to the fall of Saigon in April of 1975.

* * *

April 1967 - The Mekong Delta - South Vietnam

At 6 a.m., PT Boat-211 began its morning patrol. It was one of 250 PT boats deployed by the U.S. Navy during our involvement in this conflict. This particular vessel, PT Boat-211, was a member of the *River Patrol Force* assigned to the Mekong Delta region.

PT-211 skimmed smoothly along at 14 knots (16 m.p.h.). The twelve-man crew and three officers were all busy with their assigned duties while keeping a watchful eye along each river bank. Sniper fire was a common occurrence and a constant threat.

The rumors were that the North Vietnamese, or Viet Cong, were planning a major offensive. Which they were. But not until the following year - 1968. It would be known as the *Tet Offensive*. The scope and size of the offensive would catch the U.S. forces and South Vietnamese unprepared. This became the turning point in the long struggle between North and South Vietnam and led to the American troop withdrawal in 1975.

Weapons were now being shipped to the south along these waterways to be hidden and stored for the upcoming invasion. One of the main duties of the River Patrol Force was to stop and search all suspicious river traffic for weapons, explosives and other war materials.

These search-and-seizure tactics were very dangerous. The Viet Cong did not surrender easily. Firefights were a common occurrence. The PT boats were well-armed with *Twin-Fifties* - twin 50-caliber machine guns. A formidable weapon.

* * *

Otis Johnson was twenty-four years old from Tupelo, Mississippi. He was finishing his second tour of duty in Vietnam. He vowed it would be his last. Otis was a gunner's mate which requires special training in weapon systems. He was an expert in repair, maintenance and use of the various weapons aboard the ship.

He had enlisted in the Navy upon graduation from high school. His father, the Reverend James Johnson, and Otis both felt that it was his duty to serve the country as all the other Johnsons in the family had done previously in World Wars I and II.

Otis was a dreamer even as a young black child in the segregated deep south. He always had his plans and lofty aspirations. His vision was to return triumphantly to Tupelo as a war hero, marry his high school sweetheart, Akeesha Davis, and raise a large family.

Being an outstanding student at Tupelo High School, the young Otis also planned to take advantage of the GI Bill and go to college upon completion of his military service. His mother, Dorothy, would have wanted that. Unfortunately, she had died of complications from diabetes when Otis was fourteen.

In 1967, Otis had grown to be a handsome young seaman. He was six-feet-two inches tall and 190 lbs. of lean muscle. His eyes were a dark brown and were capable of a stare that appeared to pierce one to their core. Initially, he could be very intimidating to strangers, but once he smiled and showed a perfect set of white teeth, Otis revealed that he was really a friendly young man. His black hair was clipped short with a military *buzz-cut*. Wearing his Navy uniform and seaman's hat, the strong and smiling sailor appealed to all the ladies.

* * *

On this early morning patrol, an incident was about to happen that would change seaman Johnson's life forever.

PT-211 came upon two identical river barges moving slowly down each side of the misty river. One barge hugged the left bank, and the second barge was trailing slightly behind the first and close to the opposite right bank.

Speaking in Vietnamese, the captain of the PT boat held a loud speaker and ordered both barges to stop for inspection.

Neither stopped.

Sensing trouble, the captain radioed for reinforcements-- a combat helicopter which was referred to as a gunship or simply a *Huey*. This attack helicopter carried 2.75-inch rockets and 30-caliber machine guns. It was the one aircraft that the enemy soldiers feared the most.

The crew and officers realized that PT-211 was in danger of being caught in a possible deadly cross-fire. Their fears were confirmed. Each barge was indeed heavily armed with weapons and VC soldiers.

Before help arrived a fierce skirmish ensued. A barrage of enemy bullets whizzed past the PT boat from both sides of the river. The captain attacked the closest barge and disabled it with a flurry of machine gun fire from the twin-fifties. The second barge continued to rain down weapon-fire toward the PT boat. Fortunately, the Huey arrived and sunk the enemy vessel with two well-aimed rockets.

PT-211 suffered some minor structural damage and two crew members were wounded. A third sailor was fatally wounded and would be reported as K.I.A. (killed in action). Otis Johnson and Franklin Henderson were the two wounded enlisted men.

* * *

Otis opened his eyes as he lay on his back looking up at the early morning sky that was not quite blue as yet. There were a few white clouds moving slowly past his line of vision. Then he felt the pain in his right leg and right shoulder. This was when he realized that he was shot. Otis lifted his head just enough to see the blood seeping out from his body onto the deck. His mind began to swirl in circles, round and round before he passed out again from shock.

The medic aboard PT-211 was able to stop the bleeding from Otis's wounds with tight pressure-bandages and gave him an injection of morphine to deaden the pain.

A second helicopter had followed at a safe distance behind the Huey and landed on the river bank so that the two wounded sailors, and their slain comrade could be whisked away to the Navy hospital site in Saigon.

The following day, Otis awoke and found himself in a hospital bed. He wasn't completely clear as to what had happened. His doctor told him that he had been shot in two places and needed two units of blood. Surgery was performed on both sites. The leg wound was not a problem. It had been operated on, flushed out and sutured. The bullet had passed through his thigh without damaging the bone, nerves and blood supply. It was a flesh wound.

The shoulder was a different story. That bullet hit the scapula (shoulder blade) and caused damage to the shoulder joint. The doctors in Saigon temporarily immobilized the fracture and were sending Otis back to the States for the surgery to be done at the National Naval Medical Center in Bethesda, Maryland. He would need reconstructive surgery with bone plates.

* * *

Otis was transferred a week later and had his surgery. He would spend another week in the Naval Hospital during his recovery. During his hospital convalescence, Otis had trouble sleeping, and when he did, nightmares and flashbacks became a nightly occurrence. He often awoke perspiring heavily and in a state of panic. He could feel his heart thumping in his chest and his breath coming in short gasps as he vividly relived the terror of the firefight. The doctors diagnosed him as having *combat stress*, or as the troops would say, Otis was *shell-shocked.* He was given an honorable discharge and awarded a purple heart.

He was told by the doctors that the insomnia and nightmares would gradually subside over the next few months.

They didn't.

* * *

In fact, things got worse. Much worse. He became forgetful and had trouble concentrating for any length of time.

Arriving back home in Tupelo, there was no hero's parade. Many local residents gave him looks of disparagement. He discovered a steadily growing anti-war sentiment. Of course James, his father, welcomed him home with open arms.

The Reverend told Otis, "My prayers have been answered. Praise be to Jesus."

He also gave Otis an unopened letter from Akeesha. Otis read the *Dear John* letter as tears dripped down upon the short farewell note. Akeesha had waited patiently for several years, then became lonely. She met a young man, fell in love and was now engaged.

To make matters worse, his older brother, James Jr., had moved to Florida with his family. And his older sister, Ruth, was also married and living in Los Angeles. He especially missed his sister who took over the mother's role after their real mom had died. So Otis settled in *uncomfortably* with his father who insisted that he apply to various colleges for admission the next semester.

"The best thing to do now is to get an education and get on with your life," said the Reverend.

This was easier said than done, especially for someone who couldn't concentrate long enough to read a newspaper article or sit and watch a television program.

There also wasn't much work for an ex-gunner's mate and weapons specialist in Tupelo. It became clear to Reverend James that Otis would not be attending college or be gainfully employed any time soon. So he put him to work as the caretaker of his small Baptist church.

Otis complied with his father's wishes but not with any enthusiasm. On Sundays, he stayed home in bed. There was no way he could sit through a lengthy

Baptist service. This led to a few quarrels with his father about his lack of piety. Otis knew it was soon time to move on. But he wasn't sure as to where.

* * *

A few weeks later, a letter arrived from a Vietnam Navy buddy, Thomas Fisher, who invited Otis to visit him in New York City. Maybe if Otis liked the city, they could become roommates and share the rent on his small apartment.

Otis left with Reverend James's blessing and a paid one-way ticket to the *Big Apple* courtesy of his father. Arriving in the city, he was overwhelmed at first with the size of the tall buildings, traffic, noise and swarms of people. It was a far cry from a small town in Mississippi for a young man.

Thomas Fisher's apartment was in Brooklyn and near the famous Brooklyn Bridge. The first week, Otis's spirits picked up considerably. Several of Tom's friends, mostly Vietnam vets, would stop by the apartment. The gatherings and parties were fun at first, but the drinking and later on the drugs were too much for Otis. He never took to drink or drugs. It was part of his Baptist upbringing, and he knew his mother wouldn't approve. Otis lasted a month at the apartment and thanked Thomas for his hospitality. He also paid Tom for his stay with almost all the money that he had.

* * *

Otis had learned the subway system and found that it was fairly easy to get around the city, particularly Manhattan. So with his meager belongings in his Navy duffle bag and twenty-four dollars in his pocket, he walked across the Brooklyn Bridge, and hopped on a subway to upper Manhattan.

Otis was officially homeless as he walked alone into Central Park. After wandering aimlessly through the park for a few hours, Otis was also officially hungry. A condition that would soon become his constant companion.

He parted with one precious dollar for a hot dog and a cup of coffee from a street vendor. He placed his well-used Navy duffle bag on a park bench and started to eat his meal. Before he could partake of the first bite, a small rust-colored pooch with floppy ears appeared out of nowhere and sat at Otis's feet and wagged his tail. He ignored the dog and took a bite.

Undeterred, the little male canine hopped up onto the bench and barked hopefully for some of the hot dog. Otis always liked animals of all kinds, but no pets were ever allowed in the Johnson household.

After one more look at the four-legged panhandler, Otis asked, "Okay, do you want a bite?"

Another woof and more vigorous tail-wagging.

Otis carefully divided the hot dog into two equal pieces. The young dog eagerly ate the hot dog and bun, including the ketchup, mustard, relish and onions piled on top.

Otis laughed and carefully pet his new friend.

He then peppered the stray dog with questions.

"Where's your collar and dog tags?"

"What's your name...rank...serial number?"

With each question the small dog of mixed

breeding cocked his head from one side to the other trying to understand.

Otis laughed again as he stood up and picked up his duffle bag. He reached down and pet the dog one last time.

"Okay, see you around, I gotta get going."

But leaving wasn't so easy.

The small mixed-terrier followed closely behind the ex-seaman. Otis expected him to leave at the first opportunity for another free meal, but he didn't. He came to the gazebo by the lake and sat down to rest. His wounded leg and shoulder were starting to ache. This would happen fairly often most days. But after fifteen to twenty minutes of rest, he would be good to go again.

"Listen doggy, if you're going to keep following me, I guess I should give you a name."

More woofs and tail-wagging.

"How about a name that I can easily remember, like PT-211, or how about just PT?"

The newly-named pooch answered affirmatively.

"PT, I want you to know a few ground rules. First, I will never put a leash on you. I will share all my food with you and you're free to leave any time you want to. Okay?"

PT hopped up onto his new master's lap and began to lick his face. Otis cried out in laughter and begged PT to stop. From that day on a friendship was formed that would not be broken.

Otis and PT shared each other's hearts.

* * *

The homeless man from Mississippi kept his promise to PT, and the two wandered all over Manhattan. Otis refused to panhandle on the street like the scores of other homeless people, many of whom were also veterans. This forced Otis to concentrate and focus on taking care of his best friend.

He went to an Army surplus store and bought a small tarp, sleeping bag, a soft wide-brimmed camouflage hat and a green army fatigue jacket to wear. The store owner gave Otis a big discount because he was also a vet himself and liked the little dog with the unusual name.

He told Otis, "That dog of yours looks like he belongs in a Walt Disney movie."

Otis smiled and replied, "Maybe someday, yes, who knows... maybe someday. Let's go PT, we got work to do."

With the three dollars remaining in his pocket, Otis went into a Woolworth five-and-ten-cent store and bought two packets of pencils and two packets of pens. PT waited patiently outside. Then they walked back together to their favorite entrance to Central Park and opened their *business*.

Otis made a cardboard sign: *Pencils-$.15 each. Pens-$.30 each. Free dog petting with each purchase*.

By that evening, the two entrepreneurs sold every pen and all but two pencils. They treated themselves to a takeout from a Chinese restaurant. They also found a secluded area in the park and spread out their tarp and sleeping bag.

* * *

The next day and the following days, Otis and PT went to work selling their writing utensils and giving free pets and hugs to earn their meals. The late spring weather was unpredictable so there were days without food when business was slow. At night, during cold or rainy weather, Otis had found two shelters where he could sleep, take a shower and get a hot meal. Neither shelter minded having PT because he was so well behaved. Otis hated the shelters because they were very crowded and noisy. Most of the *guests* were addicts of some type, or mental patients that were either released early or escaped the system entirely. Other guests were just down on their luck and penniless. Theft was commonplace in the shelters, but PT made sure that their meager belongings remained untouched. A growl and a few barks made sure of that. Plus Otis still had huge muscular arms which were like his old Twin-50's—Otis and PT were left alone. So the shelters were only used as a last resort.

In time, the residents around the park knew the handsome but shy veteran and his lovable companion. Many bought pencils and pens just for the free petting. The local police looked the other way and didn't bother the enterprising business man and his partner. However, sleeping in the park was forbidden at night, and after 1 a.m. even walking through the park was not permitted.

Periodically this rule was enforced and *round-ups* took place. Fines were levied, but since the homeless couldn't pay, they were detained in jail. The sharp hearing of PT warned Otis of an impending round-up, or worse yet, from the roving youth gangs that often preyed on the homeless at night.

The seaman always had an escape route and avoided any type of trouble.

During the crackdowns, this usually meant sleeping during the day in the park and wandering through Manhattan during the evening. It was difficult to sell their pens and pencils at night, but they managed.

On most evenings, the two shared the same sleeping bag to keep each other warm. Otis's nightmares and panic attacks had decreased but still regularly plagued him. PT could sense when the bad dreams were happening and learned to wake him with vigorous licking of his face and whimpering.

During his clearer moments, Otis knew that living on the street was not the best thing for both him and his dog. But he was not sure what to do and going back to Tupelo was not an option.

* * *

June 1969 - 11 months later

After spending one year in New York City, it was time to make a plan. Last winter was too cold, business dropped off and the shelters too crowded. As usual, he discussed his options with his best friend.

"PT, we're going to have to work real hard this summer. We need to make more money so we can go south for the winter. It was too cold for me here in January and February. I'm a southern boy from Mississippi."

PT listened patiently and agreed with each suggestion with his enthusiastic tail.

Otis continued, "Selling pens and pencils puts

food in our bellies, but we need much more to get to let's say... Florida. We could go see my brother in Jacksonville. Would you like that?"

Woof-- Yes, of course.

"I'm going to need your help though. I think that if you would be willing to learn a few tricks, we could put on a dog show and earn the extra money that we'll need to get us there. Is it a deal?"

PT raised his paw and they shook hands.

"Well I guess that's your first trick."

Each day the two worked on several circus-type acts. PT was a quick learner. Besides the relatively easy tricks of walking on hind legs, twirling, hopping and playing dead, he also learned the back-flip. PT would run to Otis spring onto his chest and flip over backwards. In addition, he was adept at picking a handkerchief from his back-pocket, stealing his hat and jumping through a hoop.

Soon small crowds, mainly on the weekend, gathered to see the little rust-colored dog with the curly hair and the homeless man perform their act. Most people left spare change or a dollar bill as a thank you. Otis gratefully collected the money from his camouflage hat that lay on the ground and put it in a safe place—a zippered pocket inside his trousers.

By the end of August, they had saved three hundred and forty-five dollars.

The thrilled master told his dog, "PT, as soon as we get fifty-five more dollars, we're leaving! I can get us a ride to Philadelphia with our friend, Danny. He's got a job delivering furniture to different stores in New Jersey and Philly. After that we will have to hitch-hike south."

PT spun around a few times in a tight circle

then barked excitedly. He was apparently ready to go as well.

* * *

The big day came ten days later. Otis and PT took the subway to lower Manhattan. He was told that dogs were not allowed to ride the subway, but Otis countered with his piercing stare from his dark brown eyes. An exception was made. They then walked back across the Brooklyn Bridge to meet their friend, Danny, at the furniture warehouse where he worked. Danny was ready to leave at 4 p.m. that afternoon. He planned to stop in Somerville, New Jersey, unload some furniture, and spend the night and finish the deliveries the next day.

Danny was another Vietnam vet that had survived the war without suffering from *battle fatigue*. He sympathized with his combat brothers like Otis.

After delivering the furniture in Somerville, Danny pulled into a small motel in the nearby town of Raritan. The motel was on Route 206 near the Raritan River. Otis wanted to save his money and opted not to check into the motel for the evening. He and PT would sleep out by the river. The weather was still warm and there was no threat of rain.

That evening, Otis set up the tarp and spread out the sleeping bag. He told PT to go do his business while he crawled into the sleeping bag. Otis had hardly settled in when he heard his little dog yelp in pain.

Scrambling out of his sleeping bag, he stumbled along the overgrown path toward the river. PT continued his cries of pain.

"PT, I'm coming boy! Hold on!"

Otis was able to control his familiar feelings of panic, but just barely. A few feet from the river, he found his partner. His little dog's foot was caught in a muskrat trap. The trap was sprung and caught PT's right front paw at the carpal (wrist) joint. *It was the paw that he used the most for shaking hands*.

Otis wasn't able to see that well, but the moon was almost full and there were only a few clouds in the night sky. But he did manage to spring open the trap, releasing PT.

Picking him up, he said, "I'm sorry. I'm sorry," as his tears were mixed with anger at the trap.

Before leaving, Otis threw the trap into the middle of the river. He slowly worked his way back up the path to their camp site. Rummaging through the duffle bag, he pulled out his *Zippo* lighter that he occasionally used to make a fire. Using the Zippo for light, he inspected the injured paw. He could see that the foot was quite swollen but not bleeding.

He crawled back into the sleeping bag with his injured buddy.

"I'll keep you warm. It will be okay. I'm so sorry."

PT sensed that Otis was starting a panic attack and in spite of his pain began to lick his master's hand. Then they both settled down and waited out the long night.

"I'll get you some help tomorrow. I promise."

* * *

In the morning, PT's paw looked even more swollen, and Otis was worried it would burst open.

He put him down and the little dog was able to stand on three legs holding the injured one up.

Otis quickly rolled up the sleeping bag and stuffed everything into the duffle bag. Then picking up his injured friend, he walked out of the woods to the motel.

"Don't worry PT, Danny will know what to do."

Otis was now having trouble thinking clearly, but Danny was helpful after looking at the swollen paw.

"We got to get him to a vet. It looks like his foot is broken. There's a vet hospital back in Somerville on Route 22; I'll drive you back there. It's only a few miles."

"Thanks Danny. This guy means a lot to me," as Otis's eyes began to well up with moisture.

Danny did have a time problem. He was on a tight delivery schedule. He wouldn't be able to wait at the vet hospital.

Otis reminded Danny that he was homeless and unlike Danny he did not have any fixed schedule. His only concern was his dog. Danny drove into the parking area in front of Somerset Veterinary Group, and gave Otis his home telephone number. Otis agreed to call his friend with an update on the injured paw. He then thanked him and said good-bye.

* * *

Otis waited twenty minutes until the office opened at 8 a.m. Rosalee was first to arrive and opened the front door. She was surprised to see a large black man with a duffle bag standing there holding a small dog. Rosalee was momentarily taken aback by his unkempt appearance and military clothing.

"Oh! May I help you?"

"My dog has hurt his leg."

"Did you call? Is someone expecting you?"

"No, I don't have a phone."

"Oh! It's okay, come in and I'll get a doctor to help you."

Rosalee put Otis and PT into Exam Room 3 and gave him a new patient form to fill out. Otis filled out the form as best as he could but most of it was left blank. He was only able to fill in his name, his dog's name and the fact that his dog was a male.

His address, telephone number, dog's age, breed, vaccination history and method-of-payment were all left blank.

Rosalee collected the new-account form and was shocked that Mr. Johnson had no home or telephone.

All she could say was, "But...but are you sure?"

"Yes ma'am, I'm sure," replied Otis.

The flustered Rosalee rushed back to the office and caught me picking up my morning patient records.

"Dr. Dionne! We have an emergency in room 3 and..."

Then pausing for a moment, she motioned for me to step out of the office into the kennel where no clients could hear what she had to say.

"What is it Rosalee?" I asked.

"Dr. Dionne, I think Mr. Johnson is a *hobo!*"

Rosalee showed me the very incomplete record.

"See, no home address or telephone. I even asked him if this was true and he said yes."

For once, Rosalee had a reason to be concerned about payment, although in 1969 *hobo* was a term that was no longer used. I walked into the exam room and met my first homeless person.

I liked Otis right away and no one could not help but love his friendly, but injured dog, with two initials for a name.

Otis was quite sincere and concerned about PT. I could see that right away. Meanwhile, PT was busy licking my hand. Then starting my exam, I liked to check everything else first before concentrating on the swollen paw. The little dog could use a bath, but other than that he was very healthy.

The swollen paw was typical of a trap injury. Everything below the trap line was swollen due to the injury which was hindering the circulation. Above the trap line, the leg was normal and not swollen at all.

Turning to Otis, I explained, "We need to take an x-ray of his paw to make sure there is no fracture. Then we need to gently clean the paw, wrap it with a dressing and give him an antibiotic and some medication to reduce swelling. The former gunner's mate, now hobo, said he would wait outside until we were done.

Sandy took the x-ray while I held PT steady on the x-ray table so he wouldn't move. There were no fractures, but I was still concerned about the circulation to his toes.

I found Otis sitting on a large rock at the end of the parking lot with his duffle bag by his side.

"Mr. Johnson, there's no fracture, but it would be best if he stays in the hospital so we can check to see if his circulation returns to his paw."

Otis had a very worried look on his face both for his dog, and how he was going to pay for all the medical expenses.

I sensed his concern.

"Are finances going to be a problem?" I asked.

It seemed like a crazy question to ask an unemployed homeless man, but you never know.

Otis reached into his pocket and pulled out a small wad of bills held together with a rubber band.

"Here doc, I hope this will cover it. It's all the money I have in the world."

Just then Mike walked out of the kennel entrance and headed for Otis and myself. He had heard about the hobo in the army uniform from Rosalee, who was still in a state of disbelief.

Mike, a veteran himself, shook Otis's hand and wanted to know what branch of the service he was in. Fifteen minutes later, a deal was made between Mike and the Vietnam vet. Otis insisted on making a down-payment of twenty-five dollars as a sign of good faith, and he promised to pay the balance when he could.

Mike turned to me, winked, and ordered me to take care of the man. So now it was my turn to be shocked. This was very unlike our business manager.

Otis asked, "What time tomorrow can I find out how my PT is doing?"

"Well, my lunch hour is from noon to 1 p.m.. What if we have lunch together?"

Otis shook my hand and flashed his charming smile. He then turned and walked into the vacant field behind the hospital.

* * *

The next day we met for lunch as planned, and the day after as well. Otis was quite open and unashamed that he was homeless.

"Doc, lots of good men are homeless. They just had some bad breaks."

I really didn't know that much about the Vietnam war, other than the fact that it seemed rather senseless to me.

Otis's experience as a gunner's mate was quite fascinating.

"Doc, do you know what PT stands for?"

"Uh...patrol boat."

Smiling, he said, "Nope."

"Okay, I give up. Tell me."

"It stands for Patrol Torpedo boat."

"What! I thought just submarines could shoot torpedoes."

Otis went on to explain how during World War II, torpedoes were launched from PT boats at enemy vessels. The speed and maneuverability of these small vessels allowed them to get in close, fire the torpedo and get out quickly.

He continued on about his education and special weapons training. How he hoped to attend college, but his medical condition has put that on hold.

"The doctors think that I will get over being shell-shocked, but I'm worried about all the *Agent Orange* that I've been exposed to."

"How did you get exposed to Agent Orange on a PT boat?"

"The Army would spray that stuff all along the banks of the Mekong River to defoliate all the plants and bushes so that the Viet Cong would have no place to hide. They said it was non-toxic and harmless to humans, but I find that hard to believe. The helicopter would spray that stuff sometimes right over our boat, and it would settle all over the crew. Maybe that's part of my memory problem."

"I couldn't tell you anything about that Otis."

"Do you know how Agent Orange got its name?"

"Otis, by now you should know that I'm not hip to anything military."

"Agent Orange gets it name because it's stored in large drums that have a painted orange band around the middle. They would mix this stuff *(Dioxin)* 50:50 with diesel fuel or kerosene and spray it everywhere even on the Vietnamese crops and rice paddies." (It has been estimated that close to twenty million gallons were sprayed, until it was finally discontinued in 1971. The Red Cross of Vietnam claims that one million people have been disabled and four-hundred-thousand killed from Agent Orange.)

After lunch was over, I gave Otis an update about his dog.

"PT's paw is doing fine, all the swelling is down, but there is a problem with one of his toes--the small one on the outside didn't heal. It's dead and has to be amputated. So the surgery will be done tomorrow. I will put on a light cast to keep the area protected until we take the stitches out in 7-10 days. He can be released tomorrow evening if you can keep the cast dry."

The surgery was not difficult and went smoothly. Otis took PT into his care and returned in eight days. I removed the cast and the stitches. Everything had healed well. PT could walk normally and jumped into Otis's arms and proceeded to lick his face.

The next day Danny picked them up in his delivery truck, and they headed for Philadelphia.

That was the last time I would see my homeless friend and his cute dog.

* * *

Eighteen months later a letter arrived at Somerset Veterinary Group. Doris, who was in charge of accounts receivable, opened the letter, which contained the balance of Otis Johnson's unpaid account.

"Mike look at this. It's from that homeless man and his dog. He paid his bill in full."

"Of course he did. He's a Navy vet," Mike said proudly.

Enclosed in the letter was a lengthy thank you note and an update of their travels.

After leaving Somerville with Danny, they were picked up in Philadelphia by another trucker, who took the pair to Baltimore. Then they were passed on to yet another trucker by using the CB radio. After a few transfers from one truck to another, they reached Jacksonsville, Florida.

They stayed with Otis's brother, Junior, for the winter, and come spring they set out for the west coast-- Los Angeles, to see his sister Ruth.

Ruth fell in love with PT immediately, and introduced Otis and his talented dog to a friend who worked as a *wrangler*. A wrangler trains animals for both television and the movies.

PT landed two small parts in one movie and one television show. In addition, Otis was hired to be an assistant wrangler to learn the trade. He was also feeling better thanks to a new doctor who diagnosed his problem as *post-traumatic stress disorder*. He put him on medication to control the nightmares and panic attacks and is giving him weekly counseling.

The note ended with:

Thank you and God bless you all.
Love, Otis Johnson and PT

26

Margot

A pet wants the same things you do...
Love, Happiness and a Place to call Home.
Author

My seventeen-year-old granddaughter, Emily, was attending a month long summer program at the prestigious CAP21 (Collaborative Arts Project) in Manhattan. Upon graduation from high school next year, her hope was to attend CAP21's intensive two-year program in dance, acting and vocal performance. (At the end of the month program, the faculty at the school encouraged Emily to apply for admission - which she did, and was accepted.)

It was her first time away from home living on her own for such an extended time. We received daily updates on her classes and adventures in the *Big Apple*. She loved everything about the school and the City. Midway through the summer program, it was time for a family visit.

* * *

July 2012

Tina, our daughter Terri, her other two children (our grandchildren), Desiree and Zachary, and I piled into their minivan, and headed east from our homes in the State College area of Pennsylvania to New York. It was a beautiful Sunday morning, and we arrived just in time for lunch. My son, Ed, also took the train from New Haven, CT, into the City for a mini-family reunion.

After lunch, Emily asked if we could do something that she had been wishing to do while in New York City.

"What is it?" Terri asked.

"Well, could we... uh... walk across the Brooklyn Bridge?"

After a few puzzled looks, we all agreed that it would be fun. Tina, having been born in Brooklyn, was especially eager.

"Are you allowed to walk across the bridge?" asked the clueless grandfather.

"Of course you are Pop-Pop."

Arriving at the bridge in lower Manhattan, we saw hordes of people walking across the bridge on this beautiful day. We discovered how popular this walk had become. A raised, protected lane was built just for pedestrians. It was a festive affair for walkers, joggers, rollerbladers, and cyclists crossing both to and from Brooklyn.

As we strolled across the bridge we came to a plaque commemorating the construction of the bridge in 1883 in honor of John A. Roebling and Washington Roebling.

As we stopped to read the inscription, I asked my grandchildren, "Did you know that when I worked in Somerville, New Jersey, I met and became very good friends with Margot Roebling, a member of this family? I took care of her many dogs for several years, and we're still good friends today."

"Wow, that must have been way cool," said my twelve-year-old grandson, Zac.

After spending a pleasant day, we said our good-byes to Emily and Ed and headed home.

* * *

During the five hour car ride, my history-loving grandson said, "Hey Pop-Pop, tell us more about the Bridge and the Roeblings."

"Well Zac, I'm far from an expert, but this is what I do know. The Brooklyn Bridge is one of the oldest and largest suspension bridges in the United States. It was completed in 1883, and it connects the boroughs of Manhattan and Brooklyn by spanning the East River."

"Okay, I know all that from reading the plaque."

"Hold on, I'm just getting warmed up. John Augustus Roebling was a German immigrant, who designed several bridges. The most famous is the Brooklyn Bridge. He started his plans way back in 1868—a hundred and forty-four years ago. Everything was going well until he injured his foot during the surveying. His foot was caught between a ferry boat and a piling. His toes were crushed and needed surgery, but after the surgery he developed tetanus and died."

"Then who actually built the Bridge?"

"His thirty-two-year-old son, Washington Roebling. He was also an engineer. Washington took over because he knew all the plans and what to do. But the sad thing was Washington also became injured and sick during the construction phase of the bridge in 1880."

"What happened to him?"

"Washington was working under the river in what's called a caisson. Compressed air is pumped in so the workers can breathe. They had to construct the foundation for the bridge on the floor of the East River. Something happened, I'm not sure what, but if you come up too fast from under the water you can get decompression sickness or the *bends*. That's what happened to Washington; back then they called it *Caisson's Disease*."

"Did he die?"

"No, but his lungs were damaged, and he had to be confined to his bed. So he never was able to visit the bridge construction site again."

"Well then *who* finished the Brooklyn Bridge?"

"His wife, Emily, took over as the chief engineer. Washington taught her engineering principles, mathematics and construction from his bed. Emily Warren Roebling became the first woman to be a field engineer. So she finished the bridge for her husband in 1883."

"That's some story," said Zac.

"Then your friend Margot. How does she fit into the picture?" asked Desiree.

"Washington and Emily had a son whom they named John A. Roebling after his grandfather."

"Is Margot his daughter?"

"Sort of. It's a little complicated. When Margot was fifteen years old her mother died. Her father had medical problems and couldn't adequately look after the young teenager. So Margot was assigned a guardian, her aunt, Helen Roebling, wife of John. She was Margot's mother's sister. Five years later Margot was adopted by Helen, and she became a Roebling."

"That's a little sad," said my grandson.

"But it's also happy that her aunt could look after her," added my wise eighteen-year-old granddaughter, Desiree.

"Okay, so now tell us how you met Margot," Zac continued.

Since we had four more hours to go, I let my mind flashback to those early years at Somerset Veterinary Group and answered the question.

* * *

April 1970

The note in my office mailbox read:
Dr. D - see me before your 4 p.m. appointment-- Mike.

Looking at my afternoon appointment sheet at the 4 p.m. spot, it said: *New Account- Referral- Roebling- Peter Pan- in pain and trouble walking.*

I also noticed that the office had given me *forty-five* minutes for the appointment. My first reaction was that this must be a mistake. Dr. North and Dr. Coburn are the ones who get the referral cases, not the new kid.

It was time for another encounter with Mike. I wasn't upset about the case, but I needed to know, how did I get the referral. It was my first one, and I was flattered. Mike and I had our little meeting in the doctors' lounge.

"Doc, Miss Roebling was referred by one of your new fans, Alice Lawson, and this is no ordinary referral case. Do you know who Miss Margot Roebling is?"

"No."

"Have you ever heard about the Roebling family?"

"Nope."

Mike took an impatient drag on his cigarette and blew a cloud of smoke toward the ceiling.

"You have heard of the Brooklyn Bridge? Right?"

Happily I answered, "Yes of course."

Mike then stood up, extinguished his cigarette, and adjusted his belt and pulled up his trousers, and said, "Doc, the Roebling family built the Bridge. So don't screw up the case!"

"Don't worry," I weakly promised.

Thinking to myself, *My first referral, I should be over-joyed, but now all I am is nervous.*

* * *

Two hours later - 4 p.m.

My imagination was running wild. I was trying to picture what Margot Roebling was going to look like. For some reason, I expected a very old woman with a cane accompanied by a servant. And her dog, Peter Pan, had to be a spoiled-rotten purebred of some kind loaded with bows and pom-poms. Surely it had to be a toy breed of some type with a name like *Peter Pan.*

Walking into the room, I was quite surprised to find a charming lady only a few years older than myself. Margot was about five-foot-two-inches tall, with short brown hair, hazel eyes somewhat hidden behind a pair of eyeglasses. She was dressed in a plain blue skirt and a white blouse open at the collar. There were no diamonds and pearls, just a plain gold watch on her left wrist. She offered a pleasant and hopeful smile as I entered the room. The doctor is supposed to put the patient at ease, but in this case she was the one that put me at ease.

In her hand was clutched a manila folder with her dog's records and a larger envelope containing the x-rays. Margot stepped forward and extended her hand.

"Hi, I'm Margot Roebling, and this is my dog, Peter. I hope you can help him."

"Well, I'm Dr. Dionne and I'll do my best."

I turned and looked down at the patient who was lying somewhat uncomfortably on the floor. He was a beagle, not a small one, but a quite large, overweight, ten-year-old, tri-colored one. He wore no bows or bangles of any kind, just a simple collar.

Margot was very organized and rattled off Peter's lengthy history. I had him stand up and could immediately tell he was in a lot of pain. His back was arched, and he was reluctant to walk.

"Let's check him on the floor instead of lifting him up onto the exam table. He'll be more comfortable there."

I was also thinking about the health of my back by not lifting him up. I checked Mr. Pan and then examined the x-ray.

"Miss Roebling, your dog has symptoms of a possible disc problem in the middle of his back. This x-ray is rather hazy, and its focus is on the lower back, not the middle. So we need to take another x-ray, and we can do it while you wait."

"Wonderful, I'll do whatever you say," a confident Margot replied.

Since Peter Pan could no longer *fly* to the x-ray room, I carefully lifted the forty-plus-pounds of *dead weight* off the floor and proceeded to the second floor. Carrying dogs up and down the flight of steps was not all that much fun.

Peter cooperated beautifully, and the x-ray showed evidence of a ruptured disc and arthritic bone spurs on his thoracic vertebrae. Returning to the exam room, I informed Margot of our findings.

"Does he need surgery?" she asked.

"No, I don't think so, but we will need to change his previous medication."

"Excuse me Doctor Dionne, his medication was basically, let's wait and see what happens and feed him buttered toast!"

"Oh."

I gave him a long-acting injection of a steroid to reduce inflammation, some medication for pain to take at home if needed, and a diet to reduce his weight.

"Doctor, the diet plan will be the hardest part. Peter can be unbelievably stubborn when it comes to food."

"Yes, I know the beagle is a member of the hound family, or to be more specific, the *chow-hound family.*"

Miss Roebling laughed, thanked me and made an appointment for a recheck in ten days.

* * *

The Recheck.

Peter Pan came *flying* into the exam room--figuratively speaking of course. Holding onto the end of the leash for dear life was Margot.

"Peter slow down, you're hurting my arm!"

"So I can see that this *puppy* is much better." I smiled with a great sense of relief.

Mr. Pan passed his recheck exam with flying colors, and even lost one pound. Something that he had *never* done before. The pain and trouble walking had disappeared completely, but to be on the safe side, I gave him one more shot. Margot was so happy that she made appointments for her two other dogs, both German shepherds-- Wendy and Vicky.

So the nimble pooch and his happy mistress returned to *Never-Never Land*, and this was the start of our friendship.

Soon I was getting many referrals from Margot, who had many friends in the Bernardsville and Far Hills dog circles.

* * *

One year later - 1971

Margot had made an appointment for Wendy to check a skin and coat problem. She was accompanied by a man, whom she introduced as John DeHope. John was not a client, but came along for two reasons. First, he seemed to be smitten by Miss Roebling, and she by him. Second, he needed to check out this new vet that he was getting tired of hearing about from Margot.

John was about the same age as Margot,

maybe a little older I guessed. He was about five-foot-ten-inches-tall and 175 lbs. He had blue eyes, a broad smile and was losing his hair across the top of his head in that hopeless male-pattern-baldness syndrome. He was starting to get a little paunch in the mid-section, but still appeared to be in good shape. Margot explained that John was a well-known professional dog handler of German shepherds, and he traveled all over the country to dog shows.

While I examined Wendy, John took the opportunity to *grill* the vet with questions. I could tell that I was being *interviewed* by a knowledgeable dog person. John did not let up until he asked all of his questions to his satisfaction. I must have passed the exam because he made an appointment for his best show dog whom he called Rocky or sometimes Reno.

John left and said, "I'll see you in a couple of days."

* * *

True to his word, John returned with the most beautiful German shepherd that I had ever seen. His dog's full name was Select Champion Cobert's Reno of Lakeside. Reno would later add the title of ROM to the end of his name. The ROM stands for Register of Merit and is only given to those few dogs that have produced many offspring who have obtained the title of Champion inside the show ring.

John's first words were, "Listen, do you mind if I call you Ed? I have trouble with the *Doctor* thing."

"Sure, if I can call you John."

We shook hands, and our friendship was formed that day in the small exam room.

"So how did you acquire Rocky, or is it Reno?" I asked.

"I call him either one or sometimes just the *Rock*. And I don't own him. I'm just his handler, but the thing is, he really is my dog. At least Reno thinks he is. He lives with me, I take care of him, supervise his breedings and take him to dog shows. That's my job. I do show other dogs for other people as well, but Rocky here is my baby."

On hearing his name, Rocky stood on his hind legs and put both paws on John's chest and enthusiastically licked his face.

John laughed and made the Rock sit and said, "See how he loves me! I want you to check him over from head to toe and do blood work or any lab tests that you think are necessary. He's that important. Most people including myself consider him to be the top shepherd in the U.S. right now."

Rocky was four years old and 80 lbs. of solid muscle. He was black and tan in color. Rocky had a large masculine head, erect ears, broad chest and a long back ending in a sloping rump. His hindquarters and hind-legs were muscular and powerful.

I started my physical exam and Reno stood perfectly still as if he were being judged at a dog show.

"Ed, see how easy he is to examine? The other two things that I love about this dog is his temperament, and the way he moves in the ring. His gait is so fluid that he seems to be floating on air. Of course, Rocky makes me run my butt off in that ring as he follows right along side of me. Which reminds me," looking down at his own mid-section, "I've gained a little too much weight since I've met Margot. She's a very good cook."

John talked on and on while I checked the fabulous Reno. Then I drew blood samples for a routine profile to make sure everything was functioning normally.

"Ed, I've had his hips x-rayed, and they were certified OFA excellent (Orthopedic Foundation of America). No hip dysplasia, but we should also x-ray his elbows. So can we set that up? And so many shepherds get back problems when they get older, let's do his back as well."

"Okay, no problem. Let's do it now, then we can have lunch together while the x-rays are being developed, and the lab work is being done."

* * *

Over lunch, it was my turn to ask John questions.

"How did you get into the dog business?"

John laughed, "I'll have to give you the short version. Growing up in Newark was rough. I had very little supervision and was mostly on my own. Margot went to boarding schools, and I went to the *School of Hard Knocks*. Reaching the age of nineteen, I had to make a choice. Continue as I was doing and probably end up in some type of trouble, or enlist in the Army and try to make something of my life."

There was a bit of an awkward pause as John thought back to his youth. I knew it was best not to pry and moved on.

"So what happened in the service?"

John brightened up, "I got to travel overseas to Germany, and that's when I volunteered to work with the K-9 Corps. I fell in love with the German shepherd which was the most common breed used at that time by the Army. I read everything that I could find about training and obedience work with this breed."

"Now I want to hear about your time in the K-9 Corps."

"We had some excellent dogs to work with and Staff Sergeant Jack Dolan headed our training unit. Jack was a career Army man who was all business when it came to his dogs. He worked my tail off, but I learned one heck of a lot from him about training. Each dog was tested and trained using the German method called *Schutzhund*, where the trainers are able to evaluate each dog's capability for police work, military duty, search and rescue and so on. In order to pass the rigorous testing and training, these dogs need a strong bond with their handler and be very protective of him or her. Above all, they must all want to work and be very intelligent. They have to be strong, agile, and have endurance and a good nose for scenting."

"It sounds like you learned quite a bit about training dogs in the Army."

"I did," as he smiled proudly.

I continued my grilling of my new friend like he had done to me, "So what are your plans now?"

John paused for a moment while he reached into his shirt pocket and pulled out a pack of cigarettes.

He lit one up and said, "First, I'm going to try and give up these cigarettes. Margot doesn't want me to smoke. So don't you dare tell her that I'm having one; she thinks that I quit. Second, I'm looking to start a boarding kennel where we will do grooming and offer obedience training classes for my clients.

I even have the name already picked out for the kennel."

"What is it?"

"*The Woof and Purr Inn*," he whispered.

"That's a great name," I said.

"Well, don't tell anyone just yet. I wouldn't want them stealing the name."

"Don't worry. It will be kept secret under Doctor-Patient confidentiality."

* * *

After lunch was finished, we returned to the hospital. John took Reno out of his cage while I looked at the x-rays and read the lab results. The blood tests were all normal as I expected, but I was shocked to see the x-ray of Rocky's back.

"John, look at this! There is a small one-inch nail in Rocky's back. How did this get there?"

"No way! Let me see," he said, but the x-ray didn't lie.

There it was.

It was stuck in the thick back muscles running parallel to the spine. We could find no entrance wound or tenderness over the area. It was apparently something that had happened quite a long time ago.

"Should we operate and take it out?" asked the worried dog trainer.

"We could do that, but in doing so we might damage some muscle trying to get it out because the nail is deeply embedded. I think we should do nothing unless he becomes sore and tender over the area."

"Okay, I will rely on your judgment."

(The years went by, and that nail stayed put and never did cause any problems.)

* * *

There was hardly a week that went by that I didn't have some contact with Margot or John, either in the office or by telephone. And sometimes, I would receive a call at home like the one on a snowy evening in January of 1972.

"Ed, it's Margot. We have a problem! We have two dogs delivering puppies at the same time. John is upstairs with Pandy, and she seems to be having a hard time. Now Vicky has started contractions, and I'm downstairs with her, but I've never whelped puppies before."

"Hold it right there, Margot, I'll be right over."

I explained to Tina what was happening, kissed the kids good-night, gathered my black doctor's bag and headed out the door. It was a short drive from our home in Pluckemin to Margot's estate in Bernardsville.

I parked my car behind the house and walked in through the kitchen door. Margot didn't have to lock the doors, not with a house-full of German shepherds. Margot was in the bedroom, and I arrived just as Vicky produced her first puppy. A healthy looking female. I clamped the puppy's umbilical cord and removed the placenta. Margot began rubbing the puppy and stimulated it to take a breath. Vicky took over from there and began to lick and lick her new daughter.

I ran upstairs as John was now pacing nervously. Pandy was contracting, but no puppy was coming.

"When did the contractions start?" I asked John.

"I'd say a good hour or so ago."

Pandy was a large all black German shepherd, who was very loyal and protective of John. She had been Shutzhund trained. Since I valued all of my various body parts, I had John sit at her head and hold her while I put on a pair of latex gloves. I had to examine Pandy to see what the problem was. She had a previous litter two years ago with no difficulties, but now she was seven and approaching the end of her breeding days. I usually recommended no further breeding after eight years old.

Pandy did not object to my exam. I could feel the rump of one puppy in the birth canal but no hindlegs.

It was a breech birth.

As I was explaining this to John, I heard a yell from the bottom of the staircase.

"Ed, another puppy is coming!"

"Oh no, hold on John. I'll be right back."

I flew down the stairs and into the bedroom just in time to deliver a second puppy. Another healthy female. As soon as the puppy was out, I handed her over to Margot.

"Here you go, just rub and give her to Vicky."

I then ran out of the bedroom and back up the staircase trying to take two steps at a time until I stumbled and almost fell flat on my face. Picking myself up, I hurried back a little more carefully to help John and Pandy.

I put on a new pair of gloves and inserted my hand into Pandy's birth canal. This time I was able to work the puppy's butt to one side just enough to be able to pull backwards on one hind leg. I repeated this on the other side and grabbed the other leg. From here the puppy was now in a normal birth delivery position and Pandy gave one more strong push and the puppy entered the birth canal where I could now deliver the puppy. Fortunately the puppy was a strong, large male which John worked on while I ran back down the stairs after Margot announced, "Ed, the next one is coming!"

Two hours later, it was all over. Pandy had two large puppies, Vicky had eight. The proud father, Rocky, was downstairs in his crate and thought to himself, *Oh boy, more puppies*.

John said, "I don't think that I want to ever have two females due on the same day again."

"Me either, fella."

* * *

Margot and John were married in 1973. John moved in with his new bride. He also opened The Woof and Purr Inn as planned. John never did quit smoking, even though he tried many times. Margot became very active with the area animal shelter - Somerset County Humane Society, where she served for thirty years as the director. She rescued and placed many dogs and cats into loving homes including her own. A few hard-to-place unwanted dogs were added to the DeHope household, which kept me busy with their medical problems. I often made house calls to their home for this purpose. Tina and my three young children often came along to swim in their pool and have a picnic. All of their dogs were doted on by this loving and unusual couple. John and Margot came from very different backgrounds, but they had one common and important trait - they each had a warm heart for a cold nose.

John and Margot Roebling Dehope and "family"

John showing Author's dog, Misty

Champion R.O.M. German Shepherd, Reno

John with Reno, a.k.a. "Rocky"

27

Parker, Sudlow and Rachel the Raccoon

Any glimpse into the life of an animal quickens our own and makes it so much the larger and better in every way.

John Muir

As a child, my parents, brother and I delighted in the classic comedic duos of our day. Whether it be Laurel and Hardy or Abbott and Costello in the early movie and television shows, or later when comedy was king of the airways, I thought the best was Ralph Kramden and Ed Norton. Each week we looked forward to their hit television series, *The Honeymooners*.

It seems to me that their style and appeal was that of polar opposites-- with their obvious difference in body size to their unique personalities. The plump, scheming and excitable Ralph Kramden as portrayed by Jackie Gleason was a lovable opposite to the bumbling fall guy and not too bright Ed Norton played by

Art Carney. These three comedic duos all achieved fame and fortune. They became household names.

* * *

This story is about one more duo who were not famous or rich. Neither appeared on television let alone the movies. But they did make me laugh. David Sudlow and Festus Parker were avid coon hunters that I met one very early morning on emergency duty.

* * *

The phone call from the answering service came through at 2:20 a.m. Any call after midnight usually found me in bed and bordering on a comatose state. The phone might have rung the rest of the night if it wasn't for my light-sleeping spouse. With two young children, no noise went unheard in our household.

By the second ring, Tina started with shaking my shoulder and said, "Ed, wake up!"

This evening as the phone continued to ring, she went to stage two-- yanking the pillow out from under my head. She then turned the table lamp on for extra encouragement.

I started to mumble, "Go away, I'm awake."

Hearing these words, she immediately proceeded to stage three-- off with the covers, and one or two size 7 1/2 feet planted in any body part within reach, followed by a determined push.

On the eighth or ninth ring, I was out of bed and answered the telephone with a hoarse, "Hello." Angel, the answering service operator and telephone friend, chuckled and asked, "Did I wake you, Dr. Dionne?"

"Oh no, I was just doing some push-ups and sit-ups."

Getting more serious, Angel then said, "A Mr. Sudlow called. His dog is bleeding. He was bitten in the foot and ear."

"Okay, what's his telephone number?"

"He called from a payphone, and said he'd meet you at the hospital. And just hung up. I'm sorry."

"It's okay Angel, I'm leaving after one more set of push-ups."

We always wanted to talk to the client before meeting them on an emergency call. Some of these late night problems could have happened two days ago, and just now became an annoyance to the owner.

It was a very cool almost cold October night, and I drove our station wagon with the window open hoping to blow any lingering sleepy cobwebs from my brain. Something whispered to me that I needed to be fully alert.

* * *

Mr. Sudlow and a friend were standing outside their dilapidated pickup truck that held three large wooden dog crates. I drove past them into the employee parking area and gave a quick glance at the two men. Something was strange about them other than one was short and round and the other much taller and skinny. Maybe it was their clothing. They appeared to be identically dressed with strange hats on their heads. It was dark so I couldn't see that well.

I parked the car and entered the rear door to the hospital, turned on the lights and let my new clients into Exam Room 2. Now I could clearly see the outfits.

Halloween was a week away, but these two looked like a pair of over-aged trick-or-treaters. Their *costumes* were in fact identical. They wore matching coonskin hats with long raccoon tails dangling from the back and blue shirts underneath grayish, long furry raccoon vests. Their pants were blue jeans held up by a wide black belt with an over-sized buckle embossed with a raccoon. Each wore mud-caked, well-scuffed hiking boots.

"Thanks for seeing us Doc! I'm David Sudlow from Bound Brook," said the large in girth but short in stature gentleman. He extended his thick hand to shake mine. I couldn't help but notice his silver ring with the black raccoon in the center. He also appeared a bit out of breath, and his cheeks were sagging and very flushed. Sweat was trickling down his brow even though it was a very cool night. David took off his coonskin cap and set it on one of the exam room chairs. He was almost bald on the top of his head. His remaining salt and pepper hair was brushed back into a tiny ponytail held together by a rubber band. The ponytail was so small it didn't seem to be worth the effort. His hazel eyes were sparkling with excitement and urgency of the late night visit.

* * *

"Oh, excuse my manners. This here is my *best-est* buddy, Festus Parker. He was such a pain in the neck as a kid we called him *Festus the Pestus*."

This play on words caused Mr. Sudlow to laugh so hard that he choked and gagged on his saliva at the end of the joke.

Mr. Parker just said, "Howdy,"-- no handshake.

His clothing was a bit more raggedy and dirty than his friend. His hair was long and oily black that seemed in dire need of a shampoo. Festus had a long pointed nose and unusual eyes. The left eye was blue and the right eye a light brown. It was hard for me to maintain eye contact with him for very long. Festus was quite thin and could have borrowed a few extra pounds from David's excess baggage compartment.

I also learned that David Sudlow was called *Suds* by his friends, or more accurately his only friend, Festus Parker. He received his nickname because of the similarity to his last name, and from the fact that he liked his beer with a big head of suds on top.

Festus acquired his unusual name as a result of a disagreement between his momma and poppa when he was born. His mother, Frances, wanted him to be named after her. While poppa insisted on his name, Estis. They eventually compromised with Festus. As the talk slowed, I proceeded to make out a new patient record for their three-year-old male, blue tick coon hound named Jeb.

"By the way, where's Jeb, and what happened?" I asked.

"He's in his crate on the pickup. Festus, go fetch him for the Doc."

* * *

Festus hurried out and carried the large hound

back into the exam room and set him down onto the table.

The wounds had stopped bleeding temporarily. But one good shake of the head would get the two inch gash on the tip of his ear bleeding again. I quickly put a gauze pad on the ear, flipped it up over the top of his head, and wrapped gauze around his entire head to hold it in place.

Any head-shaking and bleeding would be sprayed around the exam room and cover the three of us with a multitude of red polka dots of blood. The bite wound on his left front paw also needed to be cleaned and sutured along with the ear. I gave Jeb an intravenous injection that would temporarily knock him out for a half-hour or so.

"How did this all happen to Jeb?" I asked while checking for any other missed wounds or problems.

David said, "Do you want to tell him, Festus?"

"Nope."

"Well, we was out coon hunting."

"At night?" I interrupted.

"Of course, when do you Yankees hunt coon?" Festus interjected and finally laughed. "Won't ketch many during the day."

More laughter this time from both of them. Maybe it was the late night or the ridiculous twosome in front of me, but I decided to join the comedy act.

"Gee, maybe that's why my luck has been so bad hunting coons! I need to hunt at night," I said and smiled.

"Doc, ya need a good dog too. Don't git nothin' but a blue tick."

"Okay, it would probably also help to git a rifle," I responded with a straight face.

More laughter.

David slapped Festus on the back and almost knocked him over onto the now sleeping coon hound.

* * *

Jeb was a mixture of three colors. His short hair coat was white and black which when mingled together produced areas of navy blue. There was tan or rust-colored patches above each eye on the eye-brow area, on his ears and several speckles of rust on the lower legs and paws. Jeb had the long floppy ears typical of hounds and was extremely well-muscled. I estimated his weight to be about seventy pounds, and he had a long whip-like tail.

* * *

I proceeded to clean the wounds on his ear and paw. "Seriously guys, tell me about coon hunting."

"Wa'll, I'll tell him Festus," as David began his hunting lesson. "Assuming you have a rifle and a coon hound, it's best to go out after 11 p.m. Coons are *knockternal* you know. And it's best to dress like us-- gives you the proper smell. We also take a lantern and a searchlight."

Festus interrupted, "You might also want to do your hunting in the woods."

Everyone laughed, but I think he was serious.

"Shut up Festus! Doc's not that dumb. We also keep our hounds on a leash until they pick up a coon scent. Then we let 'em go, turn our flashlights on and start runnin'."

Again Festus interrupted, "I run. David can't run too fast, but he clears a nice path for the way back. I calls him the bulldozer-- he just plows over small trees and bushes."

David made a fist and threatened Festus, "One more time with the fat jokes and pow-- I'm going to send you to the moon!"

I was busy placing sutures in each wound as David continued on about the proper way to coon hunt.

"The hounds will start howling and baying as they chase the coon."

For effect, Festus gave a good imitation of a hound's bay in the exam room.

"That's enough now, Festus. Let me finish the story. Raccoons have short legs and can't run nearly as fast as my dogs. But, they can swim pretty darn good though. Anyway, coons are intelligent. Actually, come to think of it, they're smarter than Festus."

"Hey, David, you're the one that's goin' to the moon!" as Festus showed his fist.

"Okay, how about a truce. Let me finish the story for Doc. So the raccoon will almost always climb a tree so the dogs can't git 'em. The dogs will surround the tree, stand on their hind legs, put their front feet up on the tree and make a terrible racket."

Another howl from Festus.

"Once we catch up, we got that coon right where we want him. We just shine our light up into the tree and take aim."

"Well, what happened tonight?" I asked while bandaging the paw and ear flap.

"Wa'll, we run into one mean, feisty varmint tonight. That coon come flyin' down that tree, head first and jumped on poor Jeb. I couldn't shoot for fear of hitting Jeb."

Festus added, "So the coon got in some good licks before our other dog, Belle, could pull that coon off. Then Jeb finished him off for good."

"Have your dogs been vaccinated for rabies?" I asked seriously.

"Of course, every year-- don't want them to go mad. I seen that once when I was a kid. My pappy shot that dog dead," David assured me.

Finishing up with some antibiotics for Jeb, I asked, "What part of Jersey are you boys from?"

At first they thought I was serious then laughed, "Are you kidding, we're from the great state of Tennessee. We both growed up in the Smokey Mountains near Gatlinburg."

"Why are you here in New Jersey, no more coons left in Tennessee?"

"No, we lost our jobs at the plant, so we packed up and came here. My aunt said they were hiring at the *Miller-Hastings* plant. So here we are. And Festus here is writing a book."

"Is that right?" I wasn't sure if I should ask the title or not, but since we were now all friends, I did.

"*Hunting the Wily Coon,*" Festus replied proudly.

"I think the *wily* part will catch people's eye. What do ya think Doc?" asked David.

"Sounds interesting, probably will make the *New York Times* best seller list."

"The what list?" Festus asked.

Before I could answer, David suggested, "Hey Doc, you should write about some of your animal stories. I bet people would be interested in that."

I laughed, "I'm not much of a writer, but may-be someday I'll write them down for my grand-kids. And if I do, you and Festus here will surely be in the book."

"Doc, I'll swap you a free copy of my book for one of yours," Festus bartered.

"It's a deal."

"Say Doc, you know when we go huntin', we don't carry much cash with us. So if we give you twelve dollars and fifty cents tonight, can we pay the rest next week?" David asked.

"Sure." Thinking to myself, *How am I going to explain to Mike that two new account coon hunters from Tennessee wearing coonskin caps didn't come back and pay their bill as promised.*

But they did.

* * *

I also thought that I would never see them again. But three months later, in the middle of January, Rosalee asked me about a Mr. Sudlow who would like to have his pet raccoon, Rachel, spayed.

"Dr. Dionne, is that possible? Do people have raccoons as pets? Do they spay them? I said that I would call him back."

"Rosalee, most normal people in New Jersey do not, but I can tell you that Mr. Sudlow is probably serious. Make an appointment for him so I can check this Rachel before I can say yes or no."

"Okay, thanks Dr. Dionne. I will. I just can't imagine having a raccoon for a pet."

The following week, it was an encore performance by Sudlow and Parker. They were both cleanly dressed this time, Festus had shaved and washed his hair, but they still wore the raccoon vests and coonskin caps. Their outfits kept them warm in winter.

Walking into Exam Room 3, I greeted my

old hunting buddies. “How’s that blue tick hound of yours?” I asked.

“He’s fine. All healed up. Festus took out the stitches for you.”

“Gee, thanks,” I quietly moaned.

“Well, here’s our little baby Rachel. She’s two years old, and we want to have her fixed.” David opened the cage and pulled out Rachel.

“And don’t worry none Doc, she don’t bite,” Festus added.

* * *

When a client makes such a promise they usually mean that they *hope* that they don’t bite. I had never been this close to and handled a raccoon before. Her fur was amazingly thick and soft. She weighed twelve pounds. Raccoons are omnivorous and will eat almost anything including plants and fruit.

They are likened to bandits and thieves because of their black mask and habit of stealing food out of garbage cans or anywhere else they can find it. They aren’t afraid either of coming on your porch or sneaking into the house or attic if need be. Their head has a short muzzle, and they have teeth like a dog or cat. Rachel’s tail had the familiar black rings of all raccoons, but it was her feet that most interested me.

She had five finger-like toes. Raccoons like to *feel* their food, often by dipping the food and their feet into water. This is not necessarily for washing the food but for increasing their tactile sensitivity located on special receptors on their feet. They don’t have a thumb like the monkey, so this limits what they can do with their feet somewhat, but they are still pretty dexterous with these *hands*.

* * *

Festus was correct, Rachel didn't bite. I could handle her easily. She was wiggly and made various raccoon sounds that I'm sure meant something. David assisted with the holding while I gave her a vaccine for canine distemper which can infect raccoons as well as dogs. I also consented to do my first raccoon spay. I told the two *night-owls* that it could be difficult afterwards.

A clever raccoon just might decide to take out her own stitches-- prematurely, before everything was healed. This would result in a big problem and a big hernia or a life threatening evisceration.

Festus and David suddenly looked worried. Even though they actively hunted and shot wild raccoons, the thought that something harmful might happen to Rachel was of concern. Giving a name to an animal, any animal, results in a more personal relationship. A raccoon is something wild that lives in the woods, but *Rachel the raccoon* is suddenly more than that because she has a name.

"What are we goin' to do about the stitches, Doc?" David asked.

"I have to admit that this is my first raccoon spay. So I was thinking about using a subcuticular suture pattern."

"A what?" asked Festus.

"Is that good?" asked David.

"All it means is that there will be stitches, but you just won't see them. They will be buried under the skin."

"Doc, you helped us late at night when Jeb was hurt, and we trust and want you to take care of Rachel," Mr. Sudlow said, and Mr. Parker nodded his head in agreement.

On the way out, Festus said quietly to David, "I hope we git her done in time."

The coonskin-capped pair stopped at the office to pay their bill and make the surgery appointment.

* * *

The following week Rachel arrived in her crate and ready for the operation. I didn't want her in the kennel with all the other animals. The noise could get her in a frightened state. I walked into surgery with Rachel and greeted Sandy, who stood there with her hands on her hips.

"Dr. Dionne, are we really going to spay a raccoon today?"

"Yes we are," I smiled.

"Before we do, Dr. North needs an x-ray on a cat right away. The client is waiting in the exam room."

"Okay, I'll put her in the back surgery room where it's quiet."

The x-ray unit and our lab shared a room adjacent to surgery. Sandy went to retrieve Dr. North's cat. I went into the lab, and said hello to Ralph, our lab technician. Ralph worked part-time. He retired as the lab tech at Somerville Hospital. He thought it would be fun to work on non-human blood samples and such.

Sandy came up the stairs with a large overweight Persian cat. She and I donned lead aprons and gloves and took the chest x-ray.

Sandy said, "I'll return this kitty back to Dr. North and then I'll help you with Rachel."

The first thing that I noticed when I walked back into surgery was that Rachel's cage was open. While we were busy with the x-ray, she had wiggled the latch on the door by sticking one of her long toes, that were more like fingers, through the cage wire. The door swung open, and out she walked!

Where is she? I thought as panic set in.

My question was answered quickly when I heard the low growling and hissing sound coming from the main surgery room. There she was perched on top of the operating table. However, she was no longer the cute, fluffy and gentle raccoon of last week.

I didn't find out until later that she had gone into a heat cycle. Which thinking back on the whole affair, I now knew what Festus meant by, "I hope we git her done in time."

The raccoon mating season starts in late January to mid-March. It was late January. During this time the females become hormone-induced, mean, aggressive, ornery and downright unfriendly to boot. Even a box of chocolates won't help!

We stood there *eye-balling* each other warily. *Now what?* I thought.

Just then Sandy walked in with a cheery, "Dr. Dionne, I'm back, let's get started."

Rachel bolted off the table, and Sandy let out a *holy* something or other.

The raccoon made it through the now open surgery door, turned left and into the x-ray/lab room.

"Sandy, go get the net from the kennel!" as I then followed Rachel into the x-ray/lab room and closed the door.

Ralph, our senior citizen lab tech, was pale and huddled in the corner. He was speechless with fright. Rachel was now on top of the x-ray table planning her next move. I had a scary flashback on the wounds received by Jeb, the blue tick coon hound.

I quietly told Ralph, "Move very slowly and silently into the dark room, close the door and stay there until I say it's all right to come out."

He nodded his head in agreement.

I waited for Sandy to return with the net, which was basically a large fishing net with a long handle that is used to scoop a big fish into a boat.

Sandy returned and opened the door slightly to hand me the net and a syringe filled with a pre-operative sedative for Miss Rachel. I held the net up like I was about to catch a few butterflies.

The *bandit* sensing trouble, decided to flee up onto the lab counter containing all of Ralph's morning samples. In a flurry of wild frenzy lasting less than a minute, every blood, urine and stool sample was knocked over, spilled and flung onto the floor. The microscope, centrifuge and other lab equipment were also knocked hither and thither.

I swung the net and missed twice causing more mess, but the third time I caught her as she leaped onto the floor. Rachel was tangled in the fish net. Before she could chew her way out, I injected her rear leg muscle.

A few minutes later it was all over. I carried her into surgery, anesthetized her, and Sandy clipped her abdomen and scrubbed her up for surgery.

Fortunately, the spay was fairly easy, and I removed those two ovaries and uterus that were responsible for the change in Rachel's behavior. As I was suturing her up, I remembered poor Ralph was still in the dark room.

"Sandy, tell Ralph it's okay to come out now. Then tell Mike we had a little accident in the lab. We need it cleaned up, and we'll have to get all new samples to run."

I didn't want to be there when Mike heard the part about new samples. After today, I was fairly sure that I might be working at the Miller-Hastings plant with Festus and David.

* * *

The lab was cleaned up. Ralph recovered after taking a day off and returned to work with a sign, *Keep Door Closed At All Times*. Mike didn't speak to me for a week, but I still had my job. And Rachel healed quite well-- no hernia.

Festus and David gave me a present of a genuine coonskin cap that they made from Jeb's little fracas with the angry raccoon. The cap was nice except for all the tooth holes from their coon hounds. And Festus and I each started writing our books.

Afterwords

Every story has an ending...

There is a statue, in a small park, located in downtown Fort Myers, Florida. The statue and park overlook the Caloosahatchie River where it merges with the Gulf of Mexico. The park is a peaceful place for visitors and residents to stroll through, have their lunch or a picnic with the family. Many prefer to just sit and gaze at the wide flowing river and tranquil Gulf. Here the sunsets are often magnificent and memorable. Pleasure boats of all types and sizes fill the adjacent marina or can be viewed skimming through the water. The park is filled with various palm trees such as the stately royal palm and queen palm. Numerous brightly colored flowers and shrubs like the hibiscus are in bloom year round.

The much admired statue is of Thomas Edison who had his winter home nearby. Henry Ford, Harvey Firestone and Edison often met in this park to relax and discuss their ideas and dreams of the future. Of course, much of the discussion centered on the relatively new automobile and how to improve it. Especially the tires.

The slow process of extracting rubber from plants in South and Central America was time consuming, expensive and not conducive for mass production of automobiles and the necessary tires.

Edison told his friends, "*I think I can* make synthetic rubber to solve your problem." His friends looked at him skeptically but also hopefully. Through much hard work and numerous failures, Edison finally achieved his promise.

Inscribed on the back of his famous statue in the park was a favorite saying of Thomas Edison. "*If you think you can-- you will. If you think you can't-- you will.*"

I copied the saying down in my notebook and used it over the years to motivate myself and other members of my family when the need arose. When it came to writing these stories, Edison's quotation made me persevere when my mind was blank and doubts were creeping in.

Acknowledgments

There are many friends and family members who made this book of short stories possible...

* My wife, Tina, was instrumental in the completion of each story, transforming each one into readable prose with seemingly unending editing.

* My son, Edward, collected all the stories and formatted the basic design of the book, plus he was my main cheerleader and encouraged me to keep going.

* Emily Dennis, my granddaughter, added her artistic talents by creating the illustrations which are at the end of each chapter and on the cover.

* Terri Dennis, my daughter, who had the patience to point out the flaws in my writing and kept revising my first story, *Eggbert the Turtle*, until it was satisfactory.

* Desiree Dennis, my granddaughter, along with her mother, Terri Dennis for meticulously designing my website.

* Zachary Dennis, my grandson, who exposed his grandparents to the wonders and mysteries of the computer and internet.

* Michelle Dionne, my daughter, who always believed that it could be written and added enthusiastically, "Just go for it, Dad."

* Kestrel and Aziza Dionne, my youngest granddaughters, who enjoy sitting on my lap to hear my wild, make-believe children stories.

* Paulyne Dionne, my aunt, who read the stories and gave me motivation with her comments.

* John and Lynda Powell, longtime friends, for all their support.

* Steve Williams, photographer, who produced the back cover photo.

* "Junior" Williams, Steve's dog, who sat patiently through the photo-shoot.

* Dr. Richard Coburn and the late Dr. Arthur North, my mentors, for their wisdom and guidance. They taught me the art of *practicing* veterinary medicine.

* A thank you to all the other relatives, friends, and strangers who took the time to read a story or two and give me feedback on their thoughts and ideas.

* And finally, a huge thank you for all the animals in this book and their owners who provided the cases and material to make the stories possible.

About the Author

Having been an animal lover since he was very young and wanting to be an *animal doctor* from the age of seven, he was one of those fortunate few who had a goal as to one's vocation as an adult.

After graduating from Binghamton Central High School in New York in 1961, he attended the Pennsylvania State University and majored in Pre-Veterinary Medicine.

He was admitted to the University of Pennsylvania School of Veterinary Medicine in 1964, and graduated *cum laude* in 1968 with a Veterinary Medical Doctor degree.

His first place of employment was with Somerset Veterinary Group in Somerville, New Jersey.

He furthered his education at the Hershey Medical Center in Hershey, Pennsylvania, on a post-doctoral fellowship.

Later, he opened his own small animal practice, Blue Ridge Veterinary Clinic in Walnutport, Pennsylvania.

He and his wife Tina have three children - Edward Dionne III, Terri Dennis and Michelle Dionne, and five grandchildren - Desiree, Emily, Zachary, Kestrel and Aziza.

After retiring, they now reside in Boalsburg, Pennsylvania, near Penn State. They have been involved in numerous volunteer activities including Special Olympics and Heifer Project International.

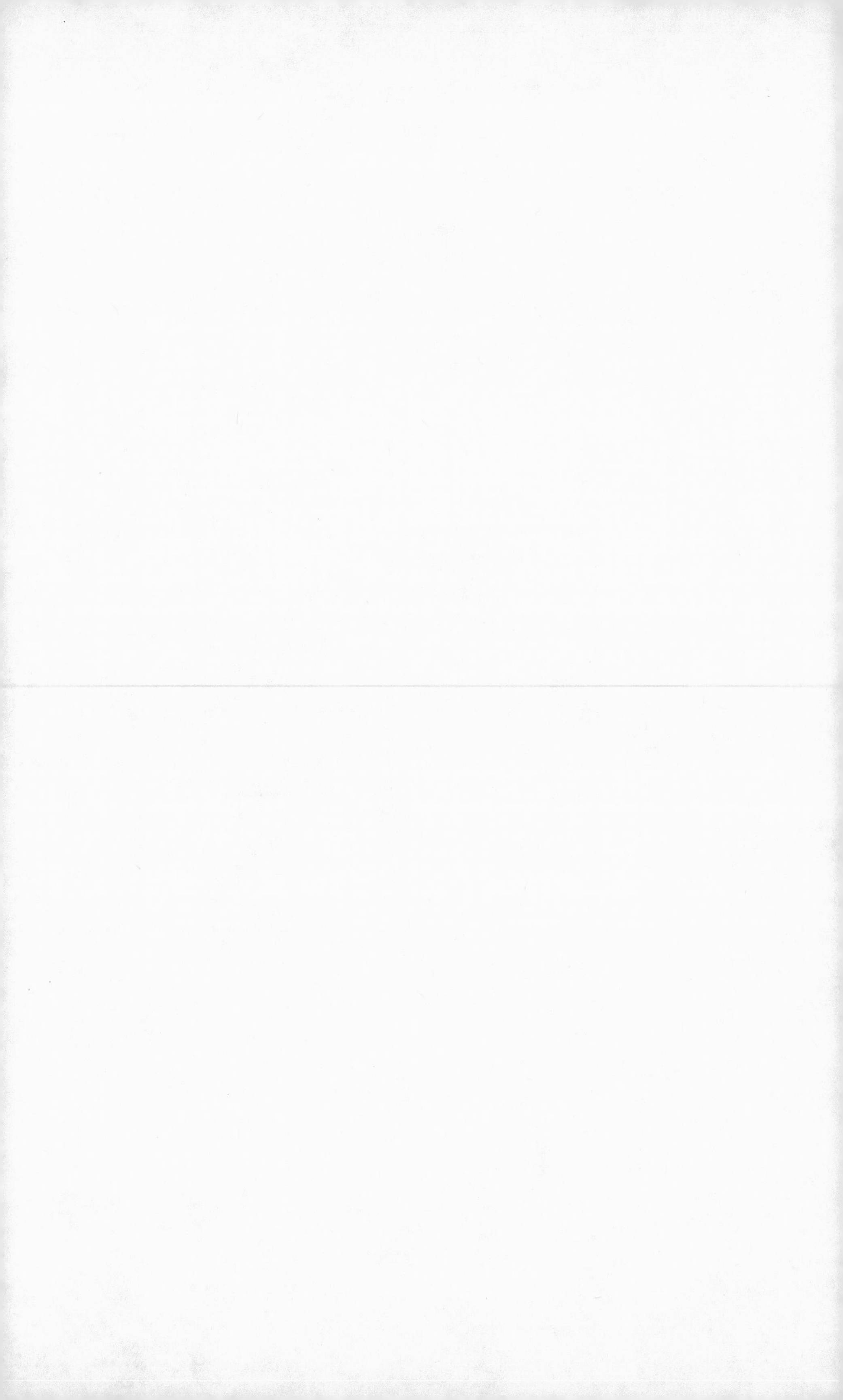

Made in the USA
Charleston, SC
05 March 2013